Work in the 1980s

Emancipation and Derogation

Papers from the Karlstad Symposium on Work

Edited by
BENGT OVE GUSTAVSSON
JAN CH KARLSSON
CURT RÄFTEGÅRD
University of Karlstad
Sweden

Gower

Published by
Gower Publishing Company Limited,
Gower House, Croft Road, Aldershot, Hampshire, England.
and
Gower Publishing Company,
Old Post Road, Brookfield, Vermont 05036, USA.

British Library Cataloguing in Publication Data

Karlstad Symposium work *(1984)*.
  Work in the 1980s : emancipation and derogation :
  papers from the Karlstad Symposium on Work.
  1. Work
  I. Title   II. Gustavsson, Bengtove
  III. Karlsson, Jan Ch   IV. Raftegard, Curt
  306'.36   HD4901

  ISBN 0-566-00862-9

Printed and bound in Great Britain by
Biddles Ltd, Guildford and King's Lynn

Contents

Foreword

Work will always be a concept of fundamental importance to man. It will, therefore, always be a fundamental area for research and development, of interest not only to academics in universities throughout the world but also to policy-makers on all levels, both regional, national and international.

All these groups were represented at the symposium, 'Work in 1984 – Emancipation or Derogation', held at the University of Karlstad, Sweden on 17-20 June, 1984, where many of the world's leading researchers in the field presented papers.

In Sweden, research on work is of particular importance, as is manifested by the creation of a special national institute – the Swedish Centre for Working Life – which works in close cooperation with the University of Karlstad. This is no coincidence since Karlstad is the capital of Värmland, a province which has been faced for some time with serious unemployment and far-reaching changes in the structure of its industry. A consequence of this has been a considerable increase in the amount of teaching and research at the University on work and working life, with the symposium as one result. It should be added that the symposium also forms a part of the 400th anniversary celebrations of the City of Karlstad.

This volume presents the proceedings of the symposium and we hope it will prove stimulating to academics, policy-makers and others, and thereby encourage further research on the multi-facetted subject of work as well as significant developments in 'real' working life.

We would like to thank all those who have contributed both financially and otherwise and thus made this symposium possible.

Karlstad, November 1984

Lennart Andersson
Vice-Chancellor
University of Karlstad

Bengt Abrahamsson
President of the Symposium
Professor at the Centre for
Working Life

Acknowledgements

We would like to express our gratitude to the following organizations, whose generous financial contributions made the symposium possible: the Bank of Sweden Tercentenary Foundation, County Administration in Värmland, Karlstad Municipal Council, Länssparbanken Värmland (County Savings Bank), Ministry of Labour, the National Defence Research Institute, the Swedish Centre for Working Life, the Swedish Council for Planning and Coordination of Research/Committee for Future Oriented Research, the Swedish Work Environment Fund, Värmland County Council, and Wermlandsbanken (Wermland Bank).

We would also like to thank all those who contributed their time and energy to make the symposium a success. Our special thanks go to the chairmen of the various sessions: Professor Bengt G. Rundblad, Professor Åke Sandberg, Professor Hans L. Zetterberg, Professor Kjell Härnqvist and Professor Bengt Abrahamsson, who was also president of the symposium; to the other members of the organizing committee: Professor Lennart Andersson, University of Karlstad, Dr. Ingrid Wahlund, Central Organization of Salaried Employees and Dr. Alise Weibull, National Defence Research Institute; to Michael Cooper and Elisabeth Wennö for their invaluable assistance in translating, correcting and proof-reading material both for the symposium and for this volume; and, finally, to Ingrid Hansson, Ingrid Lindqvist and Eva Sundberg for their indefatigable secretarial help.

Introduction

BENGTOVE GUSTAVSSON, JAN CH KARLSSON AND CURT RÄFTEGÅRD

In the invitation to the international symposium on work research held at the University of Karlstad, Sweden, we adopted the traditional approach in research on working life of considering work from two alternative viewpoints.

On the one hand, there is a tradition - the emancipation tradition - that looks upon work as being the basis for the development of the human species and human societies. It is, for example, common to attempt to define what is specific for man by means of arguments based on the fact that man can use tools and can consciously plan his activities. Further, conditions in relation to work are often used in attempts to classify societies and their development; this is the case, for example, with regard to various technologies and/or social relations of work.

On the other hand, it is pointed out that work has, at the same time, been performed under particularly degrading forms and conditions. Workers have thus been commonly exposed to various kinds of force. This fact has an etymological counterpart in that words like 'labour' and 'Arbeit' originally had connotations of toil, drudgery and slaving.

As a consequence, the subject of the symposium was framed in the form of a question: 'Work in 1984 - emancipation or derogation?'. Naturally, we did not expect an either/or answer but rather one which emphasized that it was a case of both/and.

In retrospect, as we have edited the oral and written contributions to the symposium, it has become clear that we were wrong. The question cannot be formulated simply with either an _or_ or an _and_ linking the concepts of emancipation - derogation; at least, not _if_ it is to be answered by researchers of the 1980s. Taking the majority of papers presented at the symposium into account and accepting that our choice of authors and discussants was representative of contemporary research on working life, as we think it was, we have to conclude that the question of emancipation or derogation was formulated in terms that were much too absolute and with expectations that were far too descriptive to receive an unambiguous answer.

For the reader the symposium papers, arranged simply on the basis of different thematic headings, might appear to be a collection of more or less unconnected contributions. If, however, we look for other common approaches, theoretical assumptions etc. beyond the separate contributions, certain trends become apparent, trends which we shall designate as 'the 80's approach' in research on working life.

One method of summarizing these trends is to construct a frame of reference/model which places 'the 80's approach' in the context of earlier traditions. This reveals two common features: one concerned with the relation between the research approach adopted and the problems dealt with, the other with the question of how the emancipatory and derogatory aspects of work are understood theoretically.

The researchers at the symposium seem, in the main, to represent what might be called a normative action approach. For the most part, their contributions go beyond a mere description and analysis of the problems in the different themes. They also suggest ways of achieving emancipation. Furthermore, they tend to regard emancipation and derogation as culture-related concepts. Thus, in the papers, there are no universal solutions and no absolute standard of good and bad in work and outside it.

It is these approaches, then, that we suggest are trends in current research on working life and for which we use the generic term 'the 80's approach'. As we have implied, their opposites are descriptive, analytic approaches where emancipation and derogation are looked upon as absolute concepts. A diagrammatic presentation of these dimensions will clarify the relationship between 'the 80's approach' and some other traditions in research on working life.

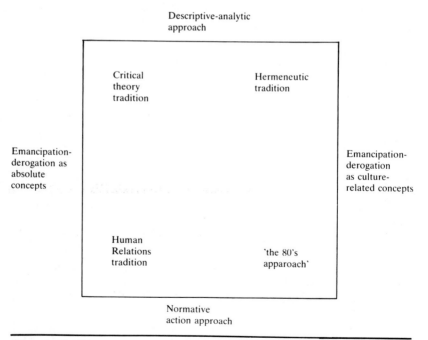

Figure 1. *Traditions in Research on Working Life*

There are, of course, no clear dividing lines between what we have designated as different traditions. However, we have marked some of the positions in the figure with key words – critical theory, hermeneutics and human relations – with which 'the 80's approach' may be contrasted. We shall attempt to illustrate our argument further by providing examples of research within the various traditions.

Harry Braverman's now classic analysis of changes in the work process is in the critical theory tradition. Braverman provides an absolute model for good work in the unity between conception and execution. The 'degradation of work' results from the separation of these two aspects, a factor which distinguishes the work organization of monopoly capitalism. However, he makes no attempt to indicate how degradation might be counteracted. He also explicitly excludes from his analysis all questions concerning the class consciousness, organization and activities of the working class.

Within the hermeneutic tradition we find, for example, occupational sociology, where Everett C. Hughes has been a major source of inspiration. This field covers such subjects as occupational socialization, occupational roles and occupational cultures; the object is to attempt to understand and describe the social relationships of an occupation and the worker's identification with his role. Emancipatory and derogatory aspects of work are considered exclusively from the horizon of the respective occupations.

As an example of research in the human relations tradition, we might mention the work done by Frederick Herzberg and his successors. A basic distinction is here made between 'hygiene factors' and 'motivational factors', the former affecting dissatisfaction but having nothing to do with job satisfaction, while the opposite is true of the latter. Furthermore, questions of emancipation and derogation are analyzed on the basis of a theory of human nature rather than as aspects of cultural variation. Finally, researchers provide a considerable amount of advice – particularly for managers – on how the work should be organized.

What we have called 'the 80's approach', which is, then, a term for the trends in research on working life discernable in the symposium material, is contrasted in the figure with the other traditions. To illustrate this further, we shall relate the various papers to the dimensions of the figure. We shall not, however, consider the contents of the papers in any great detail. Each of the symposium's sessions was concerned with a particular theme and was introduced by a discussant, who presented and commented on the papers for that theme. These 'discussants' papers', which are included in this volume, provide more detailed introductions.

Behind the idea of work as emancipation and/or derogation lies the discussion of the concept of work so central to social science, and it is not insignificant that the first theme of the symposium continued this discussion. However, none of the authors (Cornell, Karlsson and Lind- qvist, Eyerman, Tabukasch, Wallman) take such a simple dichotomization as their starting point; they go much further, emphasizing, in particular, the fact that the formulation of concepts should be linked to societal development.

As the discussant, Sven-Erik Liedman, points out, this is the symposium's most abstract theme, being part of basic research on work.

It is, therefore, perhaps natural that a direct action approach is less noticeable here.

In the theme work and technology, the culture-related approach is clearly in evidence in the way the authors deal with the relationship between technology and society. All the papers reject the view that technology is a force which is independent of developments in society. On the contrary, they emphasize the fact that technology must always be seen as part of a more complex set of problems and that it is wrong to ask whether technology as such is emancipatory or derogatory. In this respect, the papers can be considered as a contribution to the process of 'demystification' of the concept of technology. Several of them (Berggren, Edquist, Pang) take up the question of how the same technology may be applied in different social contexts.

With this basic attitude to technology and society in mind, it is not surprising that three of the papers (Berggren, Edquist, Haug) deal explicitly with the question of power and influence over the development of technology as a central aspect of the subject. Thus, we have arrived at the normative action approach mentioned above, which the discussant, Einar Thorsrud, considers to be virtually a necessity in all modern work research.

All the contributions to the theme work and culture consider various aspects of 'modernization', as the discussant, Mats Dahlkvist, points out. They stress the importance of cultural factors for the development of working life and highlight the significance of the distinctive characteristics of different cultures for attempts to evaluate alternative lines of action. Three of the papers (Anthony, Benería, Wingren) link this line of action to a culture-related approach. The fourth author (Galtung), however, holds a somewhat different view. As his discussion of the development of work is based on a typology of needs, the question of emancipation or derogation is looked at in more absolute terms.

In the theme work and education, what we have called 'the 80's approach' is apparent in various ways. Culture-relativity is found, for example, in several of the papers (Carnoy, Háber, Mathiesen) as well as in the discussant's (Donald Broady) introduction, in their discussion of how changes in qualification requirements in working life lead to both the impoverishment and the enrichment of work. This gives rise to a consideration of how different types of education and educational systems can provide the labour force with these qualifications.

Thus, there is a clear line of action in the approach; that is, an attempt is made to tackle the question of education as an emancipatory factor. In most of the papers the answer which is given is that the education provided by the general education system is basically only a reflection of the current power relations in working life. This is, however, not the only possible form of education. One paper in particular (Holmer) shows how, for example, academic education can be made part of the work for change carried out by the trade unions, by the organization of so-called research circles. The method used here is an excellent example of a normative action approach.

The authors on the theme work and power seem to have adopted a common normative approach in that they see an equal distribution of power over work as something valuable. They are also agreed that no

4

such equal distribution exists today. The line of action is clear, for example, in the argument for worker self-management (Horvat) or increased employee participation through the adoption of share-holding positions etc. (Eidem). One of the authors (Gustavsen) comments on the actual results of and the contributions made by employee representation on company boards. He also sketches the possibilities for further developments.

From an action perspective, it is also encouraging to note how the authors deal with the relationship between workers' participation and efficiency in production. It is often assumed that the participation of the many and efficiency in production are incompatible. Three of the authors (Macpherson, Horvat, Eidem) deal explicitly with this relationship without supporting the assumption of incompatibility, in fact, they argue for the opposite viewpoint. However, the discussant, Göran Lantz, seems to be more doubtful on this point. He is, however, explicit in his demand for a greater distribution of power.

In conclusion, we feel that it is worth pointing out that the papers produced for the symposium and presented in this volume completely lack those descriptions of 'wretchedness' so common in earlier research. Furthermore, they contain very little of the almost paralyzing resignation which frequently results from the exposure of enormous causal structures. They should rather be seen as part of a tradition that is concerned with ways of increasing emancipation in working life.

Part I
The Concept of Work

1 Discussant's paper on the concept of work

SVEN-ERIK WEDMAN

I have here the flattering but difficult task of opening the discussion on 'the concept of work'. Possibly it is typical that our first meeting in this symposium is about the concept of work. We are, so to say, starting from the abstract angle, and from here we have to try to reach more concrete themes, such as work and technology, or work and culture.

Although conscious of the abstractness of our topic, I shall start with an even more abstract question. The four papers that we have to deal with are not only interesting, original, and penetrating but also papers of four different kinds. This, of course, makes my task even more difficult. In one respect, however, they seem to be unanimous, namely in their interpretation of the subject of the seminar. It is about 'the concept of WORK' and not about 'the CONCEPT of work'. Nobody has, at least openly, asked: What is a concept like? What does it mean to talk about the concept of something?

Of course, indirectly, the concept of concept plays an important part in all the papers. In two of them it is overtly stated that there cannot be one concept of work but many, differing over time. In the third, two leading conceptualizers of work, Marx and Habermas, are scrutinized, and in the fourth, which is Sandra Wallman's paper, we can read that '... the concept of work will vary within one culture at a single point of history as well as between cultural systems.'

Now, let us ask the very abstract question: What does it mean to look either for a concept or for different concepts of work? One way is to make empirical generalizations in the classical empiricist manner about the kinds of work going on in a society or in different societies. The result of the investigation is dependent on whether there is any common character in all the types of work going on. Another way is to start with different theories of work from Aristotle to Habermas. A third possible way – which is, in fact, very common but which our four papers avoid – is to scrutinize ordinary language by asking questions about what we mean when we talk about 'work'. How is the word 'work' related to words such as 'labour', 'activity', 'employment', 'toil' and so on? One further possibility would be to play the role of theoretician oneself; to develop one's own theory or philosophy of work.

Here, however, I simply want to call attention to the problem which can be formulated in the following terms: Does the attempt to define the concept of work imply the conceptualization of work or is it a more passive registration of different kinds of work, or different theories about work, or different ways of talking about 'work'? Certainly, there is no simple answer.

Now, I shall go on to characterize briefly the four papers that lie before us to-day. Thereafter I shall discuss some rather fundamental questions that the papers give rise to.

Ron Eyerman's brief paper, Work: A Contested Concept, starts with the assertion that 'work means different things at different times and in different places'. Then, it traces the history of work concept from the Enlightenment to our days. (Marx plays an important part in this survey – more, I think, the so-called young Marx, who defines the human being, than the so-called mature Marx.) He also calls our attention to a concept that is not so much discussed in the other papers, namely the concept of division of labour, a notion that has dominated the discussions about the nature of work for more than 200 years. In passing, I would like to add a seemingly futile but possibly interesting question: We talk about division of labour, but is it possible to talk about division of work? If not, why not? Eyerman also takes into account the modern feminist discussions about reproduction and work. If I am right, Eyerman is more interested in taking up some of the problems concerned with the concept of work than in trying to develop his own opinion or theories. Still, he has the intention of broadening the concept of work, seeing it with Arnold Gehlen (1980), in the context of 'the "unfinished" nature of human beings'. Work here becomes a form of 'purpose-rational activity'; that means, we may add, that it is defined in a rather traditional way.

Sandra Wallman, too, tries to broaden the concept of work, developing the interesting notion of the 'work of livelihood'. This notion is closely connected to the five propositions about work that Wallman develops in the second part of her paper, the last of which is decisive. There, the 'necessary resources' are fundamental. I must admit that I am not clear about the meaning of the word 'necessary' here; are they necessary for the survival of mankind, for the maintenance of the good life of the group or the individual? Sandra Wallman says only 'necessary to livelihood' and seems to admit a certain subjectivity. According to her, the six necessary resources are: land, labour, capital, time, information and identity.

In two respects Sandra Wallman's paper adds something very important to our discussion that the other papers omit: she is concerned with unemployment and its effects, and she makes use of a broad anthropological material. She seems to have the most 'empirical' attitude to the concept of work of our six authors.

Cornell, Karlsson and Lindqvist – a troika which, for the sake of brevity, I shall call CKL – deny openly in their paper the possibility of an all-embracing concept of work. Instead, they try to develop a series of connected work concepts spread over or developed throughout history from classless society to our days. Let me quote them: 'In order to study different forms of work social science must instead develop a whole body of what we might call sub-concepts of work, based on social relations.' That means, that social relations, or rather, class relations, must be taken into account in order to develop not the concept of work in an abstract generality but a whole family of work-concepts that encompass work in its historical diversity.

I must say that I feel sympathy for the way CKL deal with the subject. Their generalization is not empirical but has its starting-point in a specific theory or perspective, a perspective that we ordinarily associate with historical materialism. The risk with their perspective could be that their survery of different social forms of work may have a certain schematic character. Furthermore, I am not quite persuaded by their treatment of the ontological method of defining work that Karel Kosîk and Marcuse have developed. To this point, I shall return.

Michael Tabukasch's paper has its strength where the other papers have their weakness - it concentrates on two very distinct concepts of work, that of Marx, the author of Capital, and that of Habermas, especially of the early Habermas. Tabukasch talks about Marx and Habermas and nothing else. His sympathies are on the side of Marx, and he polemizes against Habermas. (I am not quite sure if it is Habermas before 'Theorie des kommunikativen Handelns' or if he includes this work as well. The Habermas of to-day is, at least, less clear-cut, less one-sided than his younger ego who developed the sharp dividing line between work and interaction.) Tabukasch first of all takes account of Marx's decisive distinction between work or labour in capitalism as use-value and as exchange-value, a distinction that is connected with the distrinction between the formal and material side of commodities, machinery etc. This distinction becomes important when the task is to outline the character of labour in a post-capitalist society. In earlier works, including Grundrisse, Marx seems to assume that capitalism as capitalism shapes all the possibilities for a post-capitalist, socialist society with its socialist type of labour. The distinction between form and materia or content opens the way for an interpretation where the end of capital does not seem to be a natural inevitability and where the double character of capital and, not least, of labour under capitalism becomes clear. In his paper Tabukasch suggests the possibility of a concept of work where its double character under capital is decisive. Tabukasch, like CKL, sees work as internally related to social relations. I think that this position has to be discussed.

In this short survey, I have attempted to characterize our four papers on the concept of work. I shall now go on to say something about the general questions that these papers may give rise to.

Let me first formulate a somewhat bewildering question, namely: What is the opposite of work? What is the concept of non-work? Evidently, the opposite is not one but many. We can read in our papers and elsewhere that work is activity; therefore, its opposite is passivity, leisure. But work is not every activity; animals are active, but we do not say that they work. Here, Marx's famous old architect, who has an idea of the house to be built, which the bee has not, comes to our help: human work is purposeful activity. As so many of you are sociologists, I want to satisfy you by giving you this simple figure, where the x indicates work:

	activity	passivity
purposeful	x	
purposeless		

Now, as Agnes Heller (1981) and others have remarked, this is not enough. Herbert Marcuse (1933) and, after him, Karel Kosík (1976) have tried to delimit work from play. Marcuse says that work has a 'Lastcharacter'. I do not know how to translate this word into English but we may say that work is a burden. I think that, like Kosík, we may transcend the negativity in Marcuse's concept. The point is that man at work faces something that he has to bear or endure, he meets a reality that he cannot immediately form at will, as when he is playing.

This 'Lastcharacter', I would say, characterizes all work just as purposefulness and activity do. It is not only when dealing with nature that man's activity has a 'Lastcharacter'. Society with all its human relations is an object for human work, and this work, too, has a 'Lastcharacter'. So has the work of an artist, a painter, a writer. In all our four papers, there are quotations from Marx (this, I should say, is the unifying link between them), but I miss my own favourite Marx saying about work, namely in Grundrisse, (1973:611), where he says: 'Really free working, e.g. composing, is at the same time precisely the most damned seriousness, the most intense exertion.' Here Marx in a brilliant way characterizes the 'Lastcharacter', the burden character, of artistic work. If you allow me to be utopian for a moment, I would say that the value of work to-day and in every possible future has something to do with exactly this burden character, this 'damned seriousness', this 'intense exertion'.

So far, I have tried, (with the help of our authors), to construct a concept of work that is general and not historically determined and delimited. However, I agree with all the authors whom I am referring to here in their view that work fundamentally shifts in content and meaning throughout history. More precisely, I agree with CKL and Tabukasch when they say that the fundamental shifts have to do with the social relationships of work. Even if we say that all work means activity and purposefulness and that it has its 'Lastcharacter', this is not a sufficient definition of the real content of work, as can be easily demonstrated. Let us take the phrase: All work is purposeful. To build a house is a purposeful activity. But whose purpose? The purposeful activities of the architect, the builder, and the building workers are not identical, and the differences also depend on, for example, whether the workers are slaves or wage-earners. In short, the class relations in a society fundamentally determine what work is like in that society. The question of what work will be like in the near future cannot, therefore, be formulated only in terms of technological development. This is an old but seemingly inevitable mistake. How moving is it not to read to-day all those documents from the end of the 19th century where the effects of electricity on future work are sketched! In this very moment thousands of engineer-souls are committing the same mistake when making forecasts about work in a computer society. And we listen uncritically, just as our grandfathers listened to Jules Verne and Patrick Geddes.

In order to avoid such mistakes, I think we have to take seriously the kind of distinction that Michael Tabukasch is talking about. Here, it is not a question of work in general but work in technologically advanced capitalist societies. Work - or labour - in these societies has a double character; it is concrete work, work with its specific character or qualities, and, at the same time, it is abstract work, work that can essentially be measured in hours and days, i.e. quantitatively. We all know that work to-day is becoming more and more quantitative and abstract in character, this is, in fact, what is happening with that type of favourized intellectual work that most of us here in this room perform. This quantification is, in fact, not only what our employers but also what most trade unions are working for.

At the same time, we can see that there is another type of work – qualitative work – and I am not out of sympathy with those who, to-day, seek a new conception of work in the reproductive sphere of life. However, even there, the dual contradictory character can be seen. At least the neo-conservatives and the neo-liberals are trying to convince us that even this sphere must be quantified; housework and child care have to be paid just as wage labour.

To summarize: I have not been able here to make a direct comparison between the theses of the four papers that are under discussion. The papers are too diversified for such a comparison. At the same time, diversity and manifoldness may give rise in different ways to a fruitful discussion about the concept and the concepts of work. My own standpoint, which I have tried to make clear, is that it is meaningful to talk of a general concept of work but that this general concept is very broad and has very little to contribute to an understanding of the historical shifts in work. Here, the social relations of work must be taken into account. If we make any forecast about work in future, this is extremely important as the general traits of work have nothing to tell us about the possible future. Here, we must, first of all, take into consideration the dual character of work in our society.

2 Missing concepts of work

LASSE CORNELL, JAN CH KARLSSON AND ULLA LINDQVIST

Social science of work is characterized by the fact that the meaning of its central concept is not made explicit - and hardly even discussed. The most common form of defining work is to refrain from defining it. In the same way as a non-decision is a form of decison, a non-definition is - in this context - a form of definition. Social science has shied away from the theoretical problems by tacitly accepting the easy formula: 'Work is wage labour'. (For one of the few explicit definitions of this kind, see Dubin 1965:4).

There are, however, a number of exceptions, i.e. texts where an explicit conceptual discussion can be found. Through a survey of these we uncover three theoretical contradictions: first, activity vs. social relationship as the conceptual basis; second, an ontological vs. an empirical concept; and third, one single vs. several concepts of work. The solution that we suggest for these interconnected contradictions leads us to an overview of social forms of work through history - an exploration of missing concepts.

AUXILIARY CONCEPTS OF WORK

To be able to consider the way in which social scientists have theoretically directed their concepts of work, we have surveyed the concepts that have been used in the definitions and in the argumentations for them. We have identified a number of such 'auxiliary concepts', namely 1) activity, 2) purpose, 3) needs, 4) relations to nature, and 5) social relations. In the following we inquire into the use of these auxiliary concepts in social science of work (cf. Karlsson 1983).

Activity

There have been a few earlier surveys of scientific concepts of work and the one undertaken by Karl Elster in the beginning of this century seems to be the best known. His first conclusion was (1919:621): 'On one point the different definitions are in agreement. They recognize that "work" always is an activity'. As far as social science is concerned, this is still true: all the definitions that we have found contain some reference to work having to do with activity. Thereafter some kind of qualification is made - some activities are to be regarded as work, others are not.

Purpose

Often the activities in question are delimited by their purposefulness.

15

Using this as a defining criterion, many authors refer to Karl Marx's (1969:193) famous parable of the architect and the bee. The most pregnant elaboration is made by George Lukács (1973); the basis of his argument is that work is telosrealization, i.e. to reach a goal formulated in advance of the action. Technological positing is the essence of work.

His thesis has, however, been criticized by Agnes Heller (1981), who reminds us that all actions are teleological; Lukás regards them simply as modified versions of the work activity. Work is, further, in his interpretation a 'one-man-show', dealing with the goals of the actor. Therefore all social actions have to be explained by an analogy with individual action.

A somewhat different critique has been delivered by Peter Ruben and Camille Warnke (1979). They point out that it is seldom possible to understand and predict all the conditions for the course of a work process. In reality, work is richer than the posited goal (including the tools and their use). The reduction of work to teleological positing is thereby utterly unrealistic. In opposition, they stress the tool as the core of human work. It is through the use of tools that man wins the ability to formulate goals; the tool is the genetic precondition for teleological positing; not the other way round.

If Lukács took the extreme position that purposefulness is a sufficient criterion for an activity to be work, the Norwegian sociologist Cato Wadel places himself at the other end of the scale. He explicity denounces purpose as of relevance to the concept of work; instead, he directs his attention towards the function of the activities (1977:407, emphasis added): 'Work is human activities which can be shown to maintain, establish or change commonly valued social institutions, whether these activities have this as a goal or not. Wadel is, however, an exception; all other authors that we have reviewed use purposefulness as a part of their definition.

It should, also, be noted that a negative conceptualization provides an influential line of thought, especially in economics; work is defined by what is not its purpose. So, for example, Alfred Marshall (1907:65), who says that labour is 'any exertion of mind or body undergone partly or wholly with a view to some good other than the pleasure derived directly from the work.' Sometimes this thought is taken one step further, so that work becomes by definition disagreeable (see, for example, Lee 1980:60).

Needs

The purpose of the activities of work is to satisfy human needs for survival – this is something of a minimum program for the use of the auxiliary concept of need in the definitions. This, however, makes the picture of needs very static and limited.

Sheila Lewenhak (1980:15), for example, says: 'By "work" we mean all the multifarious processes of getting a livelihood, i.e. of obtaining food, shelter and warmth necessary for human survival'. Some authors, as Lars Ingelstam (1980:32) and Edwin G Kaiser (1966:5f) avoid indicating specific needs and instead talk of them in a general way. There is still, however, no hint that needs can develop and change.

Virginia Novarra (1980:24) puts forward a different idea when she says that 'work is directed first to survival and thereafter to making life more secure, comfortable and agreeable.' Such a line of thought is further developed by Mark A. Lutz in a pledge for what he calls humanistic economics. He starts by stating the definition of work which he says is a summary of the view in traditional economics (1980:508): 'Work is a human activity which provides the material means of survival and enjoyment of life.' His own theoretical base is Abraham Maslow's (1965) theory of a hierarchy of needs in man. He argues that today our lower needs (physiological, security) are satisfied and the higher needs (social, self-actualization) are the relevant ones. He therefore formulates this alternative definition: 'Work is a human activity which provides the means of survival and enjoyment of life.' The only difference as compared to the 'traditional' view is, then, that Lutz leaves out the word 'material'. By this simple operation a kind of dynamic is introduced into the conceptualization.

Still, we hold that the concept of needs should not be made part of the concept of work. This does not mean that we regard work and needs as unrelated phenomena. However, one cannot understand the development of human work against the background of human needs. The analysis must go the other way round (Gustafsson 1980:60): 'Only through acknowledging the primacy of production over consumption does one acknowledge the unlimited need satisfaction and the primacy of need development, for this is ultimately a function of the unlimited development of production.' The same kind of criticism can be directed towards Gerhard Brinkman (1981:18), who uses the concept of need as a basic definiens of work, not needing to be defined.

Relations to Nature

Work contains an element of a relationship to nature – that is an implicit notion in most of the texts in question. There are, however, only a few authors who let this become an explicit constituent of the actions that should be called work. One formulation is provided by Stanley H. Udy (1970:3), who regards as work 'any purposive effort to modify man's physical environment.' He is thereby trying to express a kind of lowest common denominator for work in all types of societies.

Georges Friedmann suggests a more detailed formulation, although his ambition is the same. He refers to the most famous of Marx's general characterizations of work, i.e. as 'Stoffwechsel' – metabolism – between man and nature (Marx 1969:192). According to Friedmann (1960:685) work is 'all actions that man, with a practical purpose and with the help of his brain, his hands, tools or machines exerts on matter, actions that in their turn retroact on man and change him.' But he regards this as only a partial definition. What leads him to say this is the development of a large service sector in modern societies; the activities there 'comprise types of work that, at least at a first glance, escape the definition' that he suggests. Unfortunately he does not state what one would find at a second look and the problem remains unsolved. Friedmann's concept can, however, probably be used as an operational definition of the more limited concept of productive work.

Social Relations

The last kind of auxiliary concept concerns social relations. Some authors limit their concept of work to a specific type of society or to an even more restricted context. This is, of course, a result of the aim of the research in question; Lee analyses a foraging society and has no immediate reason to give a more general definition; Robert Dubin writes a textbook on work in North American private enterprises (although he calls it The World of Work) and so on. At the same time there are authors who are looking for a concept that will make it possible to compare societies and cultures (e.g. Udy 1970 and Lewenhak 1980).

Irrespective of scope in this regard, many conceptual argumentations are built on the social relationships that the activities are associated with. One possibility is to establish in a general way the social nature of work (e.g. Novarra 1980:17ff, Wadel 1977 and Work in America 1973:3). Sometimes the social relations in question are expressed more precisely (e.g. Braude 1963:347 and Gross (1951:11). In the few examples of explicit definitions of the usually non-defined concept, i.e. wage labour, we can, however, find the most specific social relationship. 'By work', says Dubin (1965:4), 'we mean continous employment in the production of goods and services for remuneration'; he also makes clear that by remuneration he means a wage in a modern exhange economy. There arises, however, a conceptual conflict between regarding work, on the one hand, as a number of activities in themselves, and, on the other, as what is being done within the framework of a specific social relationship. In the first case, the activities of work constitute a constant throughout history and for all human beings in a given society; in the second case, an activity which is work during a certain period in history or for a certain group of people, can be something else in another period or for some other group. If you wish to analyse work, you can, in the first case, look directly for the activities; in the second case you must primarily - or, at least, also - look for certain social relations.

The problem can be illustrated by some ambiguities in Louise Tilly's and Joan W Scott's (1978:3) Woman, Work and Family. They distinguish three types of work, namely housework, reproduction and wage labour. But only the first two entities are activities; they can be defined by enumerating different tasks that are to be included in the concept: for example, cooking, washing, cleaning, and the bearing and raising of children respectively. The third entity, wage labour, is however, no task, but a social relationship. It cannot be defined by a list of what people do; it has to be built on the relation between human beings - the framework within which different activities are performed.

To take the illustation of the problem one step further, we can regard the activity of child-bearing. Many authors besides Tilly and Scott include this in their concept of work (e.g. Novarra 1980:17 and Mathaei 1982:40). Starting with the side of the conceptual conflict that is represented by activity, there is at once a difficulty; are biological processes, such as the bearing of children, really activities in the same sense as we used the term earlier? Strictly speaking they are not, as they do not depend on the human consciousness, planning of the process and so forth.

The sheer significance of the reproduction of the species is, however, usually taken as reason enough for calling child-bearing work. The importance of this 'activity' is beyond debate, but by accepting certain biological processes as work in general, there is a risk that the concept will become even more amorphous.

The discussion of female activities as work appears as a way of evaluating women. As an answer to the patriarchal ideology saying that men perform 'social' work and women perform 'natural' work, there are attempts to make those biological activities 'social' by calling them work. Concepts such as 'reproduction', 'production of life' and 'production of man' and also the idea of regarding children as 'products' ought, however, to be emptied of their hidden ideological bias. The non-defined concept of work, i.e. wage labour, is here used and accepted in conceptualizing female activities in general. This indicates a total acceptance of one type of social relationship of work as superior to all other types in history - a misguided kindness towards women in general, not just towards women in capitalist societies.

When discussing only in terms of activities, the dilemma takes the shape of a question of either/or: either child-bearing is work always and everywhere or it is never and nowhere work. If the point of departure is activities within the framework of certain social relations, the question turns into an empirical one: are there social relations where child-bearing should be regarded as work? Two possible cases can be mentioned as a preliminary answer. The first one concerns chattel slavery; if the slave woman carries her child as part of her duties in that social position, then the bearing of the child is work.

Of course this is a special case; even in slave breeding the bearing of children was in most cases not part of the duties of the slave women as such and consequently not work, but encouraged by the slave owner in other ways: allowing cohabitation (e.g. the Brazilian 'amazia', cf. Stein 1957:155f), and giving pregnant women and women with many children less heavy work.

The second case can be found in our own time. Women who have babies for other women are working; they enter a social relationship as independent producers, selling a service and a 'product' - the baby. These examples may be regarded as empirically unusual or negligible; still they are of considerable theoretical importance.

With the auxiliary concept of social relations in the definitions of work a basic theoretical contradiction then emerges. In trying to resolve it, we will utilize some features in a philosophical discourse on an ontological concept of work.

ONTOLOGY OF WORK

The Czech philosopher Karel Kosík gives the following verdict (1976: 118f) on social scientists' limited analysis of the concept of work: when they discuss the concept of work they start from analyses of activities of work, i.e. from work in its empirical forms. Thereby, however, they altogether miss the point; they do not even touch upon the problem of work. What they say is an expression of theoretical confusion, uncritical empiricism and sociologism. The question 'what is work?' is a question for philosophers; social scientists should not deal with it. A similar standpoint - although expressed in other terms - is taken by the priest and philosopher Remy C. Kwant (1960:122f).

Kosík's treatment of the problem of work is highly influenced by an early article by Herbert Marcuse (1933). In this article Marcuse criticizes the concept of work in economics; when searching for its philosophical foundations he finds that these transcend the concept. Marcuse's thesis is that work cannot be regarded as a specific activity, as is often done in economics. It is not just an activity among others; it is a 'doing' (Tun), something that permeates the life of man and his history. Work is, on this level, not defined by its object, goal, result, content, etc., but by human existence as such: work is an ontological concept.

In Kosík's philosophical inquiry he finds that the constitutive element of work is its objectivity, which means two things. First, work has as its result something enduring. The activity, the movement, is objectified in the product. Secondly, work is a manifestation of man as a practical being, as objective subject. The objectified products exist independently of the consciousness of the individual and are a precondition for the continuity of human existence – for history.

So far, however, work is regarded as equal to human doing as a whole. Now Kosík tries to delimit work as a certain kind of doing. He thereby says that work is the doing which is 'instigated and constitutively determined by extraneous purpose, whose satisfaction is dubbed natural necessity or social obligation' (1976:124; the expression is taken from Marx 1968:255). Kosík gives the following example (which is historically questionable, but which highlights the principle of interest here): Aristotle did not work, but a professor of philosophy who translates his writings is working; the reason is that the professor's doing takes place as a part of his occupation, i.e. as a socially conditioned necessity to earn his bread and butter.

On the other hand, it is not always possible to differentiate between work and free creation. What the professional craftsman or artist makes is evidently also a product. His or her doing is work and free creation concurrently (Mills 1951:222f).

But, our area of interest in this article is primarily the work concept in social science; more specifically, we are concerned with the contradiction between work as activity and as social relationship. We suggest that the first step in the solution of the contradiction is to accept that work should be considered an ontological concept. However, as a second step, this gives social science the task of determining and analysing the specific historical and societal forms of work.

This, again, raises another problem: one idea that the social scientists who discuss definitions of work seem to have in common is that one single work concept is enough. This approach has retarded both empirical and theoretical development. In fact, it has even led to such statements of resignation as 'work is a thing of such richness and complexity that it defies analysis' (Anthony 1977:312). In order to study different forms of work, social science must instead develop a whole body of what we might call sub-concepts of work, based on social relations. Thereby, the limits of the non-defined concept are also stated: wage labour is but one form of work among many others. This leads us to the conclusion: there are a lot of concepts missing, or, there are a lot of social forms of work to be analysed.

THE EVOLUTION OF SOCIAL FORMS OF WORK

In the literature there is a conventional, often implicit, pattern of social forms of work: slavery, serfdom, wage labour and a form with self-employed producers that can be called independent work. There are some reasons to maintain that these forms are main forms of work in many European societies from Antiquity onwards; still, the scheme appears to be too crude and limited when studying work historically. The social forms of work must be analysed in their historical context. The dimensions of the concepts in question cannot unequivocally be taken for granted. However, the way in which the surplus product is created and distributed, and the way that the subsistence of the primary producers is secured are important factors. Against this background, we shall make a few preliminary statements on different social forms of work in various types of societies and on the evolution of these forms (cf. Cornell and Karlsson 1983).

Pre-Capitalist Societies

The oldest social form of work which exists in classless societies can be called community-based independent work; it originates in the societies of gatherers and hunters, but it also predominates in the societies of harvesters and cultivators. With cattle breeders and nomads, and later, peasants, a form of work emerges which will prove to be very significant in the subsequent history of mankind: family-based independent work. The producing entity here is neither single individuals nor collectives, but patriarchal families. When handicraft becomes separate from agriculture, there emerges a third type of self-employment, which might be termed corporation-based, or possibly guild-based, independent work.

With the rise of class society, forced labour is established. Then a myriad of different forms of work enter the historical scene. In all of them there is a combination of cooperation relations and ownership relations (Lange 1971:39ff). The following figure attempts to illustrate a basic pattern:

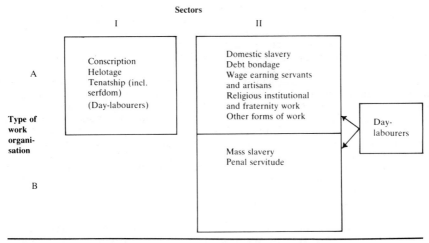

Figure 1. *Social forms of Work in Pre-Capitalist Class Societies*

In order to typologise and classify these form, the economy in such a society can be divided into two parts or sectors: one sector of subsistence producers (sector I) and another sector of big households or demesnes (sector II). Furthermore, two types of work organisation can be found. In type A the main part of the production is done in sector I, but at the same time the peasants of this sector are mobilized to do forced labour in sector II. This forced labour can be linked with or replaced by a fee, rent, or tax in kind or, later, in money. The work organisation is characterized by family-based independent work together with some form of forced labour. Here three main forms can be analytically distinguished, viz. conscription, helotage and tenantship.

Conscription means that the primary producers are obliged to perform a corvée. This was often justified by an ideology which claimed that work was assigned by a deity. Examples can be found in ancient Egypt (David 1975:102ff) and in pre-Columbian Peru (Murra 1980). If forced labour was imposed more regularly or more heavily on the peasantry, as a result of military conquest or for other reasons, a form of work ensued which - using a term from Sparta - can be called helotage (Oliva 1961). The helots - or king's slaves as they are often called - are nominally and legally slaves but they cannot be bought and sold like chattels. They are alloted plots of land to till like serfs, but their duty to do forced labour arises from their unfreedom rather than from their mode of land holding. When King Solomon was going to build the temple of Jerusalem, he had mainly two groups of workers at his disposal: the conscripted Israelite peasantry, and Canaanites and Edomites conquered by the Israelites. The latter were referred to by a term that in translation is 'the slaves of Solomon' even though it is often distorted into 'the servants of Solomon' in biblical translations (Mendelsohn 1949:96f).

The basis of tenantship, again, is a social relation where the primary producer is alloted a piece of land. In return, a rent is imposed on him to be paid in kind, money or work. A special case is the unfreedom connected with serfdom. The classical forms of tenantship and serfdom can be found in medieval Europe (cf. Duby 1973 and Hilton 1973). In an evolutionary sense tenantship is a more recent form than conscription and helotage. These three tributary forms of work should only be separated for analytical purposes; in real life they are often mixed.

In sector II within the work organisation of type A, there is also always exists a permanent work force. Here we can find very different forms of work: domestic slavery, debt bondage, wage earning servants and artisans (paid in kind or, later, also in money), religious institutional or fraternity work, and many other forms. The fact that, generally, different forms of forced labour are used here, and not wage labour, has been explained by several scholars with the argument that the idea of selling one's labour power and not oneself is a relatively late contribution to human civilization. Debt bondage, then, ought often to be seen as an unfree and covert form of wage-contract (cf. Mendelsohn 1949:29ff and Finley (1981:154).

The failure to see labour power as a saleable commodity separable from the person himself can also be traced in the conditions of permanently employed wage-earners in pre-capitalist societies. Bronislaw Geremek (1968:145) has shown that this was true among the wage-earning journeymen in the artisanate of medieval Paris. Such factors as prohibition to leave the workshop during working time and prohibition to work on one's own account or for someone else during the leisure time were reflexions of this failure.

In the other type of work organisation, type B, all production is done in sector II. The social forms of work are mass-slavery or penal servitude. Typical examples are the mass-slavery based on chattel slaves in Greece and Rome (cf. Finley 1960 and Tvarnø 1982). When discussing historical forms of work, slavery appears to be an ambiguous term, since it is often used to include everyone with an unfree status. Thereby the concept is, however, emptied of its proper meaning. There are only few societies of which it can be said that 'slavery seized production in earnest' (Marx 1969:354n) and where mass-slavery based on chattel slaves can be found. Slavery is not a social form of work of its own, but rather a constituent element in several such forms.

In both types of work organisation, A and B, there are day-labourers added to the labour force in sector II. These can be recruited either from sector I or from outside both sectors. Non-agricultural products are largely produced in sector II, but they can also, to a lesser extent, be made in sector I. In many cases such products are made by craftsmen independent of both sectors. Through history, the work organisations of type A have proved to be the most vigorous and viable. In contrast, those of type B have died out relatively fast.

Capitalist Societies

Turning to capitalism, we find that wage labour is the dominant form of work. It is based on the fact that the wage labourers find themselves in a position where they have to sell their labour power in order to get a living. This form of wage labour ought to be distinguished from that in pre-capitalist societies because it is in principle only forced by economic coercion. It should be noted that this way of looking at the matter is not only commonplace in Marxist tradition (cf. Cohen 1978:70f), but it also exists in contemporary sociology of work, even if, in the latter case, the stress is not on the fact that the workers have to sell their labour power but rather that they do so.

In capitalist societies there is a clear tendency towards an extension of the sphere of wage labour at the expense of other forms of work. In Sweden and in the United States today more than 90 percent of the 'economically active' population are wage-earners. However, not all forms of care are taken into consideration and some of the self employment that can be characterized as petty entrepreneurial-based independent work is listed as wage labour in the official statistics.

This development, however, is not entirely rectilinear. First, there are forms of work that have proved remarkably adaptable to capitalism. In peripheral capitalism, and due to special circumstances also in other cases, forced labour has had its importance in the form of mass-slavery or in some other way. Guild-based independent work has been transformed into petty entrepreneurial-based independent work. In agriculture, family-based independent work has proved very vigorous, in some cases even at the expense of wage labour (cf. Friedmann 1978). Secondly, wage labour is also, to a certain extent, curtailed; some functions are, at least periodically, brought into the sphere of other forms of work, noticeably, different kinds of care, a field where the work of housewives is important. Further, such devices as vending machines and self-service supermarkets, replace wage labour with the customer's own activities (O'Connor 1975:315). Thus, there is interaction between the extension and curtailment of wage labour within the framework of the predominant tendency towards extension.

Two different processes can be distinguished analytically. When activities and functions which were not earlier performed by wage labourers are drawn into the sphere of wage labour, we can say that they are incorporated in wage labour. On the other hand, when new activities and functions emerge as wage labour, we can talk about an establishing of wage labour.

Expansion and Reduction of Social Forms of Work

In connection with the development of social forms of work, there seems to be a fundamental problem to which a great part of the historical variations can be related. The problem is valid for those forms of work where the primary producers are deprived of part of the fruits of their work, i.e. in the conditions of class societies. It is centered on the contradictions between the survival of the workers themselves and the appropriation of the surplus product: how do the social relationships in reconstitution and exploitation relate to each other in various social forms of work? Different solutions of this problem provide a starting-point for an analysis of the historical permanence of different forms of work. The evolution can, in that respect, be seen in the light of expansion and reduction of the number of forms.

Broadly speaking the following tendencies can be distinguished: in the earliest, classless societies there are only a limited number of forms of work. With the rise of pre-capitalist class societies there arises a welter of variations in the social relations of work, i.e. an evolution characterized by a powerful expansion of disparate forms of work. But the opposite development becomes successively more pregnant – the number of forms are reduced.

In an explanation of these changes the problem cited can be used as an important part. The historically most permanent social forms of work are those which are characterized by an arrangement under which the primary producers regulate their own subsistence. The best example is family-based independent work – a form of work which emerges already in the transition to class society and which is still important in capitalism.

While wage labour dominates in capitalism and the number of social forms of work is reduced, the interaction between the extension and curtailment of wage labour indicates an essential problem connected with this form of work. The social relations of wage labour contain a delicate balancing act between the reconstitution of the labour power of the worker and the appropriation of the surplus product.

CONCLUDING REMARKS

It is only recently – in the late eighteenth century – that scientists have started to consider the concept of work in an abstract manner. The discourse has then swung between two extremes. In the middle of the nineteenth century a German economist complained that the word 'work' covered a veritable abyss of concepts; 'it is', he said, 'an overdefined word, into which so much meaning has been put that it simply does not have any meaning at all any more' (W H Riehl, cited in Elster 1919:609). Today, the concept usually has only one meaning: wage labour. Work has turned from an overdefined to a non-defined concept.

Therefore, it seems time for social scientists to direct once again more attention to the concept of work itself. It is also important that such an endeavour is not turned into an exclusively theoretical debate. Multifarious empirical studies of the social relations of work are necessary to provide social science with a much needed, but missing conceptual apparatus.

3 Work — a contested concept

RON EYERMAN

The very possibility of discussing the concept of work points to an (for us) obvious fact: work means different things at different times and in different places. To work may be a natural/human activity, but the meaning of work, both for an individual and a culture, is subject to historical change and interpretation. Such difference in meaning can be traced in various ways, but that such differences exist seems beyond doubt. In an interesting research proposal, Maurice Godelier (1980) has traced the shifting meaning of work through its representations in language. In a similar fashion, Hannah Arendt traced the evolution of the relative value placed by Western civilization on the (for her) three constitutive elements of human behavior: work, labor and action. Finally, modern sociological thought distinguishes the meaning work has for individual actors, from the function of work in a larger social context, both of which are shown to change over time.

From the Enlightenment to the industrial revolution, Europe was a battleground of competing conceptions of work. These battles took place both in theoretical and in the practical discourse of everyday life. Godelier points out that for Quesnay, the founder of Physiocracy, only agriculture was considered real work; for him work designated productive labor, and in his conception, only agriculture was productive, all other forms and the 'classes' who performed them (industrial and commercial) were merely secondary. Marx, of course, following Adam Smith and Ricardo, was to violently disagree with this conception. Like Smith and Ricardo, Marx favored a more general conception of work, thus opposing the particularistic conception of the Physiocrats. It was left to later Marxists to reintroduce the productive/unproductive distinction as a way of separating out various forms of economic and non-economic activity, and grading them accordingly. Had anyone at the time cared enough to ask the peasant, the artisan or the newly arrived industrial laborer how they conceived work, they would no doubt have heard a variety of responses, from work being the curse of God, to the noblest gift of humankind.

The common element agreed upon by these participating intellectuals, in any case, was that work is economic activity, productive of use and exchange value, and of commodities. Opposed to prior Western religious conceptions, where work was linked to salvation or to inherent virtue, in good works, this thoroughly modern view defines work instrumentally in relation to the production of material value, where the actual physical and mental activities involved in that production may themselves be valueless. Since work is that which creates value, those who work are generators of value, and, at the same time, measured - rewarded - in value terms.

27

Now, what this value consisted of and how it was to be gauged was itself open to interpretation. Those familiar with Marx's theory of alienation will immediately recognize one (negative) interpretation: when human worth and human work are measured in (economic) value terms, humans are alienated from their true being. More recently, feminist theorists have pointed out one consequence of identifying work with productive, rather than socially necessary, labor: relegating domestic unpaid labor and those who do it to a secondary status. We will return to this point.

The notion true or species being which underpins Marx's theory of alienation, as well as that of socially necessary labor contained both in Marx's theory of exploitation and in feminist critiques of economism, points to another dimension in a concept or work: the philosophical/-anthropological. In Marx's conception, work is a defining characteristic of the human being. At the level of species being, where those aspects essential to human being are elaborated, humans are distinguished from other animals by the fact that they produce - conceptually and materially - their world and themselves. In this sense, work is productive of being, and alienated work, productive of alienated being.

One need not accept Marx's theory of alienated labor to recognize how much this anthropological conception of work - as productive of social being or identity - has permeated our modern consciousness. Whether one looks to sociological studies or to everyday conversation, one's work, what one does, is intimately linked to who one is. Work, then, is a prime source of identity in modern society; as well as economic value, work produces social value or social worth - measured both in income and status. The relation between income, especially in wages paid, and social value - the relative value placed by 'society' on a particular occupation - is another area of great current controversy. Here, also, we can mention something else in our modern conception of work: the identification of work with occupation and with paid employment.

Following this identification of work with occupation many have argued that due to the nature of modern work, its increasing rationalized character, work has become less a source of identity (even where it remains the prime source of income and of value) for individuals who perform it. Where from an anthropological perspective we may conceptualize work as productive of being and culture, empirically, it can be argued, individuals are looking elsewhere for self satisfaction. In their now classic Affluent Worker studies, Goldthorpe and Lockwood, et. al. (1968, 1969) put forward the view that modern, rationalized production encourages an 'instrumental' attitude towards work, and an inward-looking, leisure and family-oriented, 'privatized' worker. Others have argued that free-time, rather than work-time, has become for many the prime source of identity and the main area of satisfaction. We can leave aside the empirical validity of such claims and be content with drawing from such arguments another dimension to a concept of work: work as a source of meaning and structure in everyday life.

The distinction between work-time and free-time made by practically everyone and anyone who works - in 'productive' paid employment, in any case - points to the importance of work (paid employment) as a source of structure, as well as placing one in the social structure (division of labor). Work activity not only orders one's day (as the division of labor orders society), but also orders one's life. Life-cycles are measured not only by clocks and coffee-spoons, but also in cycles of productive and non-productive periods, between working and non-working life. The loss of daily structure - as well as loss of status - that accompanies the loss of work is shown by several studies to be as devastating for the unemployed as the loss of income. Just the routine of going to work is itself a source of meaning and purpose in modern, secularized society. Of course, more than routine is involved in work. For many, especially in the more skilled occupations and the professions, work provides a great source of meaning, in the sense of a calling and career, as well as merely being a source of structured purpose. In addition, work is a source of friendship and social relationships, for meeting new people outside of family and neighborhood.

Thus far, we have drawn out three dimensions in a concept of work: 1) work as productive of value; 2) work as a source of individual and social identity; 3) work as a source of meaning and structure - for both individuals and societies. These dimensions are related to levels on which the analysis of work can be carried out. Work, its meaning and nature, can be analyzed and studied from micro and macro perspectives, as well as reflected up on philosophically. Just as the labor of an individual can be analyzed at the level of his/her intentions, meaning and structure, we can also analyze that same activity in terms of its organizational forms, from the point of view of institutions or a society as a whole, and, finally, from the global perspective of human civilization, as such.

Each of these levels of analysis affix another level of meaning to a concept of work. Our choice of level greatly affects our conceptualization of the issues involved. For an individual, work may be a source of income, meaning and identity in any number of variations; from an organizational perspective work may represent a set of tasks requiring coordination, according to defined goals; from a societal perspective work may be a means of social integration, necessary for the material and spiritual reproduction of a culture. Finally, work can be conceived as the means by and through which humanity distinguishes itself from nature, even raising itself through various stages of development, to an ever higher form.

For an empirical analysis of work, one could do worse than take the framework offered by Peter Berger in an essay contained in The Human Shape of Work. Here, Berger distinguishes three aspects necessary to the sociological investigation of work: the structural, the social psychological and the ideological. By structural, Berger means that every work situation (occupation) is encased within a specific structure - which can be studied from macro or micro perspectives. Work situations vary greatly he notes, in the social worlds they create and in the types of social relationships they entail. Social psychological aspects of work refer to the processes of socialization every work situation involves. 'Work' is a milieu 'which the individual enters with his (her) personality more or less widely open to its influences' (1964:232). Learning to work involves acquiring not only discipline and new skills, but also a new self-image, as a member of an occupational group or the 'working class'. Finally, ideological aspects refer to processes through which occupations present themselves and justify themselves as valuable. He says, 'minimally, the ideology will so interpret the occupation or the particular work to enhance its importance... maximally, the ideology will produce a definition of a broad segment or perhaps even all of society in accordance with the vested interests of the occupation' (op.cit.). This analysis, it seems to me, can be fruitfully applied not only to attempts at professionalization, but also to those who would organize society according to particular class interests, thus generalizing particular interests to universal status. More theoretical conceptualizations of work (and the working class) like that of Harry Braverman (1974) focus on work as a source of identity (consciousness) and collective interest. What both Berger's and Braverman's writings have in common is the identification of work with productive activity and with occupation. This way of conceptualizing work – which in itself has great empirical validity and fruitfulness – has recently been challenged from the point of view that it excludes or relegates to a secondary status the 'work' done by women in the home, a point mentioned earlier. Dorothy Smith says:

> If we started with housework as a basis, the categories of 'work' and 'leisure' would never emerge... The social organization of the role of housewife, mother and wife does not conform to the divisions between being at work and not being at work. Even the concept of housework as work leaves what we do as mothers without a conceptual home (Quoted in Gamarnikow et.al. 1983:134).

Many others – not only women – have pointed out the consequences and the shortcomings of accepting the common-sense view of work as paid employment. Alternative conceptions are not lacking, the most popular appear as some variation of 'socially necessary labor'. Andre Gorz (1982) offers a different alternative. In his view, technological development has reached a point in the West where work, as we define it, is virtually superfluous. In a way similar to Herbert Marcuse, he proposes the radical extension of free-time in liberating men and women from 'surplus repression'. The term is Marcuse's, of course, not Gorz's. Here it is not so much the concept of work that is attacked, as the conception of humanity which underlies it. Following Hannah Arendt (1958), Gorz would overturn the contemporary value hierarchy which places labor as the highest form of human activity, and which, to a great extent, forms the organizing principle around which modern life turns. I admit to great sympathy for this viewpoint.

However, neither values nor social organization respond to the wishes of social theorists. I began this paper by noting that 'work' has meant different things in different places and at different times. It is time to ask how – by what means – concepts, such as work, acquire new meanings. Surely 'work', like 'family' is a 'contested' concept, whose meaning and interpretation emerges in the interplay between theoretical and practical, commonsensical discourse. Work is not merely, or even primarily, a scientific concept. It is also a concept through which daily life is organized and understood. As such, its meaning is not subject to theoretical fiat. Although, bureaucratic fiat can certainly affect what is conceived of as work, such as when child-care came under the organization of the state and became a source of income and employment.

How, then, do concepts of work and values concerning work change? In fact, two ways have already been mentioned. The first was in reference to the Affluent Worker studies: technological change and raised living standards can affect not only attitudes towards work, but also orientations in life. For a combination of reasons, work can become less the central defining value of life and a prime source of identity. It may very well be, as Andre Gorz speculates, that such a reorientation is becoming more and more wide-spread. It may also be otherwise. A second way conceptions of work and value priorities change is through the pressure and propagation of social movements. Feminist theorists have done much to provoke reflection about our modern concept of work. The women's movement in general, and the various ecology movements have also raised debate - and consciousness - concerning some of our basic value-orientations, including the way we 'work' upon nature and ourselves. This interplay between technological change and social movements may well be sufficient to bring about a fundamental reconceptualization of the meaning of work in our time.

In conclusion, let me return to an anthropological level. Arnold Gehlen (1980) has pointed out that the 'unfinished' nature of the human being - in the sense that we are not guided by a closed world of instincts - makes that form of purposive-rational activity known as 'work', a necessary aspect of human behavior. To this may be added a similar point regarding 'family' life: human beings must develop forms of behavior regulating the care of the young. Within these two broad constraints, an extremely wide range of alternative forms of social organization is possible. It may very well be that the concept of work as it is interpreted today, and the form of social organizations in which it is embedded - which define humanity as laboring, tool-making, productive animals - is on the verge of being transcended.

4 The notion of labour: reflections on Marx and Habermas

MICHAEL TABUKASCH

It is impossible to deal with all the aspects of Marx's notion of labour in this essay. I shall sketch here only the breakthrough of Marx's dialectical materialism in the period between 1843 and 1846 as reflected in his analysis of labour. After that, I shall point out a categorial difference between the Grundrisse and Capital as far as the concept of labour is concerned, which makes the Grundrisse in this respect appear closer to Marx's earlier writings than Capital. The change in concept is accompanied by a methodological innovation in Capital, which I shall briefly depict. Habermas attempts nothing less than to lay the foundation of a critical sociology, which intends to make emancipation and the coming of age possible. His venture is as comprehensive as Marx's undertaking. It claims to mediate theory and practice in such a way, that it reaches the goal originally set by Marx more appropriately than Marx's project does. In the second part of this paper I want to examine whether Habermas's concept of labour is an improvement that reaches beyond Marx.

MARX'S NOTION OF LABOUR

We can characterize the above mentioned period of the young Marx negatively as the overcoming of Marx's 'radical essentialism', and positively as the critical appropriation of the notion of labour, as it was developed by the national economists and Hegel.

The Paris Manuscripts mark the definite abandonment of a critique of a specific reality which took its point of departure from the criterion of the 'idea' with its corresponding idealistic conception of man and the emphasis on thinking as 'true essence' (cf. Marx 1842:418f). Marx transgresses this position by relocating true essence to man as a sensuous and active being. This objective (gegenständlich) being relates to a world of 'real objects' it must appropriate. Man is seen as 'a species-being not only because he adopts – in practice and in theory – the species as his object (his own as well as those of other things), but... also because he treats himself as a universal and therefore free being.' (Marx 1844:515). This conscious and free life-activity (Lebenstätigkeit) is man's species-character and the products of his labour are therefore objectifications of his species-life. In his products man can recognize his inner essence appearing in a sensuous and contemplatable form. As a result of this productive process, man duplicates himself. Labour is a means of self-production of his species-being, whose essence thus is material activity. The objectification of labour means appropriation of nature, which becomes humanized in the process.

33

As we would expect from the exposition above, Marx's criticism centres on the concept of labour. He praises Hegel for adopting the viewpoint of modern national economy: 'he conceives labour as the essence, the essence of man confirming itself' (Marx 1844:574); but he finds fault with him for overlooking the negative side of labour, its form of alienation in the present social reality.

Marx's specific approach in the Paris Manuscripts is not an analysis of the immanent logic of capitalism as in Capital, but a reconstruction and interpretation of the 'present fact' of alienated labour as depicted in the literature of the political economists. The present state of labour - this is Marx's basic insight - follows from the essence of today's labour. 'The worker becomes the poorer, the more wealth he produces, the more his production grows in power and extent' (ibid.:511), because the labourer's product is not his, but appears 'as a foreign being... as an independent power' (ibid.). The realization of labour by its objectification is inverted into the de-realization (Entwirklichung) of the labourer (cf. ibid.:512). The consequence of the alienation of his product is the change of productive activity itself into an externalized (entäusserte) activity. Work 'is not the satisfaction of a need, but only a means to satisfy needs which are external to it' (ibid.:514). Marx denotates this state as self-estrangement of the labourer in his 'producing activity' (ibid.:515). Man's free activity is reduced to a means, if its content is nothing but the reproduction of the physical existence. In this aspect lies the alienation of man from his species-life.

It should have become obvious by now that human labour is more than the mere activity of physical reproduction or the production of material goods. Human labour produces man himself as a social being, and in its alienated form, it (re)produces labour in its specific social determination as wage-labour etc. (cf. Autorenkollektiv 1980:56) and all the social relations that go with it. In its positive determination, it is 'meaningful, lively, sensuous, concrete activity of self-objectification' (Marx 1844:585), free life-expression (Lebensäusserung) and enjoyment of life (Marx 1844b:463).

In his excerpts (1845) on F. List, Marx concretizes his view on industry, which in the Paris Manuscripts he considered to be 'the exoteric unveiling of man's essential powers (Wesenskräfte)' (Marx 1844:543), his 'sensuously perceptible human psychology' (ibid.:542) existing in the form of alienation. He criticizes the Saint-Simonist School for confusing industry's productive powers with present day industry, which has brought them to life 'without consciousness and will' (Marx 1845:181). Only after having abolished industry will they become 'powers of man' (ibid.). Industry will then have been changed into a big workplace 'where man appropriates himself, his own forces and those of nature' (ibid.:180). 'Productive forces are an end, which originates from my nature, an end in itself' (ibid.:182). Marx destroys the 'mystical glimmer which glorifies the "productive forces"' (ibid.) by stating that, in the present system, a bent back, onesided education and mindlessness are productive forces, forces which are determined by exchange value.

In the German Ideology human essence is no longer the foil against which the essence of private property can be deciphered (cf. Vergara 1974:157f). For the time being, he has no critical notion of capital at his disposal. Instead he uses instead the concept 'division of labour' with its most highly developed form, the 'world market', to sum up the most pernicious form of inverted societality (verkehrte Gesellschaftlichkeit).

After Marx - following Feuerbach - had already taken human being from its fixation in heaven back to earth and firmly established it in the real material life of man, he now removes it from the single individual, not in order to oppose it anew to men as an abstraction separated from them, but to place it in their social relations (cf. Marx 1845b:29). Marx turns further away from Feuerbach and seems to cast aside the last reminiscences of his idealist past (but see H. Reichelt 1983).

The German Ideology marks a decisive step forward in the formulation of the concept of social labour and practice, in which the social production of the individuals is the overriding factor. Material production and reproduction of human life, and not a hypostatized economic factor, are posited as the basis and driving force of human history (cf. Schmid-Kowarzik 1981:87ff).

Marx and Engels begin their argument by establishing that the physical organization of the individuals is the basic constituent of their relation to nature and that historiography has to start from this natural basis and man's modification of it. 'What the individuals are, depends on the material conditions of their production' (Marx/Engels 1846:21), on what and how they produce. From the inception of man's history up to now, three moments have existed simultaneously: 1) the production of the means to satisfy the needs (the first historical act together with the second moment); 2) and therewith the production of new needs; 3) the procreation of man, i.e. natural reproduction. As a fourth aspect, they mention the social reproduction of man. His production of life appears now as both a natural and a social relationship.

Whilst producing his life, man develops his needs beyond the original level and thus modifies his nature. Man has a history because he has to produce his life in a particular way (cf. ibid.:28). Social labour serves as the watershed that marks the starting point from which it makes sense to speak of human history. Between the forces of production, the social conditions and consciousness there exists no linear determination.

Marx's concept of the division of labour is based on Adam Smith's. But as in the Paris Manuscripts, where he goes beyond his limited under-standing by postulating that 'the division of labour is the national-economic expression of the societality of labour within alienation' (Marx 1844:557) and that it is transcendable - contrary to Smith, he speaks of the necessity of abolishing the division of labour, if one is to cultivate the individuals' gifts and faculties in all respects. 'The individuals must appropriate the existing totality of the productive forces, not only to achieve their self-activity (Selbstbestätigung), but to safeguard their very existence.' (Marx/Engels 1846:67) This is the task of the proletariat that is excluded from all self-activity. The proletariat will do away with the existing mode of labour and will allow self-activity and material life to form a unity 'that corresponds to the individuals' development into total human beings and to the shaking-off of all naturalness (Naturwüchsigkeit).' (Ibid.:68) Thus work will have been transformed into self-activity.

As the most important result of this survey of Marx's notion of labour in the first formative years of Historical Materialism, we have obtained the insight that the fundamental content of revolutionizing capitalist society centres around the concept of the transcendence of labour. A change in property relations is but a prerequisite. During these years and those to come, Marx alters first and foremost the conception of the solution, i.e. how this emancipation of or from labour can be achieved. Secondly, only a reconstruction of the 'dialectics of labour' (cf. J.P. Arnason 1976:41-55 and 1980:137-184) and not an instrumentalist reduction of the concept of labour seems to be the adequate approach to reach and transgress the level of Marx's argumentation.

Let us now turn to the Grundrisse and see how Marx critizises A. Smith's view on labour and how he contrasts Smith's negative concept of labour with his own positive one. According to Smith, the value of labour is always constant, because a certain amount of labour is equivalent to a respective amount of sacrifice of tranquillity, freedom, happiness etc.

> It seems quite far from Smith's mind that the individual, 'in his normal state of health, strength, activity, skill, facility', also needs a normal portion of work, and of the suspension of tranquillity. Certainly, labour obtains its measure from the outside, through the aim to be attained and the obstacles to be overcome in attaining it. But Smith has no inkling whatever that this overcoming of obstacles is in itself a liberating activity - and that, further, the external aims become stripped of the semblance of merely external natural urgencies, and become posited as aims which the individual himself posits - hence as self-realization, objectification of the subject, hence real freedom, whose action is precisely labour. He is right, of course, that, in its historical forms as slave-labour, serf-labour, and wage-labour, labour always appears as repulsive, always as external forced labour; and not-labour, by contrast, as 'freedom and happiness'. (Marx 1973:611).

Marx raises a number of objections to Smith. To begin with, he rebukes Smith on methodological grounds: one cannot attain an adequate concept of labour by way of empirical generalizations. Secondly, he points out a psychological aspect: man simply would not bear a permanent state of laziness. Thirdly, we can observe an anthropological-ontological dimension in his argument, which reminds us of the conception of man as a suffering being. Having his means of satisfaction outside himself in a mainly inappropriate form, he has to overcome the indifference of the external world towards his ends. In this process his needs change and it becomes more and more the individual himself, who posits his aims. The 'retreat of the bounds of nature' is effected by labour. The teleological positing makes work a 'positive, creative activity' (ibid.:614) and guarantees men's real freedom.

Marx makes plain that neither the subjective nor the objective conditions for 'attractive work' have yet been created by labour. He then distinguishes this form from play by mentioning that self-realization means in no way, that work 'becomes mere fun, mere amusement' (ibid.: 611). There are two conditions for the coming into existence of this form of material production: '1) when its social character is posited, 2) when it is of a scientific and at the same time general character' (ibid:612). The activity of the highest level of freedom is connected with the highest development of the forces of production. 'Labour no longer appears to be included within the production process; rather the human being comes to relate more as watchman and regulator to the production process itself' (ibid.:705). But in capitalism this development takes on an inverted form. Between labour that has been 'reduced to a pure abstraction and the power of the production process it superintends' (ibid.:705) has arisen a qualitative imbalance. 'The principle of developed capital is precisely to make special skill superfluous, and to make manual work, directly physical labour, generally superfluous both as skill and as muscular exertion; to transfer skill, rather, into the dead forces of nature.' (Ibid.:587) To supersede the inverted forces of production, it is necessary to strip the objective moments of production of this form of alienation. The preconditions for this appropriation are the 'absolute growth' of the forces of production and the contradiction that is inherent in this process, which will finally lead to the bursting of the relations of production.

In the Grundrisse Marx assigns to capital the function of procuring all the preconditions necessary to transform alienated labour into emancipated activity. The great historic quality of capital is to create this surplus labour, superfluous labour from the standpoint of mere use value, mere subsistence; and its historic destiny is fulfilled as soon as, on one side, there has been such a development of needs, that surplus labour above and beyond necessity has itself become a general need arising out of individual needs themselves – and, on the other side, when the severe discipline of capital, acting on succeeding generations, has developed general industriousness as the general property of the new species' (ibid.:325). Apart from the 'reduction of necessary labour time and the creation of a state, where labouring society relates scientifically to the process of its progressive reproduction' (ibid.), capital produces the subject of its overthrow and the basic character traits of the 'new man', who is going to build unalienated society (cf. ibid.:711f). The need to develop one's needs and general industriousness are thus no anthropological constants, but the result of a specific socio-historical formation.

Capital 'creates the material elements for the development of the rich individuality which is as all-sided in its production as in its consumption, and whose labour also therefore appears no longer as labour, but as the full development of activity itself, in which natural necessity in its direct form has disappeared; because a historically created need has taken the place of the natural one.' (ibid.:325) Free time then is the foundation of a further transformation of the subject, who 'enters into the direct production process as this different subject' (ibid.:712). The fully developed individual 'reacts upon the productive power of labour as the greatest productive power itself' (ibid.). The bourgeois opposition between necessary labour time and free time will thus be abolished. Nature and the historical products of man lose their objective determining power over man, and the social individual becomes capable of appropriating the material conditions of a higher form of production and labour.

We have seen that Marx overburdens capital with positive functions to guarantee (theoretically) its transcendability. When he realizes the doubtfulness of his idea of an identity between the capitalist mode of developing the productive forces and the full development of the individual in and by work – although under capitalism in an alienated and inverted, but materially realized form – after the abolition of the bourgeois separation of necessary labour time from free time, he presents a different solution.

In Capital we can find a dual aspect in Marx' argumentation which serves as a structuring principle of his method of presentation. All central concepts from commodity via the law of value and the process of production to factory and machinery are treated in this manner. He distinguishes between the form side (Formseite) and the material side (Stoffseite). He contrasts, for instance, the specific capitalist form of the process of value formation with the 'simple labour process' cleansed from all specific historical moments of determination. The form side means a presentation of the particular socio-historical aspects of the examined object, which, in capitalism, is determined by the development of exchange value. The material side refers to use value or to an object in a general, unspecific and abstract way. The difficult task of the theory is to achieve the mediation of both sides, i.e., to show the necessary forms of objectification of value. (Cf. M. Tabukasch 1978:18ff and 1980). The material side has two dimensions: an ontological and a historical one. Likewise, the form side can be divided up. It has a purely social and a specific objectified dimension.

The concept of a simple labour process shall designate the most general aspects of the material process of appropriation of nature by man to make sure that the social form determination of the means of production and labour is not mistaken for their natural absolute form. The capitalist process of production is then divided into a social labour process and a capitalist realization process (Verwertungsprozess). Thus Marx is able to distinguish between 'higher productivity due to the development of the social process of production and higher productivity due to its capitalist exploitation.' (Marx 1970:445) The development of the social labour process is not fixed to a specific historical form of production. The capitalist mode of production has its historical and logical starting point in cooperation, and develops the social side by suspending the isolation and individualization of the labourers and the labour processes. The stages of this process go from cooperation via manufacture to 'big industry'. In the system of machinery the cooperative character of the labour process is objectified in a means of labour; cooperation has thus become technologically necessary.

The capitalist mode of production turns out to be a historical necessity for engendering the social labour process as a technological necessity. It has thus become a rational process through and through and can be characterized by continuity, regularity, systematization etc. (Cf. Marx 1970:354). In this progress of rising socialization (Vergesellschaftung) of the process of production, the individuality of the directly productive worker and his possibilities to have relevant experiences of production has become trivialized as compared to the growing necessity of scientific and technological expertise.

Let us now trace the a-historical side of labour. 'As creator of use values, as useful labour, labour is therefore a precondition of existence, that is independent of all forms of society, external necessity of nature, to mediate the metabolism between man and nature, consequently of human life.' (ibid.:57) Man depends on nature in a double sense: nature as material substance and nature as a process of creation. Man himself opposes nature as a force of nature. 'By taking an effect on nature external to him through this movement and by changing her, he changes at the same time his own nature. He develops the sleeping potentials in her and subdues the play of her forces to his own domination' (ibid.:192). Marx distinguishes as the elementary moments of the labour process, the means and the object of labour and work itself. These are familiar determinations. Nevertheless in his first remark on labour, where Marx repeats his criticism of A. Smith, he signalizes a change in the positive determination of work. He no longer confronts Smith's notion of labour with an exuberant exposition of the essential moments of unalienated work. In _Capital_ he simply demands that Smith should have considered labour as a 'normal activity of life' (ibid.:61). In the chapter on the labour process he explains what this implies.

> At the end of the labour process we get a result that has been present from its beginning in the worker's mind, i.e. in the imagination. Not only does he effect a change of form of the natural; at the same time he realizes in the natural his purpose, known to him, determining the way of his doing as a law and to which he must subordinate his will. This subordination is no single act. Apart from the exertion of the organs, that are working, the purposive will, appearing as attention, is demanded for the whole period of work, this all the more the less, it carries with it the worker through its own content and the kind of its performance, the less he therefore enjoys it as the play of his own physical and mental forces. (Marx 1970:193).

Apart from the teleological aspect as the decisive determination of human labour (cf. Lukács 1973), we encounter here a degradation of labour activity itself. It loses its dimension of self-realization and 'real freedom', and we are aware of a type of non-stimulating work which demands permanent attention and subjection of the will. This characterization has nothing to do with the socio-historical form of alienated labour, it refers to labour as such, we could also say, to its ontological dimension. As far as these characterizations are concerned, the historically realized particular modes of labour may vary in degree but not in kind. Freedom exists only as a choice of ends but not as free activity. In another context in the third volume of 'Capital', Marx places the 'full development of individuality' in the sphere of consumption. He obviously has not dropped the concept of total individuality, but only shifted it to another realm – beyond the sphere of labour (cf. Marx 1972:828). This is rather a remarkable discovery, if one considers Marx's awareness of the dangers of stipulating historical conditions for absolute ones. However, it fits well into the new solution to the problem of alienated labour mentioned earlier.

There are a number of possible reasons for this shift (cf. Zech 1983:76f). The primary reason, I believe, is that Marx realizes in his analysis of the production process of 'big industry' that the transcendence of labour, as envisaged earlier, is not a necessary result of the development of the productive forces. He does not give up the idea that capital itself creates the conditions of its suspension, but only frees capital from its historical task of producing the material elements for self-realization within labour. Marx takes this step by no longer considering 'free activity' as essential to the transcendence of the capitalist mode of production, which means of course, that he has changed his concept of alienated labour.

On the one hand, we must admit that a 'utopian' element has disappeared. As a result, this theory has become more 'realistic' in so far as he no longer claims that the development of the forces of production by capital will necessarily bring about truly free life-activity. On the other hand, he considers here neither the possibility and necessity of the supersession of the existing mode of production and of labour, nor their replacement by a new mode that even assigns the dimension of freedom and self-realization not only to the process of purpose fixation (Zwecksetzung), but also to that of purpose realization (Zweckrealisierung).

JÜRGEN HABERMAS: LABOUR AS INSTRUMENTAL ACTION

Habermas critizises Marx for not clearly distinguishing between communicative and instrumental action. Marx's notion of social practice obliterates this fundamental difference. Because of a specific historical trend, significant for our time, in which the communicative processes are being reorganized according to the blue print of technologically advanced systems, we have to recognize that the unleasing of the forces of production is not accompanied by an equivalent reduction in repression. In order to prevent the danger of an uncontrolled expansion of the scientific-technological process that is about to penetrate all social spheres, we must undertake its reintegration into the communicative context. The reformulation of basic Marxian concepts in a theory of communicative action will procure the necessary categorial tools to achieve this end (cf. Habermas 1968).

Marx's fundamental mistake, according to Habermas, is the reduction of practice to 'techne'. He did not see that material production and social interaction are two irreducible dimensions of human practice. The basic constituents of Habermas's theory that structure its different levels are labour and interaction (cf. McCarthy 1978, chap. I).

According to Habermas, labour is oriented towards the disposability of the objective world. The physical-bodily constitution of man, the tool-making animal, makes up the structural element of historical-concrete labour as purposive-rational action. Labour in this sense realizes defined goals under given circumstances. It has two components: instrumental action and rational choice: 'Instrumental action complies with technical rules, based on empirical knowledge... rational choice complies with strategies based on analytical knowledge' (Habermas 1968:62). The former implies conditional forecasts which can be right or wrong, the latter, deductions starting from value systems or maxims.

In later writings, Habermas has elaborated his basic notions. He splits, for instance, strategic action from rational choice, which relates to a competing opponent 'in so far as they (the opponents, M.T.) are determined by the intention to purposive-rationally influence the decisions of the other, guided only by their own success.' (Habermas 1976:32) Purposive-rational action has a monological structure. The subjects of action follow 'each for itself (monologically) specific preferences and maxims of decision... irrespective of the question if it is in agreement with other subjects of action or not' (ibid.:33). Even if strategic action necessarily involves at least two subjects, their relationship is structured in such a way that they treat each other reciprocally as objects. Instrumental and strategic action have as their overall purpose the domination of external nature.

After having 'reconstructed' Marx's notion of labour, Habermas can rightfully claim that the act of self-formation of the human species cannot be reduced to labour. Habermas wants to avoid this mistake occurring in Marx's categorial system. For this purpose he introduces two rationalization processes: rationalization on the level of the institutional frame, i.e. of social norms, and rationalization of the subsystems of purposive-rational action, guaranteed by the scientific-technological progress. We are interested here only in the latter process. Emancipation from external nature is, according to Habermas, due to the labour process, that makes up an invariant mechanism of the evolution of the human species (cf. Habermas 1973:71).

In his Reconstruction of Historical Materialism, Habermas distinguishes the logic of development from the dynamic of development, 'i.e., the rationally reconstructable pattern of a hierarchy of more and more comprehensible structures from events... with which the empirical substrata develop' (Habermas 1976:154).

The reconstructable patterns are basic structures, which only describe the 'logical margin' (ibid.:155) of their formation process. They cannot guarantee an uninterrupted development. Yet, the structural sequences of a society in evolution are directional. In the history of technology, Habermas claims to have found a developmental pattern. It seems

as if men had projected in turn the elementary constituents of the functional circle (Funktionskreis) of purposive-rational action that is first of all fixed to the human organism, onto the level of technical means and (as if they, M.T.) had freed themselves from the corresponding functions – first from the functions of the motional apparatus (legs and arms), then from the energy-producing human body, and finally from the functions of the sensory apparatus (eyes, ears, skin) and the brain (ibid.:163).

In order to justify the directionality of the evolutionary process, Habermas introduces 'anthropologically deep-seated general structures, which were formed during the period of hominization' (ibid.:154). Man has become the tool-making animal – this implies a specific pattern of action and view of the world. Furthermore, it means an invariable relation between man and external nature, determined by the functional circle of purposive-rational action. The structure of technology is founded in the species-specific bodily organization. The development of technology 'follows a logic, which corresponds to the structure of purposive-rational and success-oriented action, and that surely means: to the structure of labour' (Habermas 1968:56). Technology and labour are inseparably connected with each other. The above mentioned structures of action constitute the objectivity of experience and bind our cognition of nature 'necessarily to the interest in possible technical disposal of processes of nature' (Habermas 1973:49). Science, technology and labour turn out to have the same basic structure determined by quasi-transcendental interests. Their development can be put into a logical order. As far as the developmental logic of technology is concerned, Habermas relies on Gehlen: 'This law refers to an inner-technical occurrence, a process, which is as a whole not intended, but this law functions behind the back, so to speak, or instinctively, throughout the human cultural history' (cf. Habermas 1968:56). Whereas the concrete historical 'pattern of the technological progress is traced out by social institutions and interests' (Habermas 1971:345).

Habermas's notion of practice has frequently been subjected to a thorough examination (cf. Weihe 1979). His extension of Marx's notion of practice (Habermas's theory is no longer class-specifically oriented) coincides with a limitation (the formation of the subject 'takes place in the medium of self-reflexion' (ibid.:71)). 'The process of institutional-ization, not directly controllable by the subjects, (and therewith that of the material production) that progresses on the level of system integration, is excluded by Habermas' (ibid.:77). To this corresponds the marginalization of the concept of labour in Habermas's theory, which is thus connected with his concept of practice. Not only is 'the practical morality, embedded in instrumental actions, with which the working subjects react upon the experience of capitalist labour activity, instrumentalized throughout' (Honneth 1980:219) conceptually excluded, but also the critical intention that can still be perceived even in Marx's ontological notion of labour in <u>Capital</u> is lost. The unity of purpose fixation and purpose realization is broken up (cf. Bahr 1970:76f). What remains for labour is at most the choice of appropriate means for the realization of a given end. As long as the fixation of ends is implicit in the concept of labour, its dialectical structure is still reconstructable. As long as we only have the choice of means but not that of ends belonging to labour, the postulate, that interaction mediated by everyday language is the only dimension accessible to humanization, bears ideological connotations.

The closed and autonomous structure of the functional circle of purposive-rational action, whose development follows an immanent logic, excludes the possibility of social change within the labour process. The dialectics of the productive forces and production relations can no longer be made fertile for a critical analysis of the work process and the production technique, on the level of concrete-historical social formations especially the capitalist one. Only in his historic-philosophical theory are the dialectics for the purpose of concretization inserted in the abstract developmental pattern. Productive forces and production relations are thus equally reduced. The latter are 'institutions and social mechanisms, determining the way in which the work force, at a given stage of the productive forces, is combined with the available means of production' (Habermas 1976:153). They regulate the access to and the control over the production process and determine the kind of social integration. The production relations cannot determine the inner structure of a concrete production process and the productive forces can no longer be conceived as expression of historic-specific ways of the appropriation of nature by concrete societies. Habermas defines the productive forces as consisting of the labour power of the producers, the technically realizable knowledge and the organizational knowledge. They indicate the degree of the possible disposal of the processes of nature (cf. ibid.). Together with the disappearance of the dialectics of the productive forces and production relations, the 'dialectic of labour' also vanishes from social theory (cf. Arnason 1980:155). In particular, Habermas's theory misses out the possibility of analysis of such a central relation as the dialectics of the labour process and realization process (Verwendungsprozess). The consideration of the supposedly formation-specific form of the social appropriation of nature, still present with Marx, forbids Habermas's approach as bad romanticism.

In the field of labour (or technology) there is no real freedom, there are at best contortions of the given developmental path caused by the social context. Labour corresponds to the compulsion of external necessity of nature and is bound at the same time to natural laws. It is the expression for a subject-object relation that is purified from all normative aspects. Its transhistoric task is the increasing objectification of nature, ending in the total separation of man and nature.

Together with the disappearance of freedom in labour, the truly creative power from technology also vanishes and therewith the possibility of its normative control. Habermas's reductionistic and individualistic notion of technology excludes extensive and essential areas of technology. It unifies the antinomic determinations of technology as instrument and as autonomous factor. Technology is, on the one hand, guarantor for human freedom, i.e. for the domination over nature, thus a controllable means, and, on the other, it asserts itself behind our backs, i.e. uncontrollably. Habermas does not transcend the technocratic ideology either in his understanding of labour, which he conceives as a mere means, or in that of technology as a neutral instrument, or in this interpretation of man's relation to nature as its increasing objectification.

It is only consequential that Habermas must lose sight of the relationship of labour and capital, which finds its production-theoretical expression in the dialectics of labour's substitution by and subsumption under capital in the sphere of production. The later introduction of the notion of 'developmental dynamics' as an empirical mechanism and a form of appearance (Erscheinungsform) cannot transcend the one-dimensionality of his conception (Arnason 1980:177f).

Presumably, the Habermasian concepts of labour, technology and science can be shown to be projections of the respective dominant bourgeois forms onto species history. At any rate, the differentations of his notion of purposive-rational action is interpretable as the reproduction of the ideal-typical structure of industrial labour (Tabukasch 1980:35f).

It would be important to analyse how the historic-specifically conceived practice-material appropriation of nature is reflected in the conceptions of world. This is, of course, not possible without the respective mediating links. For bourgeois society, for instance, we would have to analyse, beside the history of the concrete production process, the changes in the concept of labour and its ideological function (cf. for the latter, Krämer-Badoni 1978). It could turn out that the limitation of discursive will-formation to questions of the organization of social intercourse, is already for that reason insufficient, as it imputes the frame-conditions and function imperatives of society as principally unquestionable (cf. Habermas 1973:156), yet in the analysis, they might reveal themselves as historically originated. The levelling of the difference between practice and reproduction in the basis would then be a mere reflex of capitalist reality.

5 Employment, livelihood and the organisation of resources: what is work really about? [1]

SANDRA WALLMAN

This short paper begins and ends with reference to work in industrial society but ventures into comparative discussion of the concept in between. The first section considers the effect of industrial unemployment and its implications for the topic of this symposium; the second argues for a broader concept of work under the rubric 'the work of livelihood'; the third structures the expanded concept around five propositions formulated round the question 'What is work about?'; and the fourth, following on the answer to that question, summarises an approach to work which accounts for contradictions inherent in the concept in industrial society.

I   EMPLOYMENT AND UNEMPLOYMENT

Changes in technology and political economy have led to an enormous increase in formal unemployment over the last few years. The outcome is the same whether the changes were deliberately engineered or came as the unintended consequences of government or industrial policy.[2] Similarly, the way in which unemployment figures are computed makes rather little difference to the totals – although it does, in Britain at least, define individual rights to 'unemployment benefit'.[3]

Even so, much of the popular and academic discussion of unemployment in this era is concerned to apportion blame for the crisis or to design and pay for interim measures which will allow households and national economies to weather it. Few commentators can envisage the future of work as anything other than a future built around industrial employment. In that frame, admitting the possibility that there will never again be enough of it to go around is to admit despair.[4] But it is not only the pessimistic who fail to remember that full employment has been too often neither normal nor delightful, and who neglect to note that the massive economic growth which sustained it is more likely to have been the aberration of a couple of decades than the beginning of an endlessly progressive upward trend. The optimists use the same facts in a different way: they tend to believe both that 'the unemployment' will pass, and that any job in the formal economy is better than none – i.e. if we wait long enough, jobs will come back and all our problems will be solved.

Either way, these assumptions are historically wrong and politically misleading. Only by suspending them can we begin to distinguish good employment from bad (emancipation from derogation?) and to recognise what it is that employment of all sorts actually does which makes it so vital to human well-being.

45

Marie Jahoda's classic studies of unemployment have direct bearing on our efforts to understand the meaning of work. On the basis of her own and others' studies in the 1930's and again in the 1980's, she has identified five socio-psychological effects of unemployment. Turned around for the sake of argument, the same five items constitute a useful preliminary definition of work.

Thus: in the longterm,<5> people who have lost a job suffer also loss of the structure of <u>time</u>: the reduction of <u>social contacts</u>; the lack of participation in <u>collective purposes</u>; the absence of an acceptable status and its consequences for <u>personal identity</u>; and the absence of <u>regular activity</u>. (Jahoda 1982:39. Emphases added.)

These are common functions of employment, perhaps even of employment in mindless and dispiriting jobs (as ibid.:39-42), although in passing we must remember to distinguish 'between the absence of a category of experience and the quality of experience within that category' (ibid.:47). Jahoda's statement applies to employment as a category of experience. For the purposes of this discussion we would do better to apply it to unemployment and to ask what accounts for different qualities of experience amongst the unemployed.

Consider the fact that crisis of unemployment strikes different households in different ways. Why should this be so? The differences are not narrowly economic. Economic hardship is itself a matter of relative ability to get money on the side (Pahl 1980), to manipulate the social service bureaucracies (Wadel 1979), or to deploy any marketable or exchangeable items, such as skills, empty rooms or friendly relatives, which may be lying latent in the household resource system. But the experience of unemployment varies because a job in the formal economy has value beyond its wage, and because in every case it is mediated or suffered by families or households as systems, not by individuals in isolation (Fagin and Little 1984; Marsden & Duff 1975; Wallman 1984).

II THE WORK OF LIVELIHOOD

These common and common sense observations not only account for differences in the impact of unemployment, they also suggest an agenda for an expanded concept of work. Specifically, livelihood in industrial society depends on the achievement of a sense of identity and belonging (Wadel 1973, 1979; Jahobda et.al. 1972; Jahoda 1982; A.P. Cohen 1980); on the ability to differentiate us and them in apparently transient and impersonal urban settings (Hannerz 1980); and on the capacity to manage social relationships and information (Wallman 1979b intra; Paine 1970, 1974, 1976; Wadel 1979), as much as it depends on informal economic organisation inside and outside the home (Pahl and Gershuny 1979), or on some member of the household having a job in the formal economy.

In these terms the work of livelihood is never just a matter of finding or making shelter, transacting money and preparing food to put on the table or exchange in the market place. It is equally a matter of the ownership and circulation of information, the management of relationships, the affirmation of personal significance and group identity, and the inter-relation of each of those tasks to the other.

A similar expanded concept of work is implicit in studies of unenumerated economic organisation or the informal sector (as Santos 1979; Pahl 1980; McGee 1974). It also underlies recent efforts of various disciplines to monitor changes in the form and concept of employment in contemporary industrial societies (Gershuny 1979; Wallman 1979b). Two trends are clear; one is that the availability, experiences, organisation and function of employment in the formal economy is changing; the other is that the value of work outside the formal economy is increasingly widely recognised. Although the attention of political or public policy analysis tends still to concentrate on the economic values and implications of such work, other perspectives emphasise other than economic issues, so that work is seen to entail the performance of necessary tasks and the production of moral as well as economic values.

This approach to work is built on two tenets of economic anthropology. One is that the resources used in the pursuit of goals and the maximisation of benefit are not only and not always material objects. Time, knowledge, symbolic systems, skill, organisation and the goals, values and valuations of the actor are equally to the point (Belshaw 1967). The other is that the social system can be visualised in terms of spheres, domains or sub-systems - whether of activity, exchange or meaning - to which particular resources or kinds of resources pertain, and between which they can be transposed when appropriate conditions of structure and context apply. The system idea is not peculiar to social anthropology, nor, of course, is the idea of resource conversion. But the perspective of anthropology enhances it to the extent that it notices and tries to account for the fact that not everyone classifies or evaluates the same resources in the same way, and that any one person may not do so consistently (Sahlins 1974:1-39; Wallman 1979b).

This perspective allows the observation that the boundary between work and non-work need not always be drawn in the same terms, and that sometimes - as in the cases of hunter-gather people and artists alike - it is not drawn at all (see Sahlins ibid.; Schwimmer 1979). It also makes sense of anomalies in the relation between work and money. Thus: a peasant pauses in the hard labour of hoeing to say: 'I see no work between here and the grave...' (Wallman 1969). 'Work' is what he gets paid cash to do. An actor by contrast 'rests' between contracts by taking a paid job: 'It's not work, it's only for money'. 'Work' is what he identifies with. The same perspective accounts for the fact that concepts of leisure and work identity are specific to rare contexts of time and place. The Japanese are said to work at leisure, and the English to play at work. Jogging is work or recreation, sometimes it is both work and recreation. And three similar questions asked of members of the tribe Nacirema<6> would elicit three quite different answers: 'What's your job?' 'What do you do?' 'What are you into?' Non-member outsiders would not even recognise that these questions all apply to work and to work of very different sorts.

In effect when the word 'work' is used in English, only the personal or professional interests of the speaker provide the gloss. The shift in meaning is not merely careless. It follows on significant changes in the value of work itself. Three kinds of reasons account for the variation:

Firstly, the assessment of economic or moral worth depends on where, in any system, the worker sits. This is most obviously crucial because structural or status position governs the resources at his/her disposal. It is also crucial because the assessment of value is inevitably a relative assessment. The value that I put upon my work is in some part a function of what else I could be doing; what I see others doing; what I expected to be doing at or by this time; what I expect do to next year; whether my position has changed and whether that change is for the better (Wallman 1977, 1979a); whether I am prepared to sweat for the sake of my own or my children's future benefit, or I must have my returns now (compare e.g. Kosmin 1979 with Willis 1977). Migrants in any system are said to work harder and to put up with conditions that no indigenous worker would tolerate, exactly because they tend to be future oriented and to see conditions 'away', however inhospitable, as somehow better than conditions at home. All these values are governed by other things happening, or more directly, by what particular categories of people know about or think about what is happening. The (relative) value of work is therefore a function of its opportunity costs. What am I giving up to achieve this end? And of its alternative costs: How else could I achieve it? Could anyone else do it for me? One recent study used this 'third person criterion' as the defining feature of work itself: if I could pay someone else to do this task, then this is work... (Hawlyryshyn 1978). This definition is too narrow for our purposes here, but it does indicate that, insofar as the value of work depends on what else one could be doing, it is a function of information systems and creative imagination as well as of the strictures of power and competition.

Secondly, work is not always evaluated by comparable elements in the work process. This may be because not all the possible dimensions pertain to every kind of work – certainly not to all occupations. Most work can be assessed by the value of its product, but the products of social workers, service employees and politicians are always intangible and commonly without cultural definition. They depend on a recipient client in order to exist at all. Sometimes one dimension of work is identified with another. Some evaluations focus on one aspect of work to the exclusion of others – on the performance rather than the product; on the product's beauty or efficiency rather than on the time or the energy invested in its making.

Thirdly, work is not always evaluated by the same criteria. This may be because the different kinds of work are so unalike. Subsistence work and social work, artistic work and drudgery, marriage and management are comparable but not similar activities. More important, none of these evaluations is autonomous. In any one system, the value and so the concept of work depends on other elements in that system. That is as true for individuals as for social forms: the extent to which a person values one kind of effort above another depends not only on the values of the society in which he lives, but on other things happening to him or her at the time – other options, other constraints, other obligations – and the same expenditure of physical energy has different values in different domains of livelihood. These differences are readily observed in ordinary life. We may assume, for example, that the caloric value of digging so many square metres of garden is constant – at least for one individual. But its economic value changes if I dig to grow potatoes instead of ornamental shrubs; and its moral value is drastically different if, having no horticultural purpose at all, I am digging to bury stolen goods or a dead alley cat. Similar shifts can occur on the level of relationships: the moral, social, existential etc., value of the effort I put into relating to my own spouse changes if I apply the same effort to relating to someone else's partner.

III WHAT IS WORK ABOUT?

The dimension of work which come together in so many different ways are itemised in the following five proposions. They are neither exclusive nor conclusive, but may serve to focus our discourse.

Proposition 1: Work is about control – physical and psychological, social and symbolic. The primaeval purpose of work is the human need to control nature, to wrest a living from it and to impose culture on it. There can be no social group that does not 'work' at this level. Because the business of controlling nature is a matter of technical ingenuity, it is both eased and complicated by inventions of culture and patterns of organisation. The control of nature is therefore transposed into a more general need to control the environment and the business of livelihood. The working relationship between man and nature is never unembroidered, and much of the social-cultural embroidery tends to be concerned with the control of one person or category of people over another – whether direct control by means of command over the actions of others, or indirect control, achieved either by limiting their access to resources and benefits (cf. Nadel 1957), or by devaluing the resources and benefits which they have.

In the loosest possible sense therefore, people can be said to 'make' others work just as they 'work' machines, but the analogy is limited by three particular considerations. Firstly, because work involves social transaction as much as material production. Indeed its significance is more often seen to lie in the quality of the relationships involved in the allocation, production or distribution of resources than in the bald facts of material survival (Firth 1967:4). Secondly, because work is both more and less than economic activity. It 'is at one time an economic, political and religious act, and is experienced as such' (Godelier 1972:266). However instrumental or impersonal the attitude of others to his work, therefore, it is for the worker a personal experience, his relation to the reality in which he lives. Thirdly, the control of work entails not only control over the allocation and disposition of resources, it implies also control over the values ascribed to each of them. Classification of the activities and achievements of others is more subtle than the physical constraint of their actions, but it is no less controlling for that. Because the classification of work is a function of the wider political economy, the choices, decisions and rewards of the worker are constrained more importantly by the logic of the system in which he works than by the personal whim of any boss. And because the worker too is an agent, we should also notice the extent to which bosses as such are dependent on workers and vulnerable to disruption from below (Loudon 1979; Searle Chatterjee 1979).

Proposition 2: Because it is deliberate effort, directed energy, work is about incentives. In Tikopia as in business economics, an element of purpose is contained in the simplest definition of work: work is the expenditure of human energy to accomplish ends, normally with some sacrifice of comfort and leisure (Firth 1979). But as soon as we ask what the effort is for, it becomes clear that the reasons for working vary. Even in the formal job market and despite the heat generated by wage bargaining in democratic industrial systems, few would seriously argue that money is the only incentive to effort. Strike action is more often about working conditions than about wage rates, and some people go into factory work 'only' because it is more sociable than being in an office or at home, or because they want to be with their friends (see e.g. Klein

1976; Beynon & Blackburn 1972; Saifullah Khan 1979). Certainly the most serious implications of redundancy and unemployment in industrial processes are not the narrowly economic (section I above). Sometimes the incentive to regain formal employment is hard to distinguish from a pressing need to put structure and purpose back into everyday life, i.e. to direct energy, to justify effort.

Questions about incentive are usually of the kind: How can people be persuaded to make the effort necessary to accomplish particular ends? What gives them the incentive to work especially well at particular tasks and to take pride in the work they do? How is work to be rewarded when subsistence is anyway assured – whether because nature provides warmth and fish and fruit, or because a reasonable minimum wage is guaranteed by an affluent state? But the really interesting question turns the problem of incentives around: how come people tend to work as much or as little when they are not forced to, as when they are?

Proposition 3: <u>Work is about personal identity and identity investment.</u> Personal identification with the value of work is always an important incentive to effort. Contradictions in its value are common. Economically worthless work can be personally highly valued, and socially despised tasks can be a source of pride and identity (Cohen 1979: Searle-Chatterjee 1979). The fact that works of art and ritual performances are neither useful nor negotiable in exchange does not preclude their being of immense personal or social worth. Contradictions of this kind are so commonplace that the extent of discrepancy between economic and moral 'gain' can be used as a criterion for the comparison of systems of work (Schwimmer 1980).

The worker may resolve anomalies of his/her own position by identifying with only one dimension of work. Work may, for example, be defined in terms of the place in which it is done. Melanesians prefer to work 'for nothing' in the village to doing the same work for money outside (Schwimmer 1979); cleaning one's own house is unpaid work but may enhance the reputation of the cleaner, while cleaning someone else's house is rewarded in money but not in self-esteem (Piccone-Stella 1979). In other circumstances the worker ignores specific dimensions and defines himself by the lifestyle associated with a particular job. Sometimes he has no option: the efforts of white-collar workers to preserve differentials of salary and patterns of consumption are made unusually desperate by the fact that their occupations have no other locus of identity (Fred 1979).

In every case the individual can take the option of identifying with one domain of livelihood by minimising or denying his investment in others; and he can shift his identity investment from one domain to the other according to the opportunities and constraints of circumstance. The shift is probably easiest in complex industrial society, where the domains of livelihood are curiously discrete, but it is not always painless. Each domain needs attention – occupational status is not ascribed, it must be achieved; marriage must be worked at; political concern should be demonstrated – and each contributes to the composite identity structure of the individual.Too narrow a focus of effort or energy therefore creates other problems. Where over-identification occurs, it is diagnosed as pathology: anyone too closely identified with one domain of work is a 'workaholic', bound to be neglecting other obligations and probably suffering from stress (Harrison 1979). The healthy balance would seem to be a spread of effort and energy across all of livelihood so that each kind of work gets and gives its due.

Proposition 4: Work is about symbolic and productive investments in time. Inevitably, the time it takes to do a given piece of work is affected by technology because tools extend the efficiency or the energy of the worker. An item of physical work done by hand costs so much time and energy (although these costs vary with strength and skills), but if a machine is bought to do the same task, (some) human energy will be replaced by machine energy and the input of time reduced. Recently the same has become true of mental work assisted by computer, even after the time it takes to program the machine is taken into account.

Less obviously, the time value of work will vary according to when it is done. 'Overtime' can be paid at the value of 'time-and-a-half' only if it has been agreed that a specific quantity of time is worth more at particular moments in the daily, weekly, or annual cycles. On a different time dimension, personal age or time of life is pertinent. On one hand, some tasks become easier with experience and some get harder with age; on the other, the perception of amounts of time and so of time cost is not consistent throughout a lifetime: a young child feels the year between Christmases like a century, but his grandmother insists that 'the days drag and the years fly'. The difference is due in some part to changes in biological processes, but it must also reflect patterns of livelihood.

In some cultures, at least in the performance of some tasks, no time cost is computed - i.e. time, as such, appears to have no value (Wallman 1965, 1969; Schwimmer 1979). From this perspective the scope for using time as a measure of value in economic spheres without a money currency has been very limited (see Belshaw 1954; Firth 1979). Even where money values pertain, time and money often belong to different work equations: work structures time; money rewards (some) work. Remember the unemployed man in Marienthal in the 1930s whose day had no time structure and so was 'empty'. Remember too that he reported talking to his wife as an obligation, along with waking his children for school, fetching wood and eating a midday meal (Jahoda et al. 1972). It is as though, in the absence of formal employment, other activities took up the function of giving shape and purpose to his day. They 'became work' - although not, in this case, satisfying work. We could argue that they already were 'work' on the grounds that they were necessary to livelihood, but while the value of even the most essential tasks remains unacknowledged, 'hidden', those tasks will not be dignified by the status of work and their performance will score neither social nor existential points for the worker (Wadel 1979).

Ideally, if we want to know the relation between time and work we should know not only who does which necessary tasks and how long each takes, but also who chats to whom, how much time each parent spends (or thinks it spends) with its partner, with each child. While X was doing the cooking or washing the dishes, what else was happening? Was there someone else at home who should have been doing the job? What were they doing instead? It is not hard to ask an informant who plants the yams and who tends the garden, and to observe roughly how long each task takes. But we need to know also who else could have done it, and whether there was anyone else in the garden who had nothing to do with the hoeing but worked at relating to the gardener. (Procedures designed to record the context of time expenditures are reported in Wallman 1984, Chapter 3).

Work in a sociable atmosphere or work which, while accomplishing economically necessary tasks, also fulfils social obligations should be distinguished from work which has no explicit social dimension.

Finally, to bring the rest together, Proposition 5: <u>Work is the purposeful application of human energy to necessary resources. This application converts, maintains, or adds value to the worker, the thing worked on, and the system in which the work is performed.</u> This physical definition can deal with the work of economic sectors and occupational groups as much as with individual workers. It could even be made to take in the work of managers, brokers, intermediaries, artists, ritual specialists – all those whose work cannot be measured by its material product or 'use value'. In physiological terms, each is expending energy and is therefore altered by the work effort; even psychic energy burns calories. And if 'the thing worked on' can be read to include non-material resources (institutions, symbols, information), then all systems of work are energy systems. But from the social-anthropological perspective, work can never be understood as a mechanical function of energy expenditures: it is energy directed to more or less explicit goals.

These goals can be generalized as the performance of necessary tasks and the production of necessary values – moral as well as economic. The tasks of meeting obligations, securing identity, status and structure, are as fundamental to livelihood as bread and shelter. On this basis, work may be defined as the production, management or conversion of the resources necessary to livelihood – 'the sum total of capital, skills and social claims' (Frankenburg 1966). These will vary according to environment and technology and, of course, according to what is regarded as 'necessary'. But for the moment, let us assume the necessary resources to be six: the classical trio, Land, Labour and Capital (or their equivalents) are joined by Time, Information and Identity. The fact that they operate as a system means that each can be used for or converted into the other. It also means that the scope of the whole is constrained by each of its constituent parts. Ecologists have demonstrated that the viability of any system is limited by the availability of the least available resource. By this logic, the work of livelihood will be jeopardised by shortages in any one of the six domains.

IV NECESSARY RESOURCES

This view of work as the production, management or conversion of necessary resources is elaborated elsewhere (Wallman 1984). Here it is significant that the six necessary resources are analogous to the extent that they can be valued in the same variety of ways. They are also, in the right conditions, interchangeable. In other respects the two sets of three remain dinstinct. Land, labour and capital resources are not only material, they are structural. Their form and scarcity provide the framework for action by deciding which options are available in a given setting at a given time. Together they make up the objective structure of livelihood. By contrast, time, information and identity have more to do with organisation. It is these resources that decide what is done with or within the objective structure and which limit 'the conditions of possibility' Bourdieu 1977).

In so doing they account for who does better within the constraints of a single environment - who finds the opportunities, who solves the problems, and who takes best advantage of the options available.

Although this approach requires only that these non-material/ organising resources be given as much weight as the material/structural kind, there are indications that their prior importance is a characteristic of industrial society. Apter (1964) and Gellner (1982) have argued the case for identity and information, Gershuny (1979) for time. It could be that they are in their separate ways observing the limitation of the least available resource in operation: housing, services and money resources are not scarce in industrial welfare states in the way that land or labour or capital are scarce in non-industrial settings. In the latter case, society as a whole is concerned with overall shortages. In the former, there is no overall shortage; the supplies of individuals or communities are limited more importantly by impediments to distribution and access than by any poverty of the industrial system itself. Orwell saw it too. In his '1984' it was Big Brother's total control of time, information and identity resources which enslaved industrial man. Even in ours it is these dimensions of work which make the real difference between emancipation and derogation.

Notes

<1> This paper draws at length from Wallman 1982 and 1979b, and takes a good deal of its comparative material from case studies in the latter.

<2> Although of course the possible 'cure' in either case would depend on antecedent causes.

<3> Only people who fit the official unemployment category have the right to official benefit. The welfare system changes that category from time to time. People must anyway be registered as both unemployed and available for work, and it is this register which provides current unemployment figures. Inevitably some among the unemployed do not bother to register, and some may register who are employed outside the official system - i.e. in the so-called 'black' economy.

<4> This despair affects members of all age groups but is probably most damaging among the young. Some add the spectre of nuclear war to their bleak horizon - to survive one is to suffer the other. Clearly they need to be able to identify with something other than non-existent jobs.

<5> Short term unemployment is a traditional part of the industrial worker's livelihood. The effect of long-term unemployment is another matter altogether. The difference is discussed at length in Jahoda 1982, and Fagin and Little 1984.

<6> The tribe has been exoticised by inverting its name - a strategy first used in Miner 1956.

Part II
Work and Technology

6 Discussant's paper on work and technology

EINAR THORSRUD

I assume that our task is to take stock, to see what we have as a starting point for the next 25 years. Next, we ought to ask ourselves where we go from here.

The four papers to be considered do not represent a coordinated attempt to answer the two questions I have raised. But they highlight a number of significant issues. I find it necessary to link our session to the conference as a whole, with some historical reflections on power.

I think we often make life a little more comfortable for ourselves than we ought to – and we create some trouble for others – by assuming that power is something that others possess. We do not have it. We only study it. I want to stress that we as social scientists, just as much as other power groups, have misused our power, particularly by neglecting the responsibility we have of stating our priorities – of making it clear what we think 'is in the air' in our time, to which we ought to direct our attention and our efforts. Why should we not have that responsibility when we insist that others, like governments, unions and employers, should take that kind of responsibility more seriously?

To understand better what is 'in the air today' we might benefit from stating what was in the air twenty years ago. I happened to be in Yugoslavia in 1964 at the World Congress of Applied Psychology. What were the issues on which we focused?

First, we were keen to see what a political system did about the state and enterprise power structure when the country broke away from Stalinism. More specifically, we asked what happened on different levels, with investment decisions, with market relations, with work structures etc. And we compared developments in the socialist and capitalist world.

Second, we were aware that an educational revolution was coming. Did we also report some significant research on the social consequences? The answer is no, although there were numerous introductory remarks about the significance of the issue.

Third, the question of technology was not a major issue, but there were signals that a new type of choice would be available, a conscious choice of technology (a book from the Tavistock group was in preparation).

Fourth, research on industrial democracy was reported as a growing concern in Scandinavia. We were a generation of social scientists defining democracy on the basis of personal experiences ten years earlier. In

1944, we had known what it meant to live without democracy. We asked if large groups of workers did not experience something similar on the assembly line or in similar situations. In West Germany, the context in 1944 and 1964 was obviously different. In the U.S. and France, the concept of industrial democracy was not on the social agenda. Why? It certainly is now.

Fifth, a revision of our professional field was taking place. Many of us were fed up with the mass of survey and experimental studies of work satisfaction and motivation. We wanted to become more concretely and directly involved in interdisciplinary action research related to change in the social and technological conditions of work.

I mention these examples only to show that we have the power of formulating what is relevant and what is not. We have the power and responsibility of relating work to other sectors of life, to family, education, local community, to the choice of technology etc. How do we use - or misuse - or neglect to use that power? I raise this question because it has been indicated in a previous session that our domain of work is given to us by some sort of predefined professional agreement. I think this would be misleading and a continuation of the ivory tower tradition of academic life.

I will not try to outline what was in the air ten years ago in 1974. Let me just mention a major issue which the social scientists almost completely neglected at that time. Did any of us present any significant work on unemployment? Not that I know of. Did we discuss the consequences of zero-growth? No. Are we just as blind to what is in the air today as the academic world was, for example, in 1964 about the coming student revolt? Are we still blind to the fact that the meaning of work is changing? My point is that this conference should avoid falling into the trap of becoming a market place for philosophical discussion of rather irrelevant issues. We ought to focus on what is relevant for the next ten or twenty years. Now, what are the relevant issues?

What is the focus of each of the four papers we are considering? First, I would like to point to the sad fact that the papers do not report on an accumulation of research and experience on work and technology. We still suffer from fragmented, short term pieces of research. I also think the papers reflect lack of development in methods. Not much can be said about basically new approaches and methods. Has stagnation occurred in a field of research which promised so much in 1964 and 1974? My feeling is that the answer is yes, and that we are not doing much about this sad state of affairs.

I do not in any way blame the authors of the papers for this session for the fact that two important matters are missing. They have been asked to deal with other matters. How can I best select some key issues from their papers as a basis for further discussion?

Berggren's paper is based on a study of the Swedish automotive industry where he makes a very important distinction between different types of technology. The point is that the degree of choice open to designers, engineers, supervisors, workers etc is different within different phases of production even in the same industry, (e.g. in final assembly as compared to sub-assembly). It is this kind of specific clarification of the degree of choice in different types of technology that we need. Without such clarification it is rather meaningless to ask how and by whom the choice can be made.

Another important point in Berggren's paper is the implicit assumption that choice of technology is now one of the major issues not only for technologists but for trade unions and workers. I think he is fully in line with the basic ideas of a forthcoming study by OECD: What Volvo and Saab were pioneering in the 1970's the rest of the industry is now taking for granted. I think this trend is so strong that the mechanical engineering industry as a whole should pay close attention. And the same applies to social scientists dealing with the social consequences of new technology. The question of an educational revolution for millions of workers should be raised in this new perspective.

Berggren's paper makes it abundantly clear that the meaning of technology goes far beyond machinery and other hardware. For example, planning as a form of technology is fundamental in the auto industry.

Fong's paper is a timely reminder that work and technology is a burning issue not only in the West. He makes a significant distinction between the impact of technology on the developing countries with a tight labour market (like Singapore) and its impact on those with high unemployment. What he suggests is that we can learn from the New Industrial Countries the difference in terms of learning needs and opportunities, and employment consequences when new technology is introduced in countries which are on different levels of economic development. In some countries the consequences seem quite rosy, whilst, in others, increased unemployment seems unavoidable. In the latter case the labour market will certainly also push prices and wages down. So, what are the further consequences for the old industrial countries?

Having read Fong's paper we need to ask ourselves again what development is; and what role technology plays.

Haug's paper is mainly based on specific research in the process industry, from which a new set of problem classifications arises. (An account of a series of studies in the US, UK and Scandinavia raising similar key issues would perhaps be useful.)

A main point here is that the process industry has taken the first qualitative step away from mechanization towards information technology. This step was already big enough between 1965 and 1975 to redefine work for large numbers of workers and technicians. A silent revolution took place in terms of learning requirements and opportunity for autonomy, on the one hand, and centralization of control, on the other.

One of the questions which we need to ask ourselves after reading Haug's paper is: Why does it take so long for the considerable amount of experience from process technology to diffuse into organizational design in general?

Edquist's paper gives an interesting insight into the specific conditions for choice of technology in two types of economic systems (Cuba and Jamaica). Again we learn that we should be rather careful in making general conclusions regarding the consequences of new technology. In one country mechanization of sugar harvesting leads to reduced employment and lower income. In another country the reduction of the most undesirable types of work seems to be the major consequence, plus a triggering off of new and locally adapted types of mechanization.

After reading Edquist's paper I think we need to follow up his conclusions in many directions. One set of questions is directed towards the role of unions in the control of technology. Why are unions mainly active in bargaining <u>after</u> new technology has been introduced? Technocratic types of managment take it for granted that this is the only way unions and their members could be involved. But why should unions also take this for granted? In fact, unions, at least in Norway, are fully aware that it is <u>before</u> new technology comes in that they can have an impact on the major issues. This is clearly the experience gained from the new types of technology development contracts.

A second set of questions is directed towards the threefold issue of technology, learning and employment. Again, we need the specific types of studies in the four reports to pursue these issues. So far, broad surveys and speculations of a general nature have dominated research as well as public debate.

A third set of questions could be: What are the proper units for study? Should we continue to concentrate on the plant, the enterprise, the branch, or the national industry? Why do we not change our perspective and include the local community as a central unit? It is on this level that we see, perhaps most drastically, the interplay between work and technology and other sectors of life – family, school, health, local culture, etc.

7 Industrial work, technological development and new rationalization strategies — the case of the Swedish automotive industry

CHRISTIAN BERGGREN

In much social research, technology is viewed as an independent force. Common research issues in this context are 'the effects of technical development on the organization of work', 'does technology act as a force for emancipation or for derogation with regard to people's work', etc.

However, there is much empirical evidence that suggests that this is not a very fruitful perspective when looking for the factors that determine the concrete shaping of work organizations. Technology is not a social actor which designs jobs, but is merely a means, among others, at the disposal of the social actors, viz., managers and production engineers, who have the privilege of outlining production systems. In my opinion, 'strategies of rationalization' is a comprehensive concept far better suited for explaining changes in job design, for example, than 'technical development'.

Strategies of rationalization encompass strategies of capital use (for example, an emphasis on maximal utilization of machinery in contrast to an emphasis on minimal put-through times), strategies of technical development (one such strategy is the successive elimination of all human work in specified production processes), strategies of man-power use, and so on.

Managerial choices of and changes in rationalization strategies are influenced by trends in product markets and in the labour markets, by evolving new technologies and by pressures from workers and trade unions, etc.

A singularly dominant strategy of man-power use in mass production has been the concept of Scientific Management. It is noteworthy that this has not been linked to any specific technology. Instead, the decisive factor for the implementation of Scientific Management in different industries has been the production volume.

The ultimate hard core Taylorist industry has for a long time been the automotive industry. However, during the last 10-15 years this industry has made some explicit departures from this model. At the same time there has been an accelerated influx of new technology, robots and so on. The remainder of this paper will focus on the automotive industry, which provides rich empirical material to inform the general debate concerning relations between work and technology.

TECHNOLOGY AND REFORM OF WORK ORGANIZATION IN THE AUTOMOTIVE INDUSTRY

As an effect of sustained Taylorist practices, blue-collar jobs in the automobile industry have to a very high degree been reduced to extremely repetitive and fragmented work tasks. At the end of the 60's this kind of job design underwent an international crisis - not due to the introduction of new technology but due to a wave of labour resistance and revolt. Suddenly everyone heard 'the blue-collar blues' of the impoverished and degraded work in the auto factories. One famous American example was the series of wildcats at General Motors' new assembly plant at Lordstown. However, the US recession came shortly afterwards and unemployment figures rose sharply. The Blue-Collar Blues disappeared from the public scene, to be replaced by the Japanese-American race for increased productivity. In effect, Taylorist practices in the American motor industry were hardly affected.

The development in Sweden has been a bit different. Among other things, there has been pressure from a much stronger labour movement to change old practices in job design. Production engineers in the automotive industry have been spurred to test new production systems and alternative job designs that are characterized by work in semi-autonomous groups, expanded job roles, raised skill requirements, etc.

New forms of work often demand new technical solutions, e.g. new means of material handling, or the mechanization of certain operations. However, it is often the interest in the new technology rather than the technology in itself which is new. An example of this is Volvo's auto-carrier system, which was implemented in the middle of the 70's (e.g. Volvo Kalmar). Actually this system was an invention of the 1950's, but at that point there was no interest for this alternative to the conveyor belt.

We can find new forms of work organization in production processes at very different mechanization levels. At the same time there are completely different organizational designs within processes at the same level of mechanization.

Naturally there is an important correlation between the kind of production technology which is utilized and the frequency of certain work tasks. Final assembly requires a mass of standardized manual operations. The wholesale mechanization of pressing lines, on the other hand, implies that supervision tasks become salient. (A well-known analysis of work tasks, 'types of work', and technology is found in Kern & Schumann 1977.) But technology does not decide how various tasks are combined in different ways to create particular job roles. It does not decide levels of autonomy and control, etc. It certainly has an influence, however.

Today Taylorist practices are still dominant in the automotive industry. The new and important thing is that there are real organizational choices, different strategies for man-power use. Manifestations of these different strategies can be seen throughout the Swedish automobile industry.

This paper attempts to give a survey of the organizational alternatives and their distribution throughout this industry, with respect to production systems for different types of vehicles such as passenger cars vs. commercial vehicles.

The report is based on studies conducted within a sub-project of the international, MIT-initiated project, 'The Future of the Automobile', which was begun in 1981 and completed in 1984.

Data have been collected by means of interviews and observations at numerous plants within the Swedish automotive industry (cf Berggren 1983).

STRATEGIES OF MAN-POWER USE AND PRODUCTION SYSTEM DESIGN

It is possible to identify three patterns in the arrangement of production equipment and design of jobs within the Swedish automotive industry today. They are found in their most elaborate forms in final assembly. The three patterns differ from each other in several or all of the following aspects:

- degree and type of control over the production process
- character of the layout
- work content and skill requirements
- degrees and forms of cooperation among workers
- technical and administrative autonomy at shop level (by technical autonomy is understood the degree to which the work pace is determined by the workers and not by the machinery).

The historically and currently dominant 'model' is the conventional line with its distinct series layout, and centralized and detailed control. Production positions are low-qualified and fixed to the machinery or the conveyor belt. The work organization typically polarizes jobs into two different kinds.

In low-mechanized production sections, such as assembly, there is, on the one hand, unskilled, highly repetitive work on the line, and, on the other hand, inspection and adjustment jobs requiring quite a few elements of craftsmanship.

In mechanized production sections, there are simple manual operations which are residual from a technical point of view, as well as qualified and independent maintenance and set-up jobs.

Over the past twenty years, studies have pointed out several ways in which the line-system is ineffective (see van Beek 1964; Wild 1975). Nevertheless, this model enjoys the support of production management in many plants. The most important reasons for this are the following:

- The line offers production management immediate control over the flow pace. The workers are subjugated to the coercive rhythm of the conveyor belt. This gives management an illusion of reliability: 'at least the line is predictable'.

- The line allows for a simple material supply. Articles needed in assembly, etc. are delivered at few - or only one - separate stations.

- The line is a system of administration which follows established scientific management principles: detailed division of labour, high-grade specification of tasks, prior determination of operation times and strict line-hierarchy.

With the modified line, Model 2, an attempt is made to increase the effectiveness of the production system and its ability to absorb disruptions without altering the fundamental principles of design. Thus, the product flow is somewhat more loosely coupled, for instance, by installing buffers between separate stations or sections of the line. At the same time, job roles are made more flexible. However, control over the work pace and flow of work objects usually continues to be centralized. The content of the work is indeed expanded, but almost exclusively to the inclusion of more work tasks of the same kind without more than a marginal rise in the level of qualification.

Moreover, these changes often imply substantially enhanced levels of production standards, due to new balancing systems and increased pressure on the workers to compensate for disruptions and deficiencies in quality.

The strategy of man-power use behind Model 1 and Model 2 is by and large the same - viz. the one originating from Scientific Management principles.

Model 3, which represents a genuine departure from the line model, implies a shift to a new strategy of rationalization. Some, if not all, of the following features characterize work organizations of this kind:

- In low-mechanized production sections, some variation of a parallel layout has been substituted for the series connection. It could be a complete parallelization into individual one or two man stations, or a system consisting of several flows, i.e. combination of series and parallel connections. There is no centralized rate determination, either through mechanized conveyor-belts or through the central computer control of auto-carriers. Workers regulate the work pace themselves, i.e. the system allows for technological autonomy.

- There are some forms of organized collaboration between workers, usually in the shape of production groups. Thereby, it has become possible to decentralize a lot of day-to-day decisions concerning the manning and distribution of work, requisition of material, planning of the week's operations and so forth. This means that an administrative autonomy is developed on the shop floor.

- Work content is significantly expanded through the integration of tasks which demand different kinds of skills. In production departments where manual work predominates, work cycles are substantially increased. However, in an absolute sense, even these expanded work cycles remain short, usually varying between 30 and 45 minutes. In highly mechanized production sections, there is usually an amalgamation of qualitatively different work tasks, simple operations as well as maintenance functions, in the same jobs.

- Production administration is simplified. There are fewer reciprocal flows, waiting and adjustment times are reduced and the level of capital tied up in inventory is low compared with conventional systems.

Under this new strategy of man-power use, it is possible to discover a novel insight: 'Industry is forced to recruit complete human beings to blue-collar jobs, but then has only used one or two hands in most mass production work', to quote an expert in job redesign at Volvo's Gothenburg plant.

However, as far as labour-intensive processes are concerned, such as final assembly, Model 3, as well as Model 2, usually implies a significant tightening of production standards. Thus, it is possible to advocate these kinds of job designs without abandoning a fairly orthodox rationalization perspective focused on the productivity of direct manual labour.

ORGANIZATIONAL ALTERNATIVES IN THREE PRINCIPAL PRODUCTION COMPONENTS

The distribution of the three organizational alternatives varies for the different production components. There are also divergencies between production systems for different kinds of vehicles.

In the production component for pressing the sheet-metal parts, there is a positive correlation between the degree of automation and new work forms. It was not until the major part of the highly repetitive machine operation could be eliminated that it became possible to introduce qualitative organizational changes. The degree of mechanization interplays with the volume. For that reason, the manufacture of passenger cars has come further than that of commercial vehicles in the transformation of work forms in this production component. One example of this is Volvo Olofström. The operations in the mechanized press lines at that factory are built upon integrated work teams. They are responsible for the supervision of the process, the replacement of equipment as well as for the remaining manual moments, such as the removal, inspection and packing of processed parts. The new work organization has meant a substantial rise in the qualification demands on workers compared to the machine operations at an earlier phase in the development. However, there is no unequivocal correlation between automation and new work organizations. There are other examples of plants such as the Saab operation at Trollhättan where mechanization of the press-lines has not been accompanied by any changes in the traditional job hierarchy and management. In some instances, even individual piecework has been retained in mechanized press-lines.

In the next production component, that of welding car bodies and body parts, one can also find examples of far-reaching mechanization. But the proportion of manual operations here is still high compared to that found in sheet-metal pressing. Thus, the supply and removal of materials as well as the completion and adjustment of the weldings have, to a large extent, remained manual functions. Therefore, short-cycled and fragmented work which is restrained by machinery or conveyor still dominates this sphere. New systems and organizations are more often of the Model 2 type than Model 3. Conventional systems are modified while retaining a principal line layout. Examples of such modifications are the installation of buffers, U-shaped flows instead of straight ones (to make contacts between workers easier), the parallelizing of work stations at the end of flows, as well as job rotation within production groups.

Technically and economically, it is completely possible to arrange the production equipment in quite another fashion. Robot lines could, for instance, be divided into separate robot groups. To make comprehensive changes in work organization viable, it would be necessary to disengage radically human work from the short-cycled machine operations. This presupposes a more thorough-going mechanization.

The basic stages in the construction of car bodies have been mechanized to a great degree in the manufacture of passenger cars. This is also true for the making of truck cabins at Scania's new plant at Oskarshamn.

One example of an advanced work organization of the 'third type' in this production process is the tacking line for car bodies at Trollhättan. Here workers and foremen took the initiative for a matrix organization, which consisted of large teams divided into four sub-groups. In order to get a fair distribution of monotonous as well as qualified work, and at the same time, to ensure a high level of competence, each sub-group has its own area of specialization:
- robot maintenance including programming
- adjustments
- quality control
- upkeep of tacking fixtures.

Within each sub-group, workers shift between production work (mainly fixed-position loading jobs) and work within the group's speciality. Moreover, the sub-groups are responsible for the section's administrative activities for one month at the time.

A hindrance to an increase in the level of worker qualification in the system is found in an organizational fact, not a technical one. Most of the qualified work connected with the tacking line is maintenance work and this traditionally falls within the realm of an entirely separate organization which jealously guards its preserves.

Forms of work organization vary strongly among different plants. The body shop at Trollhättan is a positive example of a high technical level that has been combined with development of work organization and labour skills. Scania's truck cabin plant at Oskarshamn constitutes an example of the opposite kind. Here advanced technology (industrial robots, etc.) has been combined with severely restricted job roles. Operators are positioned between robots where they execute repetitive tasks with no possibility of influencing the working place.

The final stages in car-body processing: additional welding, grinding, fitting, polishing, inspection and readjustment, are predominantly manual.

Even here, there is a wide margin for different solutions. Saab at Trollhättan chose to introduce a parallel layout with a group-based organization in the middle of the 1970's (documented by Karlsson 1979). Volvo has retained traditional line-organization in the manufacture of passenger cars. However, a few years ago this company also started testing new approaches. One example of this new approach is a design which involves a strong emphasis upon technical and administrative autonomy, job enlargement, and the up-grading of worker qualifications. The main part of the work - welding, fitting, etc. - is performed in parallel two-man stations. Workers bring forward and send away the work object on an auto-carrier.

A minor part of the work, above all material loading, is performed 'on-line', which means more short-cycled and fixed-position work. Similar production systems exist in the manufacture of truck cabins (Volvo Umeverken).

Assembly functions continue to be performed primarily manually. The fundamental technical changes are few and far between because of the built-in resistance to mechanization in the assembly work. Such resistance is found in the complexity of the material flow, the need to use a series of different fastening techniques, the crucial importance of the inspection functions due to the proximity of assembly to the market, and the special difficulties in automatizing these inspection functions.

Today, great efforts are being made to overcome these obstacles to mechanization of the assembly in the manufacture of passenger cars. For example, automatization of specific critical operations, of certain sub-assemblies and of some sections of the heavy component assembly is underway. The most important feature here is the mechanization of parts of the gasoline engine assembly at Saab's new plant in Södertälje. Here robots have been substituted for people in a substantial portion of the assembly operations, including the heaviest ones.

Final assembly of cars, however, is not facing any great advance in mechanization. Here, the development of specialized tools and the tightening of production standards still constitute major elements in the rationalization process. (We are leaving aside the interventions to accomodate product designs to smooth production and the often very important rationalization resulting from reduction in the number of parts through model shifts.)

In many cases substantial economic gains in final assembly could be made by radically altering the work organization. The typical inefficiencies in line production, with short work cycles such as balance delays, system losses, extra handling time, etc (cf Wild 1975; van Beek 1964) could be substantially reduced and work intensity correspondingly increased. Parallelized layouts and group organization also mean increased flexibility, e.g. faster conversion to altered production volumes or new models. Finally, they allow for high quality at the point of assembly, with few or no defects being built in, and thus radically decrease the need for readjustment operations. Despite all these advantages, there are no true departures from the line model to be found in the final assembly of passenger cars. Volvo Kalmarverken, which, after all, is an example of a modified line system (an elastic line), did not pave the way for new final assembly designs in the 70's. It was not until 1982, when Saab began to redesign its final assembly at Trollhättan, that a successor to Kalmarverken appeared. The new design at Trollhättan, however, is more conventional than the original Kalmar system. The question is why? You could say that managers spontaneously tend to minimize risks (by maintaining line control) rather than maximizing gains, e.g., by pinning their faith on promising, but uncertain, innovations, such as new work organization and altered layout.

Impulses for innovation in final assembly have been greater among the manufacturers of commercial vehicles, such as bus and truck chasses. Examples are found here of plants where the line has been replaced by parallel flows operated by production groups which enjoy administrative autonomy and a substantial up-grading of the assembly work.

However, even if it is performed in long cycles (e.g. 45 minutes or more) and at a pace set by the workers, assembly work in mass production remains repetitive and predetermined, and neither stimulates personal growth nor contains any incentive for organizational development. A long-term qualification of the direct production work in assembly seems to require a much higher level of mechanization. Only then could qualitatively new work operations such as machine supervision and maintenance become an integrated part of the job.

But as in the other cases reviewed, the key factor is strategic managerial decisions about the forms of rationalization and man-power use. Mechanization in itself does not make work in assembly departments any better. This is illustrated by Saab's robotized gasoline-engine assembly. It would be possible there to distribute the remaining routine work in quite a new fashion and qualitatively improve the job content for the assembly workers. This possibility has hardly been realized. Compared with the old design and organization (from 1972), the new plant represents a regression in the organization and content of the work. The remaining manual work in the new plant is performed at rather isolated individual work stations and work cycles have been considerably narrowed. The hope is that new design will provide a better work place from an ergonomical point of view.

CONCLUSIONS

In passenger car production, the development of new work organizations tends to have come furthest in the 'middle' of the production chains. However, the limitations on designing alternative production systems appear different in a comparison of the first component of the production process – the sub-contractors – with the final component – the final assembly.

Most of the production work in the plants of the sub-contractors could be characterized as repetitive and fragmented, often taking the form of operating semi-automated machinery. Especially among the larger sub-contractors, the blue-collar jobs seem to be narrowly restricted (cf Erixon et al. 1983). These work patterns are closely associated with the sub-contractors' structurally subordinate position in the total automotive production.

The last link in the production chain, the final assembly, is the flow's nerve centre. At the same time, it is a dust bin for the mistakes of all the other production departments. All of the problems are collected here, and it is here that production management feels the greatest need for control and supervision. And in the final analysis, these are the decisive reasons for the low level of organizational innovation in the final assembly department.

Of all the plants for the final assembly of passenger car and truck chasses in Sweden, to date there is only one where the line-model has essentially been abandoned, namely, at the Tuve plant where Volvo's heavy trucks are produced. Even here it is technically possible to return to a pure line-control. On the other hand, both at Volvo Kalmar-verken (passenger car assembly) and at Scania Oskarshamn (assembly of truck cabins) it is technically possible to depart entirely from the line model.

The obstacle is not any more a mechanized pace-setter in the shape of a conveyor-belt, but rather the interest of management in detailed control over the production flow, as materialized in specific computer programs.

During all of its history, the automotive industry has been eager to seize upon new technologies devoted to higher degrees of mechanization and automatization. In this respect, the 1980's will hardly signal a break. However, the only certain consequence of this technical development is a reduction of the input of labour in relation to production volume. As we have repeatedly stressed, decisive for work organization and job roles is not technology by itself, but managerial strategies for rationalization and man-power use. In the 1980's, as contrasted to the 1960's, genuine alternatives exist in this respect. This also applies to the most work-intensive process in car production – the assembly operations. The plants of the 90's are now taking shape. Choices of strategy can and should be influenced by workers and their unions.

8 Technology and work in sugar cane harvesting in capitalist Jamaica and socialist Cuba 1958-1983

CHARLES EDQUIST

INTRODUCTION

This paper deals with the consequences for quantity and quality of employment of technical change in sugar cane harvesting in capitalist Jamaica and socialist Cuba. The role that workers and unions play in relation to technical change is strikingly different in the two countries. These differences are also examined and related to the phenomenon of Luddite machine storming and the concept of 'appropriate technology'. The latter concept has been in fashion during the last decade as the basis for a strategy to solve the huge unemployment problem in many developing countries by using more labour-intensive technologies. An empirically based critique of the notion will be presented in the last section.

What follows constitutes one section of my much more comprehensive study of determinants and consequences of technical change in sugar cane harvesting in Cuba and Jamaica from the late 1950s to the early 1980s.<1> The empirical basis for the present paper - as well as the sources thereof - is presented in the larger study.

The four most common types of sugar cane harvesting methods are:
(i)   the cane is cut and loaded manually,
(ii)   the cane is cut manually and lifted by mechanical loaders,
(iii)   the cane is cut and loaded mechanically but by different machines,
(iv)   the cane is cut, cleaned and loaded mechanically by means of combine harvesters.

The story of sugar cane harvest mechanization is strikingly dissimilar in the two cases. In the 1950s, the cutting as well as the loading of cane were exclusively manual tasks in both countries. The mechanization of cane loading started in Jamaica in 1961 and in Cuba 1964. At the present time, practically all cane is loaded mechanically in both countries, but the dynamics of the mechanization processes were quite different. As regards cane cutting, indigenous efforts to mechanize were initiated in Cuba in 1961, but these attempts did not succeed until a breakthrough came in the early 1970s. In the late 1960s the Cubans had designed an efficient harvester, but the Cuban mechanical industry was not capable of producing it. It was therefore manufactured in West Germany. In 1981, 50 percent of the cane - 33.3 million tons - was harvested by combine harvester in Cuba. This means that more cane was mechanically cut in Cuba than in any other country. All harvesters for Cuban needs are now designed and produced in Cuba, and Cuba has become the largest producer of cane combine harvesters in the world. However, these machines are considerably less productive than some of those produced in capitalist countries including the machine mentioned above, which was designed in Cuba but produced in West Germany. In Jamaica combine harvesters were tried out in the early 1970s without success, and all cane cutting is still carried out manually with machetes.⟨2⟩

The processes of mechanization in Cuba and Jamaica are closely related to socio-economic conditions. In terms of socio-economic structure Cuba was gradually transformed into a socialist society during the 1960s while Jamaica remained capitalist. Traditionally, the most important actors in sugar cane agriculture in both countries were plantations, small cane farmers, sugar workers and unions, and the state and its agencies (see Figure 1). During the agricultural reforms in Cuba in the early 1960s, the plantations were transformed into state farms. Unemployment was high in Jamaica during the whole period studied: almost 30 percent in 1980. In Cuba open unemployment gradually decreased from 12 percent in 1960 to 1.3 percent in 1970, but thereafter it grew again and stabilized at around 5 percent in the late 1970s.⟨3⟩ (See Tables 4.1 and 5.1 in Edquist 1984.)

Table 1. *Structures, Actors and Actual Choices of Techniques in Cuban and Jamaican cane harvests in the late 1950s and around 1980 (sourece: Edquist 1984, chapter 6)*

Time / Country	Late 1950s	Around 1980
	1. Capitalism	2. Socialism
C U B A	12-15 % unemployment	About 5 % unemployment
	Plantations Small cane farms Sugar workers and unions The state and its agencies	State farms Small cane farms Sugar workers and unions The state and its agencies
	Manual cut- ting and loading	Cutting mechanized by 50 %. Loading almost completely mechanized
	3. Capitalism	4. Capitalism
J A M A I C A	About 15 % unemployment	About 27 % unemployment
	Plantations Small cane farms Sugar workers and unions The state and its agencies	Plantations Small cane farms Cane cooperatives Sugar workers and unions The state and its agencies
	Manual cutting and loading	Cutting completely manual. Loading almost comple- tely mechanized.

The theoretical point of departure for the study is constituted by a combination of a structural approach and an actor-oriented one. The latter is operationalized by means of the concept of social carriers of techniques. A social carrier of a technique is a social entity which chooses and implements a technique; it 'carries' it into society. It is defined in the following way. For a technique to be chosen and implemented in a specific context or situation, the technique must, of course, actually exist somewhere in the world, i.e. it must be 'on the shelf'. But some additional conditions must also be fulfilled:

1. A social entity that has a subjective interest in choosing and implementing the technique must exist.
2. This entity must be organized to be able to make a decision and also be able to organize the use of the technique properly.
3. It must have the necessary social, economic and political power to materialize its interests; i.e. to be able to implement the technique chosen.
4. The social entity must have information about the existence of the technique.
5. It must have access to the technique in question.<4>
6. Finally, it must have, or be able to acquire, the necessary knowledge <5> about how to handle, i.e. operate, maintain and repair, the technique.

If all the six conditions listed above are fulfilled, the social entity is a social carrier of a technique. The carrier may be, for example, a private company, an agricultural cooperative or a government agency. Every technique must have a social carrier in order to be chosen and implemented. If the six conditions are simultaneously fulfilled, the technique will actually be introduced and used. In other words, the six conditions are not only necessary but, taken together, they are also sufficient for implementation to take place. This is analytically true and not an empirical hypothesis. The empirical work instead concerns determining when the various conditions are fulfilled for which actors in which structural contexts. The result of such an investigation is summarized in Figures 2 and 3. The empirical investigation as such is presented in Edquist (1984).

'Social carriers of techniques' are specific kinds of actors. The intention is that this actor concept – and the six conditions defining it – shall function as a conceptual bridge, or intermediary link, between the structure of society and technical change, to make it easier to study the interaction between techniques and society in a detailed manner.

Table 2. *Interest in Harvest Mechanization by Actors in Jamaica and Cuba (Source: Edquist 1984, chapter 6)*

	JAMAICA				CUBA		
	Loading		Cutting		Loa-ding	Cut-ting	Cutting & Loading
	1958	From 1960	Late 60's	Mid-70's	1958	1958	From 1961
Plantations	yes	yes	yes	no	no	yes	–
State farms	–	–	–	–	–	–	yes
Small cane farms	no	no	no	no	no	no	yes **
Workers and unions	no	no	no	no	no	no	yes
State & its agencies	no *	yes	no *	no	no	i	yes
Cooperatives	–	–	–	no	–	–	yes ***

yes = the actor has an interest; no = the actor has no interest
– = not relevant; i = the actor is indifferent
*) However the state gave permission to trials.
**) The larger ones had an interest in harvest mechanization.
***) The cooperatives were transformed into state farms already in 1962

Table 3. *Conditions Defining a Social Carrier of Techniques Fulfilled or not Fulfilled in the cases of Plantation Owners in Capitalist Cuba and Jamaica and State Agencies in Socialist Cuba (Source: Edquist 1984, chapter 6)*

	JAMAICA				CUBA				
	Plantation Owners				Plantation owners	State Agencies			
	Loading		Cutting		Cutting	Loading		Cutting	
	1958	From 1960	Late 60's	Mid-70's	Before 1959	Before 1964	After 1964	1960s	1970s
Interest	yes	yes	yes	no	yes	yes	yes	yes	yes
Organization	yes	yes	yes	yes	yes	?	yes	?	yes
Power	yes*	yes	yes*	?	yes	yes	yes	yes	yes
Information	yes	yes	yes	yes	no	?	yes	?	yes
Access	yes	yes	yes	yes	no	no	yes	no	yes
Knowledge	yes	yes	yes	yes	no	?	yes	?	yes

yes = condition fulfilled; no = condition not fulfilled
? = it has not been possible to judge empirically whether the condition was fulfilled or not
*) For trials only

EMPLOYMENT CONSEQUENCES OF THE CHOICES OF TECHNIQUES

The employment situation is an important determinant of the choice of technique. The decreasing general rate of unemployment in Cuba during the 1960s combined with a serious sectorial shortage of labour for the sugar harvest led to a strong interest in mechanization among all actors in Cuba. The very high rate of unemployment in Jamaica was a basis for resistance to the mechanization of harvesting among certain actors, notably the labour unions and the state. Therefore mechanization was much more of a conflict issue between actors in capitalist Jamaica than in socialist Cuba.

A mechanical cane loader and a combine harvester are capable of replacing about 10 and 30–50 manual harvest workers respectively, although these figures may vary considerably in different contexts. Therefore the consequences in terms of quantity of employment of the mechanization of cane harvesting are quite substantial; the number of jobs affected may be significant.

The quality of employment, i.e. working conditions and qualification requirements of those employed, is also strongly affected by the choice of technique in this sector; the characters of the jobs are quite different in manual and mechanical harvesting.

QUANTITY OF EMPLOYMENT

The number of professional cane cutters in Cuba decreased from almost 400,000 to approximately 80,000 between 1958 and 1970 (see Table 4.3 in Edquist 1984). The resulting shortage of harvest labour could not in the short run be filled by mechanization and therefore large quantities of workers from other sectors of the economy were mobilized, which resulted in inefficient harvesting and a very high opportunity cost.

As an alternative to mechanization and mobilization, a third possibility to mitigate the problem of harvest labour shortage could have been material incentives. Workers' wages and other remunerations of the could have been raised to stop the flight from cane harvesting. At least

74

during most of the 1960s, when the general unemployment rate was still considerable, this could have been a viable method to keep the supply of professional harvest workers higher and thereby partly solve the problem. However, this possibility of using material incentives was not practised in the 1960s or early 1970s. The reason was an ideological one. The dominant ideology in this period was to create 'the new man' and use moral incentives rather than material ones. Thus, a means that would probably have been more efficient from an economic point of view was ruled out for ideological reasons. From the late 1970s onwards – when the ideology had changed – such material incentives were used to increase the efficiency of the harvest work. Manual harvest labour was paid according to task rates and the most productive workers could earn as much as an engineer. Automobiles and other shortage commodities were also distributed to productive cane harvest workers.

Cane Loading in the 1960s

The attempts to mechanize cane cutting in Cuba failed during the 1960s. In the case of loading, however, testing started in 1963 and a viable machine was available from 1964. In Jamaica the first experiments with mechanical loaders started in 1957, and in 1961 large-scale conversion to mechanical loading was initiated. In other words, testing started later in Cuba, but thereafter mechanization developed more rapidly than in Jamaica.

In Cuba the degree of mechanization of loading increased from 20 percent in 1964 to almost 85 percent in 1970 (see Table 4.4 in Edquist 1984). In 1966, 1970 and 1976 respectively, approximately 3,700, 5,460 and 6,000 mechanical loaders were in operation in Cuba. If a mechanical loader is operated by one man and replaces 10 manual loaders, roughly 33,000, 49,000 and 54,000 workers were replaced in the years mentioned. Accordingly, the mechanization of loading considerably decreased the shortage of harvest labour. A shortage remained, however, and the mechanization of loading in Cuba did not lead to unemployment of professional harvest workers.

In Cuba the initiative to mechanize loading was taken by the state and its agencies and in Jamaica the WISCO company was the initiator. WISCO was the largest cane and sugar producer in Jamaica and a subsidiary of the British Tate and Lyle company. This, of course, reflects the differing array of actors in the sugar industries of socialist Cuba and capitalist Jamaica (see Figure 1.) In Cuba there was a consensus of interest in mechanization of loading from approximately 1961, while in Jamaica small cane farmers and, in particular, workers and unions were opposed to mechanization (see Figure 2).

The workers and unions in Jamaica had good reasons to oppose mechanization. First of all, the general unemployment rate in Jamaica was around 15 percent of the labour force in the early 1960s. Secondly, the first large-scale conversion at the Monymusk estate led to considerable redundancy of workers. Those made redundant had severe problems in finding alternative employment. One third of them had left the area within two months and another 26 percent contemplated migration to the UK.

The two cases illustrate the difference in the socio-economic dynamics of mechanization in a labour-surplus economy and one characterized by a sectorial scarcity of labour and a decreasing general unemployment rate.

In Cuba mechanization of loading in the 1960s partly and gradually mitigated the problem of scarcity of harvest labour and it created no major socio-economic problems. In Jamaica it created a lot of human suffering and social problems in addition to lowering harvesting costs for the estate owners and raising wages for those workers that could remain employed.

Cane Cutting in the 1970s

Since no large-scale mechanical cutting resulted from the attempts to introduce combine harvesters in Jamaica in the early 1970s, no redundancy of harvest workers has been caused by such machines. Accordingly, more or less the same number of manual cutters are needed today as in earlier periods.

In Cuba 50 percent of the sugar harvest in 1980 was cut by means of combine harvesters (see Table 4.4 in Edquist 1984). This has freed a large number of manual harvest workers for other sectors of the economy. For example, the number of cane cutters employed in peak periods of the sugar harvest decreased from 274,000 in 1971 to 175,600 in 1975. The quantity of cane harvested in both these years was approximately 52 million tons. In 1979 the number of cane cutters had decreased further to 126,400, although the quantity of cane harvested was 73 million tons in that year. The main explanation for the decline in the number of cane cutters was that the degree of mechanization of cutting increased from 3 percent in 1971 to 25 percent in 1975 and further to 42 percent in 1979.<6>

The detailed figures – presented in Edquist (1984) – show that the productivity of manual cane cutters increased by 84 percent between 1970 and 1979. Hence the decreasing number of cane cutters employed is not explained exclusively by the increasing degree of mechanization. The rising productivity of manual cane cutters is another important explanatory factor.

The approximate relative importance of mechanization and increased manual cane harvester productivity respectively, as factors explaining the decline in the number of manual cane cutters needed, can be calculated.<7> 126,400 manual cane cutters were actually employed in 1979. 160,875 manual cutters were 'replaced' by mechanization and 95,360 were 'replaced' by the increasing productivity of the remaining manual cutters between 1971 and 1979. Of the 256,235 manual cane cutters 'replaced', 62.8 percent were 'replaced' by mechanization. 37.2 percent were 'replaced' by increasing manual cane cutter productivity. Hence, mechanization was the more important factor, but increased manual cane cutter productivity was also of considerable importance in explaining the decline in the number of manual cane cutters needed. The 160,000 manual cane cutters 'replaced' by mechanization represented 6 percent of the total Cuban labour force in 1970.

The 84 percent increase in productivity of manual cane cutters between 1970 and 1979 may have been caused by a number of factors of varying importance. One may have been the increasing cane yield per hectare, particularly between 1972 and 1973 and in the late 1970s, since an increased yield per hectare normally increases the productivity of manual cutters. The gradual implementation of dry cleaning centers from the late 1960s onwards may also have contributed. Thanks to these, the manual cutters did not need to clean the cane stalks nor cut them into pieces.

This considerably increased their productivity. Another possible factor is that the most productive cutters were selectively kept when the number of cutters decreased. The intensity of work may also have increased due to the new system of material incentives for manual cutters introduced in the late 1970s, and mentioned earlier in this section.

My guess is, however, that the introduction of pre-harvest burning was the most important factor since burning of cane fields may as much as double the productivity of manual cane cutters. Burning was also introduced in the 1971 zafra and diffused rapidly during the years following, i.e. it was simultaneous with the rapid increase in the productivity of manual cane cutters during the first half of the 1970s.

The breakthrough in mechanical cutting could have occurred earlier if burning had been introduced in the early 1960s. In addition manual cane cutter productivity would probably also have increased simultaneously. Hence the fact that burning was introduced so late in Cuba was, with all likelihood, quite detrimental to the Cuban sugar harvest with severe consequences also for the rest of the economy.

To summarize the discussion of manual cane cutter productivity, it is obvious that there was a large potential for increasing it already during the 1960s. If the burning of cane fields and improved material incentives had been introduced in the first half of the 1960s, this potential could have been realized earlier and the negative consequences of the shortage of harvest labour during the following period would have been considerably mitigated. Accordingly, the failure to start burning and improve material incentives for manual cane cutters in the 1960s were probably serious mistakes from an economic point of view. The first was due to ignorance or rigidity and the second was related to the dominant ideology during the 1960s.

QUALITY OF EMPLOYMENT

The choice of technique also affects the quality of employment, i.e. working conditions and qualification requirements of those employed. Mechanization of cane cutting led to a considerable generation of technical skills in Cuba, which had practically no equivalent in Jamaica. These skills concerned the operation, maintenance and repair of cane harvesting machines as well as their design and manufacture. Here I want merely to add a few comments on working conditions in sugar cane harvesting as a basis for the discussion of labour union strategies in the following section.

Manual cane cutting and loading is an arduous and dirty task which hardly requires any qualifications except physical strength and power of endurance. Mechanical cutting and loading, on the other hand, require skills to use - i.e. to operate, maintain and repair - equipment of a more or less complicated nature. These tasks are also less physically demanding than the manual work tasks. Hence mechanization and automation do not always tend to lead to a dequalification of the workers and a degradation of work, as is sometimes argued.

Our example indicates, that this is not true, at least not for the mechanization of agriculture. Since almost no qualifications are needed in manual cane cutting and loading, this task cannot become dequalified.

THE DIFFERENT INTERESTS AND STRATEGIES OF WORKERS AND UNIONS IN CAPITALIST JAMAICA AND SOCIALIST CUBA

On the basis of the previous section, I will discuss below - in a comparative manner - the role, interests and strategies of the workers and unions in relation to choice of techniques in sugar cane cutting in Cuba and Jamaica. I will also relate this discussion to the notion, or rather ideology, of 'appropriate technology', which has been intensively put forward in the field of technology in developing countries during the last decade. The discussion in this section partly has the character of a generalization from the two cases (countries) to the level of socio-economic system and is therefore somewhat speculative.

In Figure 2 we can see that the workers and their unions opposed the mechanization of cane cutting (and loading) in all situations where the structural environment was characterized by capitalism and high unemployment. But as a result of the structural changes accompanied by the revolution in Cuba, the workers left the heavy task of cane cutting on a massive scale as soon as - or even before - alternative employment opportunities were created. The Cuban sugar workers and their union had no interest in opposing mechanization in the 1960s and 1970s. On the contrary, they had much to gain from it. There were no longer any social obstacles to mechanization in Cuba. In Jamaica the structure of the socio-economic system is still such that the workers and their unions must defend the machete and fight against mechanization to remain employed and fed. Obviously the same kind of actor has different interests in different structural environments.

During the last decade the concept of 'appropriate technology' has been in fashion. The background is the huge unemployment in many developing countries. To solve or mitigate this problem it has been proposed that 'appropriate', in the sense of more labour-intensive, techniques should be used instead of capital-intensive ones. I want to stress that I am here discussing 'appropriate technology' only in the sense of (more) labour-intensive techniques, although the concept may mean very different things to different people.[8]

If the labour-intensive technique is simultaneously the more efficient one, it should of course be used. And this normally also happens if the decision-making actors function rationally. If such a technique is not implemented, the reason must be that there is no social carrier of the labour-intensive technique. If there is a conflict between labour intensity and productivity, some advocates of appropriate technology still argue that the labour-intensive technique should be used. In other words, they prefer employment maximization instead of output maximization.

A combine harvester replaces 30-50 manual cane cutters. Thus the difference in terms of labour intensity is quite large between the two techniques for cutting cane. Given the extremely low wages in Jamaica around 1970, it was not profitable for the plantation owners to mechanize cutting. The machete combined with mechanical loading was more profitable in a private sense than combine harvesters in the short run. And in Cuba, mechanization was certainly not profitable - in any sense - during the ten years of failed efforts. Thus the machete created much more employment and was more profitable than combine harvesters in the short run. In other words, the choice between the machete and the combine harvester is not a conflict case between employment (labour intensity) and profitability in the short run. Advocates of 'appropriate technology' – in the sense specified above – would therefore favour the choice of the machete over combine harvesters, and they could consider their case strengthened by the fact that their strategy coincides with the interests of the workers and unions.

This strategy of appropriate technology can actually be considered a somewhat more theoretically elaborated version of the position spontaneously taken by the Jamaican workers and unions. Conversely, the Jamaican workers follow in practice the strategy of appropriate technology.

So far I have argued only in static terms. In the long run, i.e. in a dynamic perspective, the picture becomes much more complex and quite different. The following five considerations seem to be relevant in such a dynamic context.

1. If one assumes a wage considerably above subsistence level – as, for example, in Australia – it is clear that the machete is an inferior technique in terms of economic efficiency and profitability. Thus the continued profitability of the machete in Jamaica presupposes the permanence of a low wage level. There is a trend towards increasing degrees of mechanization on a global scale. Given the competition on the world market, it can, in the long run, therefore be doubted that the machete will even be efficient enough to generate sufficient income to support the people engaged in cane cutting. At the same time we know that, in the long run, increased productivity – and thereby real wages for the workers – is closely linked with technical progress.

2. To oppose mechanization in this case implies a defence of a technique requiring inhuman jobs which the workers reject even at the price of being unemployed. It gives no hope for the liberation of man from an extremely heavy, monotonous and boring job.

3. Simultaneously, the jobs created through the mechanization of cane cutting, i.e. jobs as operators, repair crew, technicians, etc. are much more stimulating and require far more skills than manual cane cutting. Thus, mechanization in this case means a tremendous humanization of production and of social life in general. This has a value as such, although mechanization also creates a basis for increasing productivity and wages in the long run.

4. It would have been ridiculous to try to stick to the machete in socialist Cuba, since people were not willing to carry out the manual cane cutting when alternative sources of income became available.

5. In Cuba mechanization of cane cutting means the beginning of a process of technical progress which will probably diffuse to other sectors of the economy. It is a part of a process of structural change of the economy. In Jamaica the choice of the machete creates no basis for a future spiral of technical change. Hence, the strategy of 'appropriate technology', as defined above, in this case implies a perpetuation of a technologically static situation.

For these five reasons, the absence of mechanization of cutting will, in the long run, lead to disastrous results for the workers. It implies a continuation of underdevelopment both of the country and of the workers. The unions in capitalist Jamaica and the advocates of appropriate technology in the sense indicated are trapped by the socio-economic system. But they are trapped in very different ways.

The workers and unions in Jamaica are, for structural reasons, 'forced' to defend the machete – an obsolete and inhuman technique offering no prospect of a better life. For them, there is a conflict of interest between employment and survival in the short run, and humanization of work and increased productivity – for a few of them – in the long run. However, if one is only seasonally employed and half fed there is only a short run. Their time horizon can be only one year or less. In other words, they are trapped by capitalism for material reasons. This is a modern equivalent of Luddism in England during the Industrial Revolution. In a socialist environment the workers are released from the trap mentioned and there is no need for them to defend an inhuman technique. Thus, in the long run, or in socialist societies, the workers have very different interests as compared to their short-term interests under capitalism.

The strategy of appropriate technology does coincide with the interests of the workers, but only with the short-term interests of workers in capitalist countries with a high rate of unemployment. In the long-run, or in socialist societies, the workers have very different interests. Thus the advocates of the appropriate technology strategy are trapped by capitalism in a very different sense. They are simply unable to think in terms of other socio-economic systems than the capitalist one. Their minds are trapped for ideological reasons since they implicitly consider this system as the only possible one and since they think of unemployment as exclusively technologically determined within this context. These are important hidden assumptions immanent in the ideology of 'appropriate technology'. They are always implicit but not always conscious. It could be argued that the notion of 'appropriate technology' is an ideological or pseudo-theoretical expression of a modern form of Luddism.

The following quotation may be illuminating in this context:

It took both time and experience before the workpeople learnt to distinguish between machinery and its employment by capital, and to direct their attacks, not against the material instruments of production, but against the mode in which they are used (Marx 1967:429).

Essentially, the differing interests of the same actor (workers and unions) in different structural environments (capitalism och socialism) and between the short and the long term in capitalist countries, boil down to a problem of distribution of income. And the main means of distributing income is – in these cases – economic rewards from employment.

In Cuba the problem of distribution was gradually mitigated during the 1960s through a decrease in unemployment and through the implementation of a welfare system. Employment was offered to those previously unemployed, and to many of those employed in sugar cane agriculture through expansions of other sectors in the economy. Partly, this alternative employment was productive and partly it implied lower productivity in these sectors, i.e. disguised unemployment. But the problem of distribution was mitigated in the sense that practically everyone was given a reasonable income and some degree of social security.

Accordingly, if the problem of distribution could be alleviated for example through employment expansion in other sectors - under capitalist or socialist conditions - the sugar workers and unions in Jamaica would have no interest in opposing the mechanization of cane cutting. If the problem of distribution cannot be solved, the workers and unions will continue to oppose mechanization.

In a survey covering 35 cane growing regions, it has been shown that there is a strong correlation between the standard of living of agricultural workers and the degree of mechanization of sugar cane harvesting. Although the study says nothing about the causal relationship, it shows that a low degree of mechanization goes with a low standard of living and vice versa. (Fauconnier 1983). This places workers and unions in an extremely difficult dilemma. If they are not successful in their resistance to mechanization - because of a weak position of power - it will have disastrous consequences for most of them in terms of increased unemployment in the short run. If they are successful, it will have disastrous effects for the workers in the long run - in terms of the permanence of a low, or even decreasing, real wage level as well as extremely heavy and monotonous work. Hence the prospects for cane harvest workers in Jamaica are not bright.

The most viable long run strategy for the workers and unions is not to fight the machines as such, but to transfer their struggle to the social and political level. This would, of course, include a fight for securing compensation in case some workers should be replaced by machines. However, it must also include a struggle as regards the power over how to introduce and use the harvesters. The workers should fight for the power to control the pace of mechanization themselves. In this way they could make sure that mechanization is introduced only gradually and at a rate that will never exceed the shortage of labour. In this way, not a single worker would be put out of work by the machines, but the workers would still benefit from the gradual mechanization in terms of higher wages and better working conditions. In a country like Jamaica where the unions are very strong and much of the cane production is state-controlled, such a power struggle should have better prospects than in many other capitalist sugar cane producing countries.

The problem discussed in this section certainly also has its parallels in industrialized countries with increasing structural unemployment, simultaneous with the introduction of increasing numbers of computers and robots.[9] At the same time, however, the discussion here illustrates that unemployment is not principally technologically determined, as those advocating 'appropriate technology' seem to believe. [10] On the contrary, unemployment is - just like income distribution - first and foremost a socio-economic and political problem.

Notes

[1] The study as a whole will be published by Zed Books (London) in early 1985. The title is: Capitalism, Socialism and Technology - A Study of Cuba and Jamaica (Edquist 1984). It is an attempt to

investigate in detail the differences between a capitalist and a socialist country with regard to causes and consequences of technical change in a specific economic sector. The intention is to illuminate various issues related to technical change, of general importance also for other countries, in particular those of the Third World.

<2> The details of this story are presented in Edquist (1984).

<3> In the early 1980s it decreased somewhat again.

<4> If the condition of information is fulfilled for an existing technique, this does not mean that the technique is available for the social entity. The latter must also be able to gain access to the technique in a physical sense, e.g. by purchasing it.

<5> These conditions are elaborated upon in (Edquist & Edqvist 1979: 31-32), where the concept was theoretically developed in a rationalistic manner, and defined. Some minor changes have since been made in relation to the presentation there. The conceptual framework is also partly based upon Edquist (1977) and Edquist (1980). It is specified in detail in chapter 2 of Edquist (1984).

<6> The detailed figures and their sources are presented in Table 7.8 in Edquist (1984).

<7> This is done in section 7.4.1.2 of Edquist (1984).

<8> In Edquist & Edqvist (1979) various meanings of 'appropriate technology' were discussed and a critique of the concept was presented.

<9> In the industrialized countries the subject of job reductions in industry due to the introduction of industrial robots is very much discussed. According to our estimate, the total stock of robots in the OECD countries taken together was 62,000 by the end of 1983. If one robot replaces two workers, the number of jobs lost, in all OECD countries was much smaller than the number replaced by cane combine harvesters in only one small Third World country. Hence the job replacement potential of robots is much smaller than that of harvesters. The estimate of the number of robots installed is taken from Edquist & Jacobsson (1984) which deals with the diffusion of electronically controlled capital goods in the engineering industry, i.e. numerically controlled machine tools, industrial robots, computer aided design (CAD) systems and flexible manufacturing systems (FMS).

<10>In Palmer, Edquist & Jacobsson (1984) we have discussed the relation between technical change and employment in more depth. The problem was analyzed at different levels of aggregation such as machine level, firm level, industry level, national level and international level. One conclusion in that study was that unemployment is much more a political-economic problem than a technological one.

9 Automatization as a field of contradictions

FRIGGA HAUG

TECHNOLOGY IN QUESTION

To ask whether technology acts as a force for emancipation or for derogation with regard to human labour is to give technology a sort of self-determined place which it does not deserve. Technology is not a subject. Nevertheless, it is a means and, at the same time, a condition, a possibility, a hindrance to acting and working.

Technology is in itself historically and socially determined and constructed. There is no technology as such. Domination and certain understandings of the so-called man–machine relation are built into machines. In engineering we find two justifications for the construction of machines:

1. Traditionally, humans are conceived of as systems of stimulus and response. Workers are perceived as beings who are added to machines. From machines signals are sent to those beings, who have to act safely, reliably, quickly, exactly etc. One can easily recognize this as an underlying principle of automated machines and even as part of the philosophy underlying the humanization of labour. At the same time, it is easy to see that this perception of the worker as an appendix to the machine not only justifies the idea of techonology as a subject, but is also far from perceiving and using the workers' specific human capacities.

2. If we want to construct machines in such a way that specifically human forces are put to use and allowed to develop, one of the first tasks would be to give them enough information on the ongoing working process. This would change the usual information on the state of the process into historical information on the process, which would allow its future to be predicted. This line of engineering is connected, for example, with the name Kelley (1972). His ideas on machines are based on a concept of man as the only being who can choose, plan and invent. Machines therefore have to deliver data which allow man to make decisions (for a closer analysis see Haug 1982:18 ff; and Projekt Automation... 1981:240 ff).

TECHNOLOGY AS A CHALLENGE

Under the given circumstances, however, we also have to develop the ability to act and to make the best out of given machines under given relations of production.

Such an analysis is overshadowed by increasing unemployment. There is a certain coyness in speaking of hidden possibilities in new information systems, if one cannot offer a solution to unemployment at the same time. In an important conference on work reduction held by the largest German union (IGM – metal-workers) in Sprockhövel, in January 1984, Oskar Negt indicated that trade union politics in the age of automation must develop strategies which are based on the unemployed. With respect to Marx he outlined a positive understanding of automation as a force which allows an understanding of work as creative, rather than wearisome and stressful. The social relations of production, however, are in opposition to the productive forces. Increasing unemployment (here he cited employer predictions that in 1990 they would only need 20% of the workers employed in order to produce the same amount of commodities) would make the social relations of production a last obstacle to freedom and somehow make the unemployed a new revolutionay subject: 'Class conflicts of the traditional kind still determine social life to some extent; but they are traversed by a new line of fighting: it is the fight of living work against the overwhelming power of dead work, which is objectified work in societal machinery' (Negt 1984). Negt's views are in a certain sense congenial because they promise the ability to act and a solution to the problem of unemployment at the same time; still, they are a bit abstract because they do not tell us how the forces of the unemployed and those still working could be united.

Obviously we must understand unemployment as a decisive signal, as an alarm which indicates a need for basic changes. The question remains whether new technology of the given type, the average automatization, confronts us with working conditions which have fatal consequences for the workers in terms of their class consciousness, their health, their knowledge, their self-fulfilment etc. or whether it can be used to alter society in the long run and to create more human work.

Up to now, research projects on automatization are (at least in our country), generally speaking, either technology-centred (e.g. Horst Kern och Michael Schumann, to mention the most influential ones in the Göttinger institute 'Sofi') or task-centred (here the Munich research centre 'ISF' and the name of Burkard Lutz, or the Frankfurt 'IFS' should be mentioned). Both approaches can generally be seen as one-sided with complementary implicit assumptions; in the one case, it is supposed that technology is immediately translatable into activities; in the other, that tasks can alone determine what has to be done. Thus they assume, for example, that domination fully determines work.

RESEARCHING THE CONSEQUENCES OF NEW TECHNOLOGY

To avoid this one-sided emphasis, our research group (Projekt Automation und Qualifikation, PAQ) has developed a theoretical guide for empirical research which we call activity-oriented, and which we want to recommend for any research on work. If we want to find out what possibilities workers have for acting, we have to know what a worker is really doing, when working. For this purpose we have to carry out a multi-level analysis.

First we analyze the demands of the forces of production or, more precisely, the demands of the technological equipment. It is fairly easy to find out the typical demands of automated workplaces:

- to avoid disturbances and remove them
- to optimize the process
- to change the process to make new products
- to introduce new technology.

But knowing this, we still do not know what, for example, an operator is doing when fulfilling those demands. They are not identical with the practical activities.

Our next research step leads us to the tasks, as the employers define them. Tasks attempt to define a whole set of activities. Normally they include the state of the class struggle, because the demands of the unions are in a way part of the definitions of the tasks, as the employers can define them. This concerns, for example, responsibility, qualification, conditions, time etc. Divisions of labour, domination, exploitation are transformed into tasks as well as the demands of the productive forces insofar as the employers understand them. Yet tasks are far from being identical with workers' activities.

Empirical research has to determine how the workers themselves translate the demands of both the productive forces and their transformation into tasks by the employers into activities. We understand work as an active behaviour in its own sense, active in terms of the demands of the process of production and the definition of tasks.

To do research in these three steps has the advantage of combining several factors and of avoiding three problems common to industrial sociological research:

- the exaggeration or neglect of technology
- the exaggeration or neglect of exploitation and class struggle
- and finally the exaggeration or neglect of the
  workers' autonomy.

If one observes how workers act in the work arena in a field of tension whose poles are determined by the productive forces on the one hand and by tasks on the other, one can discover how they deal with hindrances or how they hinder themselves, discover new possibilities for taking action, invent new forms of learning and co-operation, master the process and overcome the most urgent obstacles. We can see that work is mostly done in an overdetermined grey zone of informality.

THE DIMENSIONS OF ACTIVITY

We need further categorial instruments to study this relation of technology and work. In our research group we differentiated activities in four dimensions. These dimensions of activities are orientated according to human development: motivation - cognition - learning - cooperation.

Here it is important not to concentrate on one of these dimensions but to study their interrelationships where the changing of one element alters the others and, at the same time, disturbs the balance for the whole. Thus we think of development as a process of crises and breaks, of deconstruction as a possibility and necessity for construction. (The interrelationship of the dimensions of activities has lately been worked out by Klaus Holzkamp in his most recent book, 1983:249 ff). To study a single dimension separately leads to the well-known theories which have long dominated industrial sociology, such as the dequalification or polarization-theory (known in Sweden as the degrading-upgrading debate). To concentrate on one dimension during research makes the researcher rather easily a very conservative warner against any changes at all. Here the mere fact that there is a demand for a change in cognition, for example, looks immediately like depravation, because it always means at the same time, that the knowledge which has been used up to now is no longer valid. Only if we study the homogeneousness of the different dimensions of activities can we detect the new type of human work.

As an illustration, I will give a short example: In some plants in the chemical industry we found a division of labour between operators who only worked at the control boards and other workers who walked around, observed the installations and carried out mechanical repair jobs (we call them 'Rundgänger'). The latter were obviously less qualified than the former, their work was more physical, they had to report their observations to the operators and they were not much respected. This divison of labour was broken in other plants. Here the operators switched places with the men outdoors at regular intervals. There was a spontaneous estimation that those operators would feel less qualified, because they had to perform these low graded tasks. But there was no doubt that the operators loved to go out, to look after the installations, that they felt more competent than their colleagues who only worked at the boards. Since this work out of doors was not very qualified according to usual standards, there was only one possible explanation for the change of the operators: the task of going around, looking after the installations and doing some repairing had altered its meaning, when built into another activity - operating. It was no longer merely routine work, but was at the same time part of a learning arrangement, because it showed on a lower level the construction of the very process which was operated from the board. At the same time it was a way of moving the body, which is very little used when operating (cf. Projekt Automation... 1980:169f).

WORKERS' ACTIVITIES BEYOND POLARIZATION AND DEQUALIFICATION

Meanwhile the dequalification and polarization debate has come to an end, at least in West Germany. Although it still practically determines the politics of the trade unions, its most influential protagonists Kern and Schumann have altered their position. Now they speak of the new type of production with the increasing importance of higher qualified work and a tendency for unskilled labour almost to disappear (see Kern and Schumann 1984). At any rate, this tendency is no longer a prognosis, which was met with very great scepticism when published by us in 1975 (see Haug et al. 1975:90), but is generally accepted. I shall give an example from the chemical industry in West Germany, where the employers' association published the following data: since 1955 the percentage of unskilled labour has drastically diminished. Whereas in 1955 every third worker was unskilled, it is now every tenth. The percentage of highly skilled labour (Facharbeiter) has increased to 64%.

In our empirical studies, we found the workers to be occupied with three main sorts of activities, which were not defined in their tasks and which should be examined more closely; they tend to support development of the workers and hence an automatization project from below. These are:

1. Activities to promote the development of production

    These occur primarily during the construction of installations and/or while beginning work on new machines or new programs; the usual task for automated labour to optimize a process needs in itself an activity which demands the capacity to develop the productive forces.

2. Activities intended to develop the cooperative relations

    Workers in automated plants often transgress the official division of labour. They start informal cooperative relations and there is a sort of arrangement of mutual criticism in order to improve work, which was formerly tabu.

3. Activities intended to develop the self (learning activities):

    These can be defined as 'playing with the installations', which is both forbidden and tolerated by employers. They can also be seen as a sort of private learning process: taking installation plans home for example, although this is forbidden.

All of these activities are ambiguous – they often strengthen competition among workers, make single workers the accomplices of the employers or provide in themselves a basis for exploitation. Nevertheless, we believe that these various forms of self-determined activities in the production process are important. They allow us to develop a more realistic picture of the worker than one which assumes that labour, for the worker, is only a means to an end. Such a realistic picture does not assume a mere instrumental (and thus stress-producing) relation between workers and work and can be of use when attempting to develop an alternative policy based on support within the industry. For this we have to understand workers as people with an interest in doing good and useful work.

CRISES, RUPTURES AND CULTURE

The more one realizes that the change in production methods called automatization appears as a crisis, the greater the necessity of looking for support for a positive automation policy. Automation is a technological revolution, it completely changes the normal way of working; it makes all work data-processing i.e. brainwork. Hence it evokes insecurities, anxieties, disorder, break-downs etc. Former knowledge and abilities are questioned. Learning arrangements – such as 'learning by doing' – are no longer applicable and, above all, former structures of solidarity and resistance – for example, the habit of collectively withholding labour – collapse. Even those habits which formerly regulated the use of energy are no longer adequate, are threatened. (For a more detailed analysis of this aspect of the necessity of a new health-culture for automated labour, see Projekt Automations-medizin 1981:234 ff).

In this situation we experience a complete change of the productive forces while the social relations of production remain the same. The necessity arises of constructing new structures of activities and of changing the culture which enables the workers to work. All these changes question the structure of the social relations of production; they are always concerned with domination. This can be illustrated by using the example of the division of labour: mental vs. physical, male vs. female. First of all, automation questions the division of mental versus physical labour, which was the basis for class separation for centuries. There is no physical labour after automatization. In another sense however physical strength has also been the basis for the subordination of women, for the gender-specific division of labor.

In data-processing those typically male virtues, which formerly allowed a 'superiority' over women, lose their power. This shift takes place in a structure of hierarchical division of labour along domination lines. Boundaries of competences are jealously protected by masters, foremen against the staff; the gender problem is woven into this hierarchical line. Masculinity is both a symbol of domination and a right to a more responsible job and, on the other hand, a sign of physical strength, which condemns a huge group of men to the lowest positions; in this respect, unskilled labourers reproduce themselves as a strongly exploited group, whereas this very oppression is their male identity articulated against women (see Willis 1977).

All of these different features form a structured domination/subordination pattern in which workers gain a certain ability to act. Differentiation from other groups of workers – skilled as opposed to unskilled workers; men as opposed to women; natives as opposed to foreigners etc. – even hostile ones, is part of this ability to act. The relations among workers have become an important field of research and intervention in two respects:

- in a general sense, as a field which has to be studied with the goal of a united working class capable of altering its situation collectively.
- and particularly in the case of automatization, as a field whose structures are breaking down. This means, among other things, that solidarity among the most class conscious workers – the skilled labourers – who form the core of the workers' organisations, is being corrupted. In this threatening, uncertain situation, privatization and isolation appear as a sort of rescue. Old structures are defended – even by the unions – and the fights are lost against the vigour of the new productive forces. But this situation is not merely chaotic, a losing battle. As we have seen, a great number of these old structural features are not only self-protecting obstacles to automatization – as virility against women and, at the same time, against office jobs; or physical work against intellectual work as part of class consciousness; they are also the obstacles to liberation, to unified action by all workers, to the possibility of increased ability to act.

Thus, new technology does not determine social consequences as such, but it does alter the conditions under which workers are used to living and acting. In a broad sense, therefore, cultural work becomes an urgent political task, especially for unions. Automatization in this respect means the chance and necessity to work against sexism, racism and ageism – all obstacles to acting on the possibilities provided by this new way of working. Cultural work has to help construct new types of identity, including what is assumed to belong to privacy and what to business, changing the perception of masculinity and feminity, of intellectuals and foreigners. We need a picture of the automation worker which offers a new basis for workers' pride, for self-fulfilment in labour and serves human interests in useful and good labour.

But it is not only the workers' own sense of identity which hinders them in utilizing the chances automatization offers. Under existing social relations of production, all possibilities, which ought to be grasped are, at the same time, generally contradictory. All progress appears as a regression or a hindrance. To utilize the chances automation offers means to simultaneously loosen and tighten the grip of existing power structures. For a humane automatization project it is, therefore, very important to really comprehend what is going on in order to be able to support workers on crucial points.

AMBIGUITIES AND CONTRADICTIONS

I will try to sketch some of these contradictions which correspond to the dimensions of activity mentioned above since they are the starting point for both workers' and employers'/management politics in automated labour.

Learning: For our purpose, I cannot work out a theory of learning and its meaning for human beings. With reference to Critical Psychology (e.g. Holzkamp 1983:121 ff) I can only state here that learning through activities as a lifelong necessity of development is a specific human trait. Thus we can judge work as inhuman if it does not provide an opportunity to develop oneself, to learn. In this respect, a huge amount of work – all routine and partialized work – can be valued as prehuman. Human capacities refer to planning, inventing, decision-making. Human work should thus be organized as a continuous learning arrangement. As mentioned above, automatization is a sort of working environment which incorporates learning into every-day work. We see this, for example, when new installations are set up. But the construction of new installations is, at the same time, an instrument used for integration and singularization by employers.

An analysis of thirty cases (nearly half of our sample cases used this special arrangement for the new workers in the automated plants – see Projekt Automation... 1980:153 ff) led to the following thesis:

Participation in the building of new installations, though a non-theoretical type of learning for a later mainly theoretical type of work, has the desired effects of forming certain attitudes because: the new team is selected from above; the staff in the form of a squad is organized in a rather military way – work is exception, test, risk; workers learn as a chance to develop and because of this, they accept overtime and sacrifice their leisure time in order to study; they experience a personal sense of satisfaction when everything functions: during this process old solidarity structures break down between those who are selected and those who are not; the new team experience themselves as heroic, as adventurers of production, polarized against those who failed; success is connected with collectives in which personal development is possible; this sort of self-determination includes its exclusion from determining or participating in the goals of production; it is not the interests of wage labour that form the basis for the new community but rather production as such.

This can be effective because the new situation in automated labour is both a chance for the worker and her/his collective self-fulfilment and for the employer, who can unite with the workers' interest in good, collective and developmental work.

Even the above mentioned habit of secretly taking plans and other informative material home to learn in the evening is, in one respect, a very human activity, a form of taking one's own development into one's own hands. On the other hand, it not only saves educational costs, which should be granted by the employers, but it is also directed against colleagues and is a form of competence born out of the fear of being rejected or failing.

Under existing social relations of production the very human activity of inventing new ways of producing is contradictory - it helps rationalize work places and increase profit.

Knowledge: Knowledge is a very crucial point. Its reservation is part of the functioning of domination. The division between physical and intellectual labour allowed domination to be based on intellectual labour, the subordination of the 'hands' to the 'head'. As far as automated labour is concerned, this very division of labour is no longer possible in the old way. The knowledge needed by a worker to operate an installation undermines the connection between knowledge and domination. The conscious relation to the process as a whole is necessary. Workers have to optimize and plan. The planning process demands social rather than profit-oriented criteria if it is to be carried out by the workers themselves. Workers' pride in their work and the desire to produce useful things are, at the same time, a basis for appropriating the necessary knowledge and carrying out this longterm work with automated machines as well as for getting adapted to given conditions and existing social relations of production. If workers are asked to decide the amounts of different products, as we, for example, experienced in an oil plant, they tend to develop privatizing actions due to the private character of the production as a whole: The different shifts start with different ways of riding the installations, competing against each other; they keep secret certain data instead of making them available to all. But, in fact, generalization is one basis for a project of alternative working from below without domination.

The ability to oversee and direct the whole production process within the given relations of production gives the workers the chance to harmonize existing contradictions. In an energy plant, for example, we found workers very much convinced that they cared about the provision of electricity for the town, conceived as light for families and electricity for the underground to take family fathers home; this perception allowed them to avoid the problem of pollution, which was a daily threat to the environment.

Thus, knowledge is not in itself a guarantee of thinking, feeling and acting in a socially responsible way. Within our social relations of production it can also strengthen the private character of producing and production.

Cooperation seems to be a very clear case especially when vertical divisions of labour become less useful even for making profit. The idea that workers would be happy about such a development and grasp the chance to work without hierarchies results from a misunderstanding of the state of the working class. Divided into a lot of different groups articulated against each other, skilled workers in particular feel really threatened by this destruction of hierarchical structures. Once their advantages over unskilled labour, over foreigners and women are destroyed, their whole identity is threatened. For new possible ways of cooperating to be accepted, cultural changes will be necessary.

Motivation: The question of why workers reserve a great part of their labour has been the main question of industrial psychology and sociology for a long time. Taylor, Fayol, Majo, Lewin, Lauterburg, Gellerman etc. are names which stand for different schools of management knowledge concerning the motivation of the workers. How can workers be influenced to really work to the limit of their strength and ability? Automatization has put this question on a quite different level, a phenomenon which has hardly been recognized up to now. Using the example of programming, I want to show that the question is no longer how to get workers really involved in their work, but more the other way round: how to help them not to be obsessed by it.

Problem-solving activities have a tendency to become independent from boundaries like working hours or, more generally, the division of leisure time from working time. The programmers we met were really fascinated by their computers. They tried to resist and experienced their machines as a threat to their privacy since they forgot time, meals, money, and families. Thus the very human quality of really being engaged in a task is, at the same time, desired and fought against. Programmers do not protest against the private form of production but against its encroachment on the private side of their lives. In the end, due to a specific half responsibility usual in capitalist plants (or even in the state apparatuses), our programmers shifted the problem to a longing for more domination. Hence they interpreted the machines as dangerously seductive and asked for praise from their bosses whom they nevertheless considered incompetent. They expressed the demand for socially meaningful work in terms of verbally given personal affection. I think it is not overinterpreting to judge that the possibilities and chances for the programmers in our sample were transgressed and partly destroyed by their being members of our society. One of the effects of our system is the privacy of the workers, which we have to take into account. This means that their personalities are formed within this society and thus the division of private freedom vs alienated jobs is not only reproduced by them but also defended against dissolution (for a more thorough analysis see Projekt Automation... 1983:12-47). Thus they criticise capitalism by acknowledging it. They shift their interest to persons from whom they expect social integration from above.

I shall close with a short summary of some contradictions we met when studying the effects of new technology:

1. Automatization makes wearisome, boring, monotonous, routine work disappear. This allows work to be experienced not as coerced but as creative, useful activity.

2. This alters the relation between working time and leisure time, the latter having been a well defended island of meaningful activity and therefore one of the victories of the working class against capital.

3. Another consequence of automatization is a new pulling together of several divided operations. It is the basis for another type of

cooperation which is less hierarchical and makes possible different relations between the working groups (men towards women, qualified towards unqualified, natives towards foreigners).

4. Furthermore, automatization does away with a Taylorist division of tasks and therefore with totally unqualified labour. This disappearance of unskilled labour presents a challenge to formerly skilled labour because of the latter's privileged position. It is, at the same time, a chance for more workers to do qualified labour as it creates increasing unemployment due to the existing social relations of production.

5. Automatization makes it possible to work in a learning arrangement.

6. Finally work is directly experienced in terms of societal responsibility; this means that nonsocial purposes (like mere profitmaking) are more easily recognized and could be refused. The means of the workers to do so increase as the production process becomes scientific.

All of these almost utopian perspectives, however, are not automatically given. On the contrary, if we just watch and let things happen, large-scale unemployment, breakdowns and destruction among those still working are the most probable consequences. Automatization is a challenge. It demands a lot of joint energy in changing society and its members in particular. Social sciences should be one part of this energy. The traditional division of labour with its domination, class exploitation and oppression of women and minorities (like the old, the young, foreigners) has to be overcome. In order to do this, we need strong organisations and a cultural revolution which includes them at the same time.

10 Employment, skills and technology

PANG ENG FONG [1]

INTRODUCTION

Since the Industrial Revolution two centuries ago, the impact of technology on employment has been a controversial issue. In the last two decades as a result of the microelectronics revolution and its far-reaching effects on employment and productivity, the issue has attracted the attention of policy-makers not only in industrial countries but also in newly-industrialising and developing countries. Governments in industrial countries, especially those growing slowly and suffering from high unemployment, fear that the quickening pace of technological change arising from the increasingly widespread use of computers and robots may displace workers and drastically change future employment patterns and opportunities. They worry that computer-based technologies will erode skills, diminish the meaning of work, and intensify social conflicts.

In some of the newly-industrialising countries, namely the four fast-growing East Asian countries - South Korea, Taiwan, Hongkong, and Singapore - the policy emphasis is different. These countries, all of whom enjoy full employment and are short of all types of workers, are promoting high-tech industries as part of their restructuring strategy. They are not as concerned as industrial countries with the labour displacement effect of computer-related technologies, but in sharpening their competitive edge in world markets, and upgrading skills.

Unlike the industrial and the newly-industrialising East Asian countries, the developing countries, most of whom have large labour surpluses because of rapid population growth, want 'appropriate' technology, i.e. technology suited to their labour-abundant economies. Their development priority is job creation through rapid industrialisation, not job quality, preservation or displacement. But their ability to attract labour-intensive firms from developed countries may be undermined by computer-based technologies that are sharply reducing the capital costs of production relative to labour costs and so making low-wage labour a less important factor in relocation decisions.

Whatever its development level and strategy, every country has to grapple with difficult social and economic issues raised by rapid technological change. In an interdependent world economy, how each country tackles the problems and promise of technology, especially that spawned by the microelectronics revolution, will influence not only its own future but also that of less developed countries. In particular, how industrial countries, the major creators of new knowledge and technologies, handle technological change will shape the ways newly-industrialising and developing countries view and use new technologies.

93

For example, if they cannot minimise the adverse social and economic effects of new technologies, this is bound to influence the attitudes of developing countries to new technologies.

This paper deals mainly with the impact of technology on employment and skills at two levels. Though its focus is largely on the experiences of industrial countries, its analysis is also pertinent to developing countries because their employment patterns are also increasingly affected by information-based technologies. The paper is concerned at the macro level with the employment effects of technological change, particularly that associated with the introduction and diffusion of computers and robots into factories and offices. At the micro level, it analyses how technology interacts with organisation to create new work patterns and behaviour. The paper also speculates on the types of skills and organisations that are likely to emerge from the spread of computer and information technology in this century.

TECHNOLOGY AND EMPLOYMENT

In industrial countries, over a century of economic expansion has shifted the working population first from farms to factories and then from factories to offices. In the process, the main form of labour has changed from manual work to machine work, and from machine work to paper work. With the advent and spread of computer-based technologies, many forecasters (e.g. Naisbitt 1982; Jones 1982) predict that work in the future will be increasingly abstract and computer-mediated, dealing with symbols in electronic networks rather than with physical things like machines or paper. They argue that computerised operations in plants and offices will render redundant not only large numbers of industrial workers but also office workers who perform routine and repetitive tasks. Jones, for example, foresees the emergence of a post-service society characterised by declining industrial and office-based service employment, the increasing irrelevance of work as we know it today, the rise in new types of deliberately time-absorbing work such as leisure and do-it-yourself activities, and more tensions between the information-rich, who are employed and well-paid, and the information-poor, who are unskilled and living on state welfare. Jones's analysis refers to industrial countries, but applies as well to newly-industrialising countries as they become more affluent and develop into service-based economies.

Jones's vision of a world where most goods and services are produced by information technologies and robot-manned factories overstates the transforming power of microelectronics and underestimates the capacity of economies to create new jobs as technological change destroys old ones. It is one thing to suggest that the trend towards an information society is accelerating due to the diffusion of computer technology, but quite another to extrapolate from this trend a radically transformed information-based society with few industrial and office workers and much time-absorbing work.

Historically, employment in industrial countries expanded with rapid technological change - the mainspring of economic progress and the source of the high living standards industrial countries enjoy today. The rise in demand-sensitive tertiary activities (transport, storage, retailing, tourism, entertainment, personal and professional services) and primarily information-based employment (teaching, research, telecommunications, office work etc.) has more than matched the decline in industrial employment. In the 1970s, this increase in service employment, however, was not enough to absorb the large influx of postwar babies into the job market.

When computers were first introduced into office applications in the United States about two decades ago, pessimists predicted large-scale, permanent displacement of clerical workers. The reality was rather different; the growing use of computers has been accompanied by the doubling of clerical employment in the U.S. since 1960 (Riche 1983:14).

Several factors explain why computers have not displaced large numbers of clerical workers in the U.S. or elsewhere. First, the volume of work expands with economic growth, offsetting jobs eliminated by computers. Second, computers create opportunities for new activities, e.g. the preparation of more timely reports. Third, they require new workers - system analysts, programmers, keypunch operators etc - to service and use them. Finally, they generate new jobs in manufacturing for engineers, technicians, and operators.

Technological change has not led to widespread unemployment in newly-industrialising countries either. In Singapore, for example, rapid automation and mechanisation in the expanding export-oriented electronics industry have not reduced total employment; the number of jobs created by the industry's increasing output and scale of production far exceed the number of jobs destroyed by capital-labour substitution (Lim and Pang 1981:52). If anything, the phenomenal growth of the industry, which is dominated by multinational firms, has increased demand for all types of workers, aggravating domestic labour shortages and encouraging firms to automate and mechanise further.

Historically, the impact of technological change on employment has varied by industry in advanced countries. It has not always been in terms of computer technology or automation. Mechanisation, use of larger capacity equipment, and faster machines have also changed skill requirements. Some industries, such as electronics, banking, tourism, air transportation and telecommunications, with greater application of technological advances have recorded impressive employment and productivity gains. Others, like shipbuilding, textiles, garments, and footwear have grown slowly or declined, not so much because of the direct effect of technological innovations but because of competition from imports, and failure to modernise.

Though its general effect is positive, technological change inevitably causes dislocations because its impact falls unequally on different groups of workers. In particular, computer technology and automation have weakened the demand for unskilled and semi-skilled workers, and increased the demand for specialists, technicians and white-collar workers. Worldwide redeployment of industry may further reduce the demand for unskilled labour in industrial countries; for competitive reasons, developed-country firms such as those making electronic sub-assemblies and components and other labour-intensive products have to relocate to low-wage, stable locations. Protectionism and new technologies that drastically cut the need for labour could slow worldwide industrial restructuring. Even so, many newly-industrialising countries, such as Taiwan, Hongkong and Singapore will continue to lure foreign investors from developed countries with attractive investment incentives, industrial peace, low-cost suppliers, and disciplined workers.

Since the early 1970s, industry's contribution to employment growth in industrial countries has been nil or negative. In newly-industrialised countries, industrial employment expansion was exceptionally rapid in the 1970s, but has slowed in the last few years. In these countries, as in the industrial countries, it is service employment in the government sector, transportation, financial and business services, personal and professional services that has grown fastest in recent years.

In industrial countries, the changing pattern of job supply associated with technological change may reinforce the long-term trend of rising unemployment that has developed because of increasing institutional rigidities, loss of economic dynamism, and ageing populations. Industrial workers displaced by import competition and/or computer-related technologies will not take, or cannot fit into, lower-paid jobs in the tertiary sector. Many are geographically immobile and cannot or will not move to areas where tertiary employment is expanding. They are also costly to hire in terms of wages and benefits compared with women and young workers. Thus the shift towards service employment will induce more women to enter the job market while prolonging the unemployment of displaced workers. Moreover, it will raise frictional unemployment since turnover is faster in services than in industry.

Other features of the labour market make it less likely that technologically-induced structural unemployment will decline in the foreseeable future in industrial countries, even if there is sustained economic expansion. New entrants into the job market are increasingly better-educated and, partly because of unemployment benefits and changing values towards work, are more able and willing to wait longer for the job that meets their aspirations. Government policies on social insurance, training, sickness benefits, etc increase the fixed component of labour costs with the result that these costs are increasingly rigid and are not responsive to changing market conditions.

While the prospect in industrial countries is one of rising technological unemployment in the manufacturing sector, that in newly-industrialising countries is one of rising demand for unskilled labour, assuming their growth momentum does not slacken because of a new world recession (Lim and Pang 1984). The newly-industrialising countries believe that high-tech industry will create a demand for highly-skilled professionals and technicians and curb the demand for unskilled, especially female, labour. In fact, high-tech industry, especially the manufacturing operations they promote, will be for many years to come intensive in the use of unskilled labour. In many products and processes, rapid technological change, short product life-cycles, small series and customised production, make automation difficult and uneconomic. Unskilled labour is the most flexible factor of production, since it can be retrained and redeployed more easily and quickly than a new machine can be designed and manufactured. It can also be profitably employed in small-scale and fluctuating production.

TECHNOLOGY AND SKILLS

Computer technology will change the demand for skills in the future. Some writers (e.g. Evans 1980; Jones 1982) believe it will radically reshape occupational and organisational patterns. They envision that advances in microprocessor-based technologies such as robotics equipped with vision and touch capabilities will eventually displace most industrial jobs, even those now performed by highly-skilled humans who control and guide machines (Evans 1980:148). Even in the area of office employment, an area where computers have created many clerical, maintenance, and technical jobs, new computer technologies, as they become increasingly more 'intelligent' and flexible, will displace large numbers of clerical workers now engaged in routine and repetitive tasks of entering and compiling data. As low-cost quality-rich information systems become available, the demand for middle managers whose work consists of compiling, assessing and presenting information will also decline. With sophisticated high-quality data systems, top managers will be able to make decisions without relying on inputs from middle managers. They will be able to analyse more information from different areas and assess more quickly the consequences of different business decisions. They will become of necessity less specialised in outlook and will need to develop 'helicopter' skills to help them evaluate the broad picture.

Some forecasters believe that, besides reducing the demand for middle management, the spread of high-quality information systems will lead to the decentralisation of decision-making and the emergence of smaller work organisations (Jones 1982:91-95). Opportunities for home-based computer-linked work will increase, reducing the need for commuting and for large offices in cities. Bureaucracies will wither. Work arrangements will become more flexible, job sharing more feasible. Power will be increasingly concentrated to a small number of persons who control the development of software and direct the transfer of information into knowledge. The medical, legal, and teaching professions will decline in status and importance as computer technology demystifies them and makes them more accessible to laymen. But jobs on the low-end of the socio-economic ladder - packing, cleaning, truck-driving, serving - will rise in importance as they cannot be economically displaced by technology, at least in this century. The information-based economy will need only a few people to produce the goods and office-based services required to satisfy the material wants of the population.

Microelectronics technology will continue to expand in range, capacity, and reliability in the future. Its price will continue to fall while its power increases exponentially. This does not mean that there are no limitations to its capabilities and that it will transform beyond recognition the economic landscape of industrial countries. In the first place, microelectronics technology will have great impact only where pure information processes are involved. Where a physical process is involved, its potential will not be as great; computer programmes can instruct a machine to cut metal but the cutting itself is a physical process whose improvement will depend on such factors as advances in materials and process technology, and better machine design.

Secondly, present manufacturing methods limit the potential of microelectronics in key industries in advanced countries. Futurists tend to see manufacturing as one undifferentiated sector. In fact, there are three types of manufacturing - mass production (e.g. automobile assembly, home appliances, consumer products), customised production (e.g. aircraft assembly, oil rigs, ships), and batch production (e.g. machine tools, computers, and computer peripherals). In mass production, capital equipment is highly specialised; the production process is highly automated and capital intensive, and raw materials account for a very high proportion of manufacturing costs. These characteristics of mass production limit the potential of electronics, which can reduce the cost of control systems but will not alter the basic features of mass production.

In customised manufacturing, the production run is small and the labour skills required highly specialised. Its processes are difficult to formalise. This means that until low-cost, flexible and sophisticated robots are developed, it will be difficult to change the nature of customised manufacturing radically. It is in batch production manufacturing that microelectronics has the greatest potential; microelectronics can remove organisational bottlenecks in production planning, design, and scheduling and so greatly increase productivity. It has made possible in batch production flexible manufacturing systems that raise productivity spectacularly while greatly reducing labour requirements. Such systems are, however, still embryonic. Also, batch production accounts for less than half the manufacturing value-added in industrial countries. So even if flexible manufacturing systems (which involve besides robots, numerically-controlled machine tools, automatic conveyance, storage, inspection and computerised control systems) become widespread, it seems unlikely that, by the end of this century, steel-collar workers will displace most blue-collar workers. According to one estimate (Bylinsky 1979:96), robots will have replaced no more than 5% of the blue collar workers in industrial countries by the year 2000.

Though it will be many years before robots can deal with unstructured manufacturing environments, their use in industry will continue to spread. And how fast they diffuse will depend on their cost and capabilities. So far, they have been mostly employed to perform dirty, dangerous, and physically demanding work such as welding and painting, work that human beings are only too happy to let robots take over. But as their costs drop and become competitive with those for human labour, they will be used in more and more manufacturing operations. In capital-intensive industries, such as automobile assembly, computer manufacturing, consumer electronics and others where maximum use of capital equipment is economically necessary, they will work two to three shifts, displacing much more labour than automated machinery and mechanisation. Robotic technology will have its greatest impact when robots equipped with sight and touch can operate in flexible environments.

Robots in the future will make many industrial skills redundant. At present, their design does not capitalise on the skills and knowledge of industrial workers. But there are no reasons why sophisticated robotic systems cannot be designed and developed to make use of acquired human skills. In industrial countries, robotic design has been largely left to the engineers, with unions and workers having little influence on the introduction and diffusion of new technologies that affect skills and employment. The response of unions to robots has been essentially defensive: they have viewed robots as a technological innovation. They have demanded that management gives advance notice of new technology, minimises technological labour displacement by using normal attrition to reduce the workforce, provides training for affected workers, and cuts working hours to spread employment.

Contrary to the views of futurists, who see robots displacing most industrial labour and creating massive unemployment, the main social problem created by the use of robots is retraining, not unemployment. Robots improve the productivity and competitiveness of firms, encouraging their expansion and enabling them to pay higher wages to workers. Robots, like any other labour-saving technological change, can destroy production jobs, but they also create new jobs for maintenance workers, programmers, and operators in robot manufacturing plants. The challenge in the future is to retrain workers that robots displace, and provide those still in industry with new skills to enable them to work with new technologies.

TECHNOLOGY AND WORK ORGANISATIONS

Technology not only changes employment patterns at the national and international levels, it also creates new work patterns and behaviour. Information systems based on computer technology, in particular, have changed the way people act and relate to each other at the workplace. Increasingly, office and, to a lesser extent, factory jobs are dependent on large-scale information systems. So far organisations have used these systems to simplify and rationalise routine tasks in high-volume operations. Their objective is to improve the quality of work in terms of accuracy and timeliness and the quantity of work in terms of scope and coverage. The effect of these systems is to formalise the skills and knowledge of workers into programmed decision rules. As a result, workers often have less room for individual judgement.

With the spread of information technology, work is increasingly carried out at computer work stations. The worker manipulates symbols on a display screen, rather than objects like machines or paper. The computer mediates his work, making it an abstract activity that nonetheless demands focussed attention. The long-term social impact of widespread computer-mediated work is not known. Some reports (Zuboff 1983; Clutterbuck and Hill 1981:94-123) suggest that its impact varies greatly with skill level and the type of job. For some workers, e.g. keypunch operators, computer-mediated work is deskilling as well as boring and unchallenging. For others, e.g. managers, instant access to more information means more conceptual skills and knowledge are required to analyse the greatly increased volume of information available. They have to learn to imagine how tasks could be reorganised to take advantage of the new opportunities that information technology offers.

Besides changing skill requirements, information technology changes an organisation's environment. The volume of transactions expands as information technology increases the organisation's capacity to take on new tasks and make additional demands on workers for more reports and activities. The rhythm of life in the organisation speeds up with increased activity and feedback. But not all the additional tasks and activities that information technology makes possible add to productivity. Much of it in fact takes on a Parkinsonian character - the volume of work expands to fill the information processing power available.

Information technology will slowly reshape the structure of organisations. There will be proportionately fewer middle managers and clerical workers as a greater proportion of their responsibilities are transferred to information systems. But the change will be gradual. The pyramid form of organisational structure will remain dominant because of bureaucratic inertia and the power of affected groups to resist change. Even so, information systems, as they spread, will encourage other less hierarchical forms such as matrix and diamond-shaped organisational structures to emerge.

Information technology, if not introduced with adequate understanding of the way people work in organisations, can create a regimented environment. Managers may resist it if it limits their freedom to make decisions, or increases the measurability of their work. Clerical operators will resist it if they perceive that management is using it to increase their work load while diminishing their sense of mastery over their work environment.

Information technology alters social interaction patterns. By making the computer terminal the primary focus of interaction, it makes clerical workers who used to work in groups feel isolated. Because it encourages remote supervision through visual displays, it can increase clerical workers' feelings of powerlessness. Also, because it is organised to replace human judgement with impersonal decision rules that dictate the pattern and order of work, it becomes more like a source than an instrument of authority.

Information technology can also enlarge the range of interaction of managers: it makes it easy for them to interact with managers in other parts of the organisation. By the same token, it can give top management access to the same data that lower-level managers have. This could inhibit the willingness of lower-level managers to take risks and lead to an overflow of information to top management. The quality of decisions may suffer as a result.

Information technology has implications for managerial control. In industrial work, managers focus on controlling physical activities. In office work, their focus is on interpersonal behaviour, communication, and teamwork as the keys to high productivity. But with computer-mediated work, they will need to focus on ways to improve mental concentration and learning; new conceptual skills will be as crucial as interpersonal skills to high productivity in an information environment. Much more than with office work, managers will have to understand the kind of skills information systems require, and increase opportunities for workers to learn, retrain, and manage themselves.

With information technology, as with other technologies, the important questions are political, not technical: who controls technology, and for what purposes? Technology is, after all, not an autonomous or neutral force. The value and meaning of the applications of technology depend on management's objectives and philosophy. In designing applications of information systems, management can decide to use the flexibility and remote access capability of the systems to give workers increased control and freedom. Or it could design applications to deskill workers and supervise their work performance closely. As with previous technologies, information technology can be used to degrade work or to maximise the potential of human beings, freeing them from tedious work and enlarging the possibilities for satisfying activities.

Technology does not impose rigid skill requirements; many types of skill structures are compatible with a given technology (Wilkinson 1983: 82-92). Organisations do not have to react passively or adapt defensively to it. There are many examples of innovations that improve both plant productivity and the quality of working life (Walton 1974). Further, economic factors alone do not determine completely a firm's choice of technology or the work organisation that must go with the chosen technology (Davis and Trist 1974). The political and social processes that operate in an organisation set the context for the choice of technology. They make technological change and the nature of work organisations a negotiable issue to be resolved between management and workers.

TECHNOLOGY, GROWTH, AND THE FUTURE OF WORK

At both the macro and micro levels, adjustment to technological change has always been faster and less painful in an expanding economy. In the 1960s, when the industrial economies were growing strongly and enjoying full employment, both firms and workers adjusted well to automation and mechanisation (Weber 1967). Expanding firms were able to reallocate and retrain workers affected by labour-displacing technology. Retrenched workers were absorbed into productive employment in other growing industries or regions. And governments, because they had sufficient resources, were able to provide well-paid public sector employment to many new entrants into the job market as well as support educational and retraining programmes for displaced workers. In the past decade, growth slowed in the industrial countries, straining their ability to create public sector jobs and to maintain welfare programmes. This slowdown – the basic causes of which are related to the maturation of industrial economies, population ageing, the growth of the welfare state, changes in values towards work and economic growth, and international economic instability – has intensified the adjustment problems of industrial countries, particularly those in western Europe, to technological change and international competition. In many industrial countries, protectionist measures have provided temporary relief to the problem of import competition, but they have only delayed the urgent task of economic restructuring which is vital to faster economic growth.

Unless the industrial countries recover their growth momentum, they will find great difficulties adapting to the employment patterns that the microelectronics revolution is shaping. In the future, employment in high-volume production operations in industry and offices is likely to continue declining. New jobs will be found largely in time-absorbing activities including personal services, entertainment, recreation, and tourism, the productivity of which is hard to measure. Education and public services are potentially great absorbers of workers, but the ability of governments to provide jobs in these areas depends, in the final analysis, on economic growth.

In newly-industrialising countries – which are, in terms of development level, about where the industrial countries were in the early 1960s – adjustment to technological change has been fairly smooth and painless, thanks to rapid economic growth. In Singapore, for example, the government provides numerous incentives to encourage firms to automate, computerise, and mechanise as part of its ambitious industrial restructuring strategy. Workers retrenched by technological change and government economic policies in such industries as textile, tyre manufacturing, sawmills, car assembly have found new jobs easily in expanding industries such as electronics, transportation, and financial and personal services.

Changing patterns of employment have implications for the meaning and future of work in industrial and developing countries. In industrial countries, as computer technology shrinks industrial employment, and as service employment (arising either from new technologies or, more likely, from the further growth of time-intensive activities) expands, more opportunities for challenging and rewarding work will develop. These opportunities mesh with the rising aspirations of increasingly better-educated workers, who place great value on the intrinsic reward of work. However, even for such workers, work is not necessarily their central life interest, though the status, security, and satisfying social relationship associated with working are important to them. The trend towards more service employment will probably be accompanied by rising unemployment among the poorly-educated, who will have severe problems adapting to the service economy. For these workers, other alternatives to work, e.g. job sharing, non-market activities, early retirement etc. will need to be devised.

In developing countries, industrial expansion has created mostly unskilled jobs. Many of these are filled by women workers with little education and low aspirations, who have to accept the tedium and discipline of factory work. Work for these women entering the modern sector for the first time is an economic necessity, as it is also for the many others who have to eke out a living in the employment-elastic informal sector. As economic progress takes place in developing countries, values towards work will change, as they are already beginning to do in the newly-industrialising countries where people are showing increasing interest in non-monetary rewards of work, the environment, and cultural pursuits.

CONCLUSION

Technological change, for all its ill effects, is the bedrock on which the economic well-being of countries rests. While it has destroyed many jobs that offer satisfying, challenging work and created regimented, authoritarian work environments (with the objective of raising productivity) in both the industrial and service sectors, it has also expanded opportunities for rewarding employment in many areas including teaching, R & D, the arts and entertainment. The new information technology reinforces the trend away from high-volume industrial employment and expands opportunities for mentally challenging work. It has the potential, if managed wisely, to liberate large numbers of men and women in both industrial and developing countries from the dull and unsatisfying work they do today, and to foster more democracy and participation in work organisations.

Notes

<1> I am grateful to my colleagues, Stanley Richardson and Barry Wilkinson for helpful comments and suggestions.

Part III
Work and Culture

11 Discussant's paper on work and culture

MATS DAHLKVIST

WORK AND CULTURE

'Work' is always carried out in a social setting: either directly in cooperation with others, or indirectly through a larger societal context, for example a market. Further, no social setting is possible without communication, language, belief-systems and pictures of 'the world' (Parsons & Smelser 1956; Therborn 1980). Thus, 'work' is impossible without some 'culture'. Equally evident is the fact that changes in the mode of 'work' will contribute to changes in 'culture', and vice versa. To approach 'work and culture' in 1984 is to approach societies that are not only 'industrial', 'capitalist' and 'modern', but perhaps even 'post-industrial', 'post-capitalist' and 'post-modern' (Bell 1973; Dahrendorf 1959; Inglehart 1977). Not surprisingly, we thus find as the common theme in the following contributions – the problem of 'modernity'.

MODERNIZATION AND THE CULTURE OF WORK

The Loss of Community

In 'traditional' society, work was done in the realms of 'the household'. It is typical that the social theorists of the 17th century, Thomas Hobbes and John Locke, do not see any distinction between 'the family' and 'the enterprise'; consequently, they do not have any concept for independent wage-labour either, but talk only of 'servants' (Hobbes 1651:255, 285; Locke 1690:130f, 157f). With early 'modernization' – the introduction of capitalist, commercial and manufactural-industrial social relations – the 'household' begins to dissolve. This is the starting-point for Gustaf Wingren.

In the first place, the close family-like tie between 'master' and 'servant' is broken, and gradually evolves into the depersonalized antagonism of 'owners' and 'workers'. In the second place, the community of the family is broken in the sense that the working person – be he entrepreneur, employee or worker – actually leaves home to 'go to work'. Thus, 'family-life' and 'work-life' are established as distinct social spheres (Habermas 1962). In the third place, the distance between producer and consumer is increased; there is no longer personal contact between the craftsman and his customer. 'The market' widens, and is constituted by a whole network of merchants and middlemen and depersonalized exchange-transactions. We could go on, but the story is well known (Polanyi 1956; Heckscher 1955; Marx 1867; Hilton 1976).

The Loss of Identity

The transition from 'traditional' to 'modern' society is often said to result in the individual's loss of identity. This argument is found in Johan Galtung's paper. In traditional society work is executed with 'identity' and 'unity'. There is unity with nature, with fellow workers and fellow consumers; and the realm of the market and exchange is limited. Nature and persons are insubstitutable; every person has a special skill or role, hence a stable identity. But the insubstitutability also imposes a ring of oppression on the individuals; they are condemned to be where they are, Galtung holds.

In 'modern' society work is executed in quite a different milieu. Pieces of nature, bits of technology, persons, pieces of know-how can all be brought from all parts of the world, everything and everyone is substitutable. Hence we find a large degree of loss of identity, but also a great deal of alleged freedom, although freedom-in-alienation.

Johan Galtung compares Western societies with Japan. He holds that the superiority of Japan is due to the invincible and unique combination of Buddhism, Confucianism and Shintoism that rules Japanese culture. This gives the Japanese labour-force a work-culture of collectivity, authority, belonging, devotion and a common goal; values that cannot be found in the West. The situation in Western societies, Galtung suggests with implicit and explicit reference to Dürkheim, Marx and Weber, is rather to be described with the notions 'anomie', 'alienation' and 'the iron-cage of rationalistic modernity' (Dürkheim 1960; Marx 1867; Weber 1946, 1947).

At this point I would like to insert a parenthesis of methodological criticism. You could assert equally rightly – or wrongly – that also in the West we have a culture of devotion, belonging, communality, and common goals. This would be the unique combination of Protestant work-ethics, Christian righteousness and socialist collectivity and solidarity; a really invincible mixture. To put it briefly, I think Galtung states his case in too simple a manner. Further, he compares Japanese reality – at least alleged reality – with Western theorists. The correct comparison, of course, must be Japanese reality with Western reality; and this is a far more demanding program. But let us leave this and return to our argument.

Re-winning Community

Is Galtung's picture of Western societal culture, as a mixture of 'anomie-alienation-iron cage', correct? I think this is really open to question. Peter Anthony holds that, at least as far as enterprises are concerned, the alienating 'iron-cage' is a totally misleading conception. Enterprises have never been such depersonalized, instrumentalist, and rationalistic bodies as is maintained in the theory of organization, and the like. They, in fact, function as communities, in that they are social networks of tradition and narrative. Perhaps the stockholders use them for profit-making; but the 'culture' of both management, employees and workers is something quite different (and here, I both sharpen and widen the position). Keeping clear of holistic simplifications, Peter Anthony has, I think, made an important point in opening up the closed conceptual universe of the alienating 'iron-cage'.

Liberating Possibilities

A similar attack on the pessimistic view of industrialization and modernization is made, from another standpoint, by Lourdes Benería In a critique devastating of Ivan Illich's stupidities concerning gender and sex, she concludes with an attack on Illich's romantic and pessimistic social philosophy as a whole.

Although critical of many traits in industrial and capitalist societies, Lourdes Benería finds it useless to tell fairy-tales of a rosy past in general, and of the relation between the sexes in particular (as if chastity-belts and female drudgery had never existed). On the other hand, she points to the actual liberative capacities of present society. Benería is, of course, very conscious of the two-faced character of female 'liberation' concerning jobs or household-work; nevertheless, she sees cracks in the wall.

Linking Optimism with Realism

I think it is high time to join in an attack on the all too common pessimistic outlook on capitalism and industrial society. (Why is it so that such pessimism is more often found among sociologist friends, than among fellow economists or political scientists?) I do not mean that these societies are without faults - quite the contrary. But the faults should not blind us to the point that we do not see actual progress and liberative capacities. And I am really not talking about wishful thinking. I am talking about theoretical concepts operationalized into rigorous empirical research. It is far too easy to accept 'alienation' and 'iron-cage' as axioms. Thus 'optimism' needs a more elaborated conceptual frame-work to be theoretically meaningful and empirically fruitful.

A PROPOSED CONCEPTUAL FRAMEWORK

Spheres of 'Everyday Life'

The paradigm of the alienating 'iron-cage' argues as if all social relations in contemporary societies were 'capitalist' or 'modern'. This is most evident in 'Marxist' writings where contemporary society is often referred to as the capitalist system (Dahlkvist 1978, 1982). I would rather suggest that 'capitalism' and 'capitalist' relations - in the proper sense of the word (Marx 1867; Weber 1946, 1947; Friedman 1962) - is only one of several types of social relations in contemporary Western society; perhaps also a diminishing type. This means that the prevalence of actual alienation, 'iron-cage' meaninglessness, oppression, loss of identity, lack of health in various senses, etc., cannot be blamed on capitalism alone; and certainly not in every individual case. This also means that we are not odd, if in many life-situations we do not feel alienated at all! We, and others, perhaps in statistically significant numbers, may at times feel unoppressed, full of identity, and even find ourselves meaningful; be it at work, in the family, towards a friend, with regard to the public good, or in the struggle for a better world.

Furthermore, we should not think of there being only one 'everyday life'. It consists, in fact, of several social spheres, different social networks into which the individuals enter during the 'everyday'(Ahrne 1981; Therborn 1980; Habermas 1962). Most of these spheres are not necessarily oppressive, but rather designed for, or at least containing, meaningful communality and common purpose. Thus, we can conceive of these spheres as possibilities for identity and belonging; or as the anthropologist Sandra Wallman put it in her typical Anglo-Saxon fashion: 'individuality-options'.

The most obvious spheres of 'everyday life' (i.e. system-like social networks) in contemporary Western societies are:

a) the work-place (a most important one);
b) social and political organizations and committees (such as trade unions, political parties, old or new social movements);
c) cultural and leisure activities (sports, choirs, clubs, churches, cultural associations etc.);
d) housing estates (neighbours, shops, bars, schools etc.);
e) family and relatives (including Christmas, christening, marriage, birthdays, funerals and the like);
f) friends, this very modern and urban phenomenon.

Whatever we may say of social spheres like these, the social relations between the actors are not solely capitalist. They are of different natures. Even at the work-place the 'capitalist' relations, such as the relations to foremen or to machines, are only part of the network. But the relations between the wage-earners are not, in any sensible notion of the term, 'capitalist'. Quite the contrary. In many cases – too many from the viewpoint of the 'iron-cage' paradigm – we find bonds of solidarity and a preparedness for collective organization.

But, of course, we do not only find community, solidarity, identity, meaning, and belonging. We also find isolation, oppression, alienation and meaninglessness. The advantage is that the framework does not beg the question, but leaves it an open empirical matter to decide which one is the case, or in what proportions.

The same is true of the relationship between the sexes. In all these spheres we can find established patterns of ideas and roles which place men and women in certain, often unequal, positions. But it is important to look at these matters as open empirical questions. It is equally important to recognize that the struggle/cooperation between the sexes concerns different matters in the different social spheres; and that advancement in one sphere does not automatically imply advancement in others. It would, then, be unfruitful to ask for the explanation of 'the oppression of women' (or men); the causes and battlefields are multifarious (Foucault 1976; Barret 1980; Habermas 1962; Millet 1971).

Forms of Organization of Social Production

The spheres of 'everyday life' are, of course, embedded in the larger framework of society, and its forms of societal organization. Since the 16th and 17th centuries, 'state' and 'capitalist economy' have constituted the main form of societal organization in the West. Nowadays, 'the state' increasingly conducts and administers 'economic' matters, such as housing, transport, energy, education, and health; not to mention direct enterprising (Galbraith 1967; Shonfield 1965). This means that the social economy of today is not really constituted by capitalism alone. On the contrary, the total production of goods and services is provided by bodies with different kinds of ownership, where the amount of 'public' or 'private' power and control differ.

The main forms of societal production are:

a) capitalist corporations, neatly divided into: 1) large, 2) small;
b) one-man enterprises (simple commodity-production, with no or few employees);
c) producer's cooperatives, including union-owned companies;
d) consumer's cooperatives, including cooperatively owned housing;
e) 'public sector' agencies (health, education, transport);
f) community-owned enterprises;
g) state-owned enterprises;
h) household work (perhaps on a level above, or below, the others).

In a country like Sweden, capitalist corporations do not employ more than 40-50% of the labour-force, (and I did not have to exaggerate these figures too much!) The 'public sector', including communal and state-owned enterprises, employs between 30-40%. And the final 20% is divided between the others. Whatever we may call it, it is not only capitalism. It is rather, in the real sense of the word, a mixed economy.

Politics, Economics, and History

From the point of view of history, this is a transitional society. It is actually leaving the exclusive dominance of capitalist institutions behind, as the works on 'the growth of the public sector' or on 'the welfare state' suggest in their empirical results (Flora & Heidenheimer 1981). I thus take a position that differs from the proponents of the perspective 'welfare-capitalism', who consider the transition to 'socialism', not as something going on, but as something to be awaited (Korpi 1978, Himmel-strand 1981; Therborn 1984; Giddens 1973). I also, consequently, consider the theories of 'monopoly', 'state monopoly' or 'late capitalism' to be fundamentally wrong, since they see the present societies as holistic totalities rather than pluralistic combinations (Poulantzas 1968; Boccara 1972; Mandel 1975). My theoretical perspective on contemporary society as a combination of several forms of societal organization, and, consequently, of contemporary history as a transitional epoch, is elaborated in a forthcoming study with the title 'The Mixture of the Mixed Economy' (Dahlkvist-Nordlöf 1982).

In this study, we do not see politics in Western societies as a question of distributional struggle. Nor do we see them as the administering of conflict-free societies, as the theory of 'the end of ideology' suggests. Nor do we see them as the technical administering of the 'highest' stage of capitalism, where politicians are caught in the spider's web of capitalist ideological idolatries. Rather, we see contemporary politics as a struggle, and a serious and intense struggle, about the fundamental institutional framework of society; a struggle about 'the mixture of the mixed economy'. Consequently, we do not see history as inherently uni-directional as proponents of the theories of 'modernization' or 'historical materialism' often suggest. Rather we see history as a relatively open question, possible to roll back, or, at least, open to alternative futures, as answers to the problems of today (Dahlkvist 1982; Østerud 1978).

As in the case of the spheres of everyday life, contemporary politics, socio-economics and history suggest demanding empirical tasks. To investigate this social reality, with the use of adequate theoretical and empirical tools, should really be a more meaningful and non-alienating endeavour than merely to assume the axiomtic notions of 'meaning-lessness' and 'alienation'.

12 The metamorphosis of management, from villain to hero

P. D. ANTHONY [1]

I am going to begin this story (the word will turn out to be well chosen) with a very brief and inadequate account of a recent work in moral philosophy. Alasdair MacIntyre, in After Virtue, a study in moral theory, could be said to argue that the culture of Western Society, in the sense of 'a spirit which informs the way of life of a people' has been destroyed and that one of the principal agents of that destruction has been management. This has followed from a state of affairs in which there is no longer any possibility of moral exchange or of the evaluation of moral judgments. The argument from here will be set out in three stages: first, an attempt to explain MacIntyre's case; second, within an acceptance of that broad argument, a distinction which seeks to establish that MacIntyre's account of management, while persuasive and understandable, is mistaken; third, an attempt to re-interpret management (in ways that may seem bizarre) and to restore, no less, the culture of Western Society (an attempt that may seem as ambitious as it is absurd).

MACINTYRE'S ARGUMENT

As the result of the 'enlightenment project' man has been made individual and autonomous, freed from the external authority of traditional morality. But the price paid for this freedom is the isolation of man from the medieval and classical relationship with a social and moral network. There is now no authority at all. Each individual now speaks unconstrained by divine law, natural teleology or hierarchical authority; 'but why should anyone listen?' Each of us sees ourselves as an autonomous moral agent, but each of us is engaged in manipulative relationships with others.

> Seeking to protect the autonomy that we have learned to prize, we aspire ourselves not to be manipulated by others; seeking to incarnate our own principles and stand-point in this world... we find no way open to us except by directing towards others those very manipulative modes of relationships which each of us aspires to resist in our own case. The incoherence of our attitudes and our experience arises from the incoherent conceptual scheme which we have inherited. (MacIntyre 1981:66).

The process of moral exchange has been replaced in modern society by a fictitious, moribund exchange conducted in terms of 'rights', 'protest', and 'unmasking'. The current climate of 'bureaucratic individualism' means that characteristic debates are between individualism making its claim in terms of rights and organisations making claims in terms of utility. Both are incommensurable fictions. 'The mock rationality of the debate conceals the arbitrariness of the will and power at work in its resolution'. Protests are almost always a negative reaction against 'the alleged invasion of someone's rights in the name of someone else's utility'. No one can ever win an argument or lose it, 'hence the utterance of protest is characteristically addressed to those who already share the protestor's promises... they rarely have anyone else to talk to but themselves' (MacIntyre 1981:69). 'Unmasking' is the process by which the hidden, covert motives of will and self-interest are expressed as lying behind and 'explaining' overt moral statements. These charades in which moral discussions are imitated but not engaged in are the result of the doctrine of emotivism in which moral statements are deemed to reveal only the feelings or sentiments of those who make them. Hence, settlements of moral disputes become impossible except by reference to non-moral grounds. So, moral exchange becomes impossible.

These characteristically modern activities are carried on, says MacIntyre, by the three 'central characters' of modern society: the aesthete, the therapist and the manager. The third is allotted the greatest importance by MacIntyre. In a world reduced to the exchange of moral fictions, managers rely upon their own peculiar fiction, the claim to 'possess systematic effectiveness in controlling certain aspects of social reality' (MacIntyre 1981:71). Managers claim to be morally neutral, effectively engaged in the pursuit of means to ends decided by others. But the contrivance of means is a central part of 'the manipulation of human beings into compliant patterns of behaviour; and it is by appeal to his own effectiveness in this respect that the manager claims authority' (MacIntyre 1981:71). So, the notion of effectiveness is used to sustain and extend managerial authority. Expertise, while claimed to be morally neutral, is used to justify authority and social control, which is argued to have a moral foundation.

The manager is engaged in a masquerade based upon a moral fiction, his claim to authority is built upon sand. MacIntyre has no difficulty in disposing of the two purported foundations of the claim; that the manager is engaged in a domain of morally neutral facts in which he is expert and that he is able to arrive at law-like generalisations, to be scientific. The claim to be scientific may, in fact, be a little more complex than MacIntyre acknowledges, but the refutation of that claim, simple or complex, is well-established and widely acknowledged. He ends this argument with the conclusion that the claim to managerial expertise is a modern illusion.

> The effects of eighteenth century prophecy have been to produce not scientifically managed social control, but a skillful dramatic imitation of such control. It is histrionic success which gives power and authority to our culture. The most effective bureaucrat is the best actor. (MacIntyre 1981:102).

I shall return to that attribution later but, in the meantime, MacIntyre implies that certain characteristics resided in traditional, pre-enlightened society, that they are characteristics of philosophical accounts before moral and political exchange was destroyed and that they are necessary to any community which will not become corrupt or, in the terms from which we set out, are necessary to the maintenance of culture. The first part of his explanation is sociological and the second philosophical, although an essential part of his thesis is that sociology and philosophy are dependent upon each other.

In the first, he distinguishes between 'practices' and 'institutions'. A practice is 'a coherent and complex form of socially established cooperative human activity' (MacIntyre 1981:125) which realises goods (values, not commodities) which are internal to that practice, concerned with standards of excellence, human conceptions of ends and goods. Bricklaying is not a practice, architecture is; planting turnips is not a practice, farming is. Internal goods are judged by those engaged in a practice but their achievement 'is a good for the whole community who participate in the practice'. External goods, on the other hand, are the object of competition in a distributive exchange with winners and losers. Practices require institutions to carry them forward. But there is a tension between the two. The practice is always vulnerable to the competitiveness of the institution. Practices are concerned with internal goods, they depend upon institutions which are concerned with external goods. Practices would be (are) swamped by institutions were they not sustained by virtue.

In this second part of the explanation, MacIntyre identifies three essential virtues, soon to be joined by a fourth. The virtues of justice, courage and truthfulness sustain practices and maintain our search for the good in overcoming the dangers and threats of acquisitiveness. They are also necessary to the maintenance of a community which, like practices, depends upon the fourth virtue, tradition. A living tradition is a socially-embodied argument about the nature of the goods constituting that tradition. It emerges from the past, from history, is conducted in a narrative, and confronts 'a future whose determinate and determinable character, so far as it possesses any, derives from its past' (MacIntyre 1981:207).

The creation of human communities, political activity and work were once conceived as practices. Not now. When work is put to the service of impersonal capital, separated from everything but survival and institutionalised acquisitiveness, the practice of work ends. '"Pleonexia", a vice in the Aristotelian scheme, is now the driving force of modern productive work' (MacIntyre 1981:211). The means-ends relationship of work has become external to the goods sought by those who work. In our terms, not MacIntyre's, the culture of work has been destroyed.

THE MISINTERPRETATION OF MANAGEMENT

This account of MacIntyre's thesis is quite inadequate because it is set out in a work of enormous scope and richness and of great importance. The following criticism, not of the argument, but of his account of management is delivered with due humility.

MacIntyre leaves us with a world in which moral exchange has become impossible and moral philosophy derided. One of the most important agents of this destruction is management, a characteristic modern activity which exemplifies current vices rather than virtues and which contributes to our isolated confusion by trading in myths and fictions. In order to identify MacIntyre's misunderstanding of management I am going to provide an outline of two 'theories' of management, the first I shall call 'official theory' the second 'real theory'.

113

Official Theory

This is the explanation of managerial organisation and managerial behaviour as rational, purposive, goal-directed activity, structured so as to facilitate the achievement of business or economic goals. Insofar as management is conceived to be related in any way to wider social concerns, they are derivative of those business objectives so that what is good for General Motors is, ipso facto, good for the U.S.A. To the extent that social or political demands impact upon management's pursuit of economic goals they can be recognised as a part of the environment (which may include the aspirations of trade unions or the requirements of racial legislation) imposing a wide variety of claims upon managerial attention in arriving at a pluralist (and utilitarian) accounting which is still directed at the achievement of business objectives. It is the classic account of managerial organization, frequently refined and elaborated, symbolised by organization charts and backed up by a considerable (and partly ineffective) effort to equip and sustain effective managerial performance and expertise. The focus of attention has moved from the machinery of control in 'scientific management', to the recruitment of social science, the motivation and involvement of 'human resources' and organisational development.

The official theory is the dominant explanation of management behaviour, partly because much of what MacIntyre says about it is correct, including his philosophical explanation of why it has come to be dominant. It is dominant because of the conjunction in which both monetarists and Marxists stress the importance of economic drives as providing the rationale of behaviour, particularly of capitalists and their managerial functionaries. In both accounts, behaviour which is not economically directed and rationally planned came to be seen as deviant. In this way, the official theory (both in its writers and in their radical critics) comes to be hortatory rather than descriptive, concerned with the way managers ought to behave rather than with what they do.

For this reason the official theory begins to encounter some problems with the real world. The first of them arose when, as the result of the well-known Hawthorne Experiments, the inhabitants of the bank-wiring room and thereafter, the whole of subordinated labour, had to be dismissed as deviant, excluded in some way from the formal organization, bent upon pursuing its own irrational ends. The next was more alarming, in that it came nearer to the managerial home. The whole corpus of research on supervisors and foremen confirms that this 'front line of management' as it was once described, is now to be seen as 'the lost managers' also to be excluded from the formal organisation in that their behaviour cannot be accounted for in terms of rationally-determined, goal-directed activity (Child and Partridge 1982). The official theory has been dented to the extent that it has been forced to recognise a culture of work which resists and reacts to the formal attempts to control it. But what if this gradual emergence of deviance and decay does not stop there?

Real Theory

Explanations of management are no longer consistent and cohesive. Over the last ten years or so, and with increasing empirical evidence to support it, a view has emerged which suggests a different explanation of managerial organisation and behaviour. Several general conclusions emerge from those researchers who have concerned themselves with a descriptive rather than a prescriptive account of managers. They spend most of their time, sometimes up to 90% of it, in talking (Stewart 1983). Their conversations are frequently brief, unscheduled and apparently disorderly. Their conversations are directed widely and cannot be comprehended within any formal organisational chart (Kotter 1982). They create, particularly the most successful managers, wide personal networks with subordinates, subordinates of their subordinates, people in other departments and in other establishments (Kotter 1982). They maintain these networks by systems of obligation and independence, sometimes by behaviour which must be deemed deviant by any reference to formal requirements (Dalton 1959). Much of their behaviour can best be described as political in character. They construct their own agendas, schedules, plans for resource allocation and often regard the formal network of objectives and controls as irrelevant or unrealistic. They are men (they are usually men) of wide and considerable abilities and their success must be explained by reference to a relationship between their own personal development, the complex context of their firms, and their intimate and detailed knowledge of its historical development and operations (Kotter 1982).

The result of the development of this 'real theory' of management has begun seriously to challenge the 'classical' or 'official' theory of management organisation and it raises questions about the direction of current management education and development. It is possible that it has even more fundamental implications. The whole foundation of classical management theory has been economic and Weberian, even Marxist. In any of these perspectives, the business organisation has been seen simply as an extension in scale of the entrepreneurial business. Managers are engaged in a rational pursuit of business objectives, engaged in the co-ordination and control of subordinates, sometimes acknowledged to be only partially included in the pursuit of these goals. But real theory suggests a different, more anthropological account. It is in this sense that MacIntyre misinterprets management; he describes it as it ought to be, not, perhaps, as it is. And if it is not as it ought to be there is the possibility of rescuing it from his dire conclusions.

THE RE-INTERPRETATION OF MANAGEMENT

The remainder of this discussion is speculative to the point of fantasy. The excuse for engaging in it is the damage to social relationships done by MacIntyre's telling criticisms. It stands in a long and pessimistic tradition of European thought which has never diminished since the onset of capitalism, has familiarised us with the concepts of alienation and anomy and has driven some to the despair of terror or withdrawal to escape from it. MacIntyre's attribution of cause is to the whole mode of philosophical practice but he makes management an important instrument by which that philosophy, or what passes for it, is applied to the world. We have established, I hope, that he might be wrong about management. Can we also establish that it acts in a quite different way, that is has aspects which are positive in the maintenance of social relationships?

He told us, if you remember, that the best manager or bureaucrat (he seems to use the terms interchangeably) is the best actor, that histrionic success is what gives power and success to our culture. That assertion was intended as an indictment. What happens if we take this to be an accurate description? To anticipate the conclusion before it has been reached, I am going to suggest that managerial organisations are best or most accurately run as communities in which histrionic success or story-telling, is a practice essential to the community's survival and well-being. We are going to be fortunate, in short, if it turns out to be true that the best managers are the best actors.

Let us take acting and narrative as being closely associated with each other, if not synonymous; acting is, after all, the dramatic exposition of a narrative. MacIntyre has a great deal to say about narrative. It expresses and passes on a community's living tradition, expresses the values that hold it together, begins in its history and points to its future. It also defines the community, its narrative relates only to the community and can be expressed only by its members (frequently, only by its oldest and most respected members). MacIntyre cites Barbara Hardy who points out, in a discussion of George Eliot's Silas Marner, that the activity in the public house 'The Rainbow', 'is not just cleverly contrived entertainment and "distraction" but a self-analysing drama of the community from which Silas has been excluded. The drama consists of telling and listening to stories which are a part of the history of the parish'. Marner's being allowed to tell stories in 'The Rainbow' is 'a first step towards that social restoration which is the subject of the novel, and the society into which he steps is that of the communal story, the annals of the parish to which he will belong' (Hardy 1975:135). And of Thomas Hardy, she says, 'a remarkable feature of Hardy's story-telling is the way one tale breeds another, as if the community recognised narration as a ritual necessity. So the community pours forth its benign autobiography' (Hardy 1975:202).

The importance that MacIntyre ascribes to narrative and history in the maintenance of a community relates to anthropological studies of small communities. Redfield speculates as to whether one 'could write a book about a little community in the form of a generalised biography?' (Redfield 1960:55) and he adds, significantly from our perspective, that to use this biographical account would make it difficult to describe technology as an organised system of operations or to use concepts like ecological system and structure. Referring to his 'history' of the community of Chankton from 1880 to 1948, he notes 'the aesthetic unity of the tale, by the suspense and resolution of the problem the people set themselves' (Redfield 1960:102-103). And he wonders whether 'it might be possible to say something about the history of a little community from the inside view. Such a history would be a people's own story as that people have come to conceive it. It would show how a group conceives its unity in relation to time' (Redfield 1960:110).

Is it possible to conceive of managerial organizations in the same terms, as communities supported by history and traditions which are carried on by narrative and related to a culture?

There are two considerable problems and one explanatory advantage in taking this unlikely view. Let us deal with the problems before coming to the advantage.

The Economic Problem

To see managerial organisations as communities is 'unlikely' because it flies in the face of what they are commonly conceived to be; organisations constructed to pursue economic ends, profits. Once again, where Marxists and monetarists agree there seems little room for doubt. I shall briefly suggest that there are real reasons for doubt.

To suggest that the ultimate end and purpose of an organization is the achievement of economic ends does not necessarily and immanently connect those ends to the everyday behaviour of its inhabitants and it certainly does not establish that those ends 'explain' that behaviour. In one sense, all organisations have to serve ultimate economic ends in order to survive. This is true of hospitals, monasteries and universities. But the ultimate and absolute importance of economic survival does nothing to 'explain' the goals and the values which realistically concern their inhabitants. In the ultimate we all have to die but that prospect, absolute and important though it is, does not condition or even influence the way that most of us live. I have suggested that the growing body of empirical evidence that supports 'real theory' sustains the views that managers behave in a quite different and sometimes contradictory way to what could be expected from an 'official' view which sees them as rationally deployed and directed in the pursuit of economic goals. Profit and economic survival are, of course, ultimately absolute goals for organisations like I.C.I., but it is quite likely, even probable, that many line managers, more functional managers, and most administrative and professional personnel work, in reality, in quite a different milieu. It is not as unlikely as at first sight it might seem that managers are engaged in a social, political, cultural network.

We certainly know that they talk for most of their time. Do they engage in narrative? Some certainly do. Many senior managers end the working day in the office or in a bar, surrounded by their subordinates, while they narrate the day's events in a way that makes sense of them. The most junior managers make little contribution, perhaps like Silas Marner, because they have not yet been admitted to the community nor yet allowed to tell its tales. As we are told in a recent study of the rhetoric used by management, management can be seen 'as a sub-culture, i.e. a social collectivity whose members share a set of implicit and explicit meanings acquired through innumerable communicative exchanges'. Management's oral tradition is 'a means by which culture is generated, maintained and transmitted from one generation to another' (Gowler and Legge 1983:199).

The Problem of Identification

If we were to accept that managerial organizations can be seen as communities, in some ways seen more realistically thus than as economic institutions, there are problems in identifying the community. In the first place this is a problem commonly found in social anthropology, it explained that study's early predilection for small, isolated, peasant communities as a focus of study. The more specific problem about management organisations is that they appear both to be complex and to be bifurcated. I shall defer the problem of bifurcation, the split between managers and those thay manage, who are deemed often to be outside managerial organisation but to be employed by the company.

The problem of complexity in management refers to vertical fissures between functional departments and specialists, and lateral divisions between 'top' , 'middle' and 'lower' management. As it happens, a neat and tempting solution to this problem is available. We could very easily suggest that the relationships between these compartments are precisely the way in which the tension between the organisation as a formal, economic, goal-directed concern on the one hand, and a community on the other, is handled. We could then explain quite persuasively that the board of directors, aided by the functional controllers in financial accounting and cost control departments, maintain the formal direction of the organisation towards the achievement of economic goals against the erratic and wilful tendency of the rest of the inhabitants to create for themselves a community.

It might, thus, make sense to think of managerial organisations as communities, concerned with cultural transmission by means of narrative, history and tradition and constrained within an economic context represented by certain personnel, senior managers and functional specialists engaged in tasks of control.<2> That would appear to be a reasonable compromise between 'official' and 'real' theory, allowing each its due place with supremacy accorded to the final hegemony of economic control. 'Real' theory is an account of what organisations are; 'official' theory an explanation of what their controllers wish them to be.

But there are suggestions that 'reality' is more pervasive than even this compromise view would suggest. If any management specialism qualifies as the functionary of capital it must surely be that concerned with the apparatus of financial control. That, after all, is where the 'bottom line' is defined and drawn. In a recent discussion of the relationship between management and management accounting, Earl tells us that the function of accounting information systems 'is seen to be the provision and maintenance of stability – of ensuring both organisational order and organisational continuity. It is suggested that accounting is a key element of the culture by which organisations (or societies) are held together and survive' (Earl 1983:123). And he goes on to say that

> there is strong evidence that management accounting systems, rather than embodying and facilitating the normative goal-setting, goal-directed and goal-achievement management paradigm, frequently are used to make sense of past actions and decisions taken, thereby discussion rationales and goals retrospectively... This use of accounting procedures in a sense is retrospectively writing the organisations's history (Earl 1983:125).

He argues that there is little evidence that the application of accounting techniques result in financial success, considerable evidence for management's subversion of them so that 'many accounting pratices are rituals that modern organisations devise in order to protect themselves from uncertainty' (Earl 1983:126). Still further, he says, the very language of accounting creates the organisation's culture by the use of rhetoric composed of constructs like 'profit' and 'bottom line', the 'harshest no-nonsense management watchword' which 'is even more imprecise than profit' (Earl 1983:128).

This is indeed to suggest that our compromise view is too weak, that not only are the controllers a part of the managerial community but that they are essential to its maintenance by contributing to its culture, its narrative and its history.

I have proposed that it is conceivable to regard managerial organisations as communities, that MacIntyre's account understandably mistakes them to be the way they have so often been described. What are the consequences for his argument of that mistake? Let us now return, with suitable levity, to the restoration of Western Society from the disarray in which MacIntyre left it.

CONCLUSION

It cannot be done, of course. MacIntyre's attack is directed against the modern European philosophical tradition and its separation from sociology. But management is made the focus of that attack, the agent of manipulation, the purveyor of myths in support of its own aggrandisement. If management is not as he sees it then there may at least be some grounds for hope.

His critcism of management is entirely justified in terms of what it has claimed to be or, more precisely, of what managerial theorists have said of it. But if management organisations are communities in all the manifest ways that have been suggested, then we could reach conclusions different from his. To repeat the earlier question: What if it turns out to be true that the best managers are the best actors, the best story-tellers? What if there is a culture of management? The maintenance of communities and the relationships of work were once 'practices', in MacIntyre's terms, supported by the virtues and sustained by a narrative tradition. Then they were destroyed and one of the principal agents of that destruction was management, ruthless in its pursuit of acquisitive goals. But, if managers behave precisely like the members of communities they were deemed to have destroyed, the very fortress from which the attack was launched is undermined. Management itself can be seen as the very 'practice' which it has been mistakenly described as attacking.

What prevents us from seeing management in this way is not the way in which managers behave but the way in which they have been described as behaving. About that MacIntyre is entirely right; about managers he is wrong. The false description of management behaviour could, in fact, be described as an extension of the 'enlightenment project' but, in this respect, at least, it seems to have failed. It may be that managerial organizations, like those old, besieged, working-class communities (in coal and steel, what is left of them) are irreducible bastions, like them except that management, because of its very centrality in our society, is infinitely stronger.

There are also consequences for the distinction always drawn between the managerial members included in the organisation and the proletarian subordinates who are in part excluded or alienated from it. The official theory must face the facts of shop-floor deviance which managers must wrestle to control. But if managers and industrial subordinates are both engaged in a community, both at odds with the organisational construct that encloses them, there is some prospect of restoring the relationship between them. In fact, the extent of that relationship and the nature of their co-operation may be much more considerable than an economic, goal-directed view of the enterprise can deem to be imaginable. The traditional division into two sides may not appear to be so realistic if one of the sides is not so committed to the values which it has been understood to impose, unsuccessfully, upon the other. If both are seen to be engaged in the culture of work, both enclosed in a community, then the theoretical relationships between them may begin to appear as a practical managerial responsibility instead of a futile attempt to bridge the chasm of alienation.

If managerial organisations are communities engaged in a 'practice' then they contain the seeds, not of their own destruction, but of potential renewal and social growth. They have certainly been inhibited from seeing themselves in this way and, therefore, from any prospect of effective social development. The explanation for that inhibition lies in the false model that has been constructed of managerial organisations as essentially economic institutions. That model is a ridiculously inflated reification of economic behaviour, at best only a partial account of human activity, exaggerated and made into the basis for explanation of managerial behaviour. The dangers of this process are rightly identified by MacIntyre but they are dangers that are partly discounted once we recognise that it does not serve to explain what managers actually do.

There are two practical steps to be taken in getting ourselves out of this impasse. The first is to stop deceiving the managers, to begin to give them an accurate rather than an idealised (if that is the right word in this context) account of what they are and what they do. The second is to change the manner in which they are educated and trained for what they do. There is already some evidence of considerable uncertainty about the traditional direction of management education. Some disquiet about American versions was voiced by Professor Leavitt in his 1983 Stockton Lecture to the London Business School: 'The decline of American management is closely correlated with the rise of the American business school'. In the British context, confusion becomes understandable when we are told that

> the modern manager is often confused. He is not quite sure how to behave and there are many times when he is torn between exerting strong leadership or permissive leadership behaviour. With this in mind, the programme represents an attempt to integrate different behaviours. (Kerslake and Radcliff 1980:48-49).

It would, in fact, be surprising if there was no pessimism about management education when the received view of what managers do, upon which their education is based, is wrong. It is no great exaggeration to suggest that managers are taught that what they do is bad behaviour which they must correct if they are to survive and prosper.

If managers are members of communities, engaged in their maintenance, in the practice of political skills and in the elaboration of systems of mutual dependence and obligation, their education should recognise the skills they use and the concepts they need to develop. They need to understand the ideas of responsibility, authority and justice. In short, managers should be educated in the virtues which they exhibit in the practice in which they are engaged.

Notes

<1> I would like to acknowledge the co-operation of Dr. Michael Reed in developing the argument in this paper and the helpful suggestions made by Professor G.F. Thomason. I am also grateful to Dr. Barrie Daniels for her help in the discussion of narrative.

<2> It would be stretching things a bit to suggest that there could be an adaptation to management of Redfield's distinction between the little tradition and the great tradition; the former represented by the mass of unreflective managers, the latter by the reflective overlords of organisation sustained by the high culture of the management educational priesthood.

13 Meditations on Ivan Illich's *Gender*

LOURDES BENERÍA

INTRODUCTION

Among the many questions to explore in any discussion of 'Work in 1984', there is the issue of including gender dimensions in our analyses and conclusions. Is work in 1984 different for men and women and, if so, in what way? Why is it that, despite the policies that many countries have adopted to eliminate discrimination in the labour market, we observe a stubborn permanence of the wage gap between men and women and, in some cases, even a tendency for the gap to increase?[1] What are the interconnections between gender and the division of labor? To what extent does gender determine the placement of workers within the labor hierarchies prevalent in different types of productive structures? To what extent can we say that the division of labor between the sexes creates relations of domination/subordination between them? What connections can we trace between work, culture and gender?

I have chosen to deal with some of these questions within the context of discussing Ivan Illich's book Gender, which raises a series of controversial issues that have angered feminists. Given Illich's status and reputation in the international community, the book is likely to have a wider readership than other works dealing with women's issues. It is therefore important to discuss the questions that he raises. This paper is not intended to be a review of his book nor a repetition of previous critiques.[2] Instead, it concentrates on issues related to the theme 'Work and Culture' included as part of this conference. I will first review Illich's central thesis, followed by a critique of some basic arguments in his analysis; I will then deal with some of the key concepts used in the book. The last part of the paper returns to the questions posed above about gender and the nature of women's work.

ILLICH'S THESIS

Illich's basic message may be summarized as follows: Once upon a time, there was a kingdom of 'vernacular gender' where the sexes were separated and complementary – in response to the natural order of things. Tools were 'gendered' and the sexual division of labor well defined and unquestionable. However, the Europe that emerged between the 11th and the 18th centuries, went through a period of 'broken gender' in which tools became more inter-exchangeable between men and women and the two spheres of gender less clearly separated. Finally, from the 18th century on, the reign of 'economic sex' appears with the rise of individualism, industrialization and the use of machines that can be used indiscriminately by men and women (i.e., tools that are not

121

gendered) and with what Illich calls the transition from 'patriarchy' to 'sexism'. The result is that despite 'unisex' tools, 'economic discrimination against women appears when development sets in' (Illich, p. 65). His conclusion is that 'the struggle to create economic equality between genderless humans of two different sexes resembles the efforts made to square the circle with the ruler and straight edge' (p. 66). The implication of this message is that 'peace between men and women, whatever form it may take, depends on economic contraction and not on economic expansion' (p. 16). This solution therefore is very much along the lines developed by Illich in his previous books, Deschooling Society and Medical Nemesis, that is, the need for humankind to roll back economic growth and industrialization in order to eradicate the negative outcomes of this process.

Illich develops his thesis in a very unconvincing way despite his effort at illuminating his points with long footnotes and the citing of an extensive body of literature. There is, for example, a basic contradiction in his argument: if tools have become 'unisex' instead of 'gendered', it would appear that the basis for the equality between men and women has been created. Yet, for Illich the opposite has taken place; for him economic discrimination sets in with industrialization. The gendered world of the past was not 'discriminatory'; it kept men and women in their natural spheres. In addition, for Illich, equality between the sexes is an impossible goal; he, in fact, proclaims that 'The ideal of unisex economic quality is now dying' (p. 17). Although economic equality has rarely been advocated as 'unisex', for Illich the ideal seems to be that of a gendered society that 'bespeaks of complementarity' (p.4; emphasis mine). I will return to this subject below.

Arlie Hochchild has called Illich 'the ideologue in scientist's clothing' (Hochchild 1983), an expression that captures very well the reader's reaction to his book. On the one hand, he makes use of a great deal of the literature on women that has appeared during the past fifteen years. For example, he relies on this literature to show that the wage gap between men and women has not narrowed over time, or that women perform a high proportion of what Illich calls 'shadow work', that is, the unpaid work of the unreported economy. Yet he mentions this literature in a way that its richness goes unnoticed and without giving much credit to it. To illustrate, there is very little that is new in Illich's analysis of 'shadow work' other than the name. Many authors have talked before of the underestimation of women's economic activities, and the extensive debate of the 1970's on domestic work generated a rich and insightful exchange.<3> Illich ignores it and proceeds as if his analysis was breaking new ground.

Of the literature that Illich does use, he often shows little under-standing, as with the case of the writings dealing with the concept of reproduction, the significance of which he seems to miss all together. Thus, Marxists do not call shadow work 'social reproduction', as Illich states, even if some of the activities that are not part of the market – as childrearing – can be included in social reproduction. In the same way, feminists did not 'discover' reproduction, nor the distinction between reproduction and production (p. 35); they have instead found this distinction, made initially by Engels, instrumental in analyzing that sphere of human activity that had largely been ignored by conventional thinking and which they found useful in dealing with their concerns. The ignorance (and arrogance) with which Illich speaks of these issues adds nothing to a body of literature which has opened up new dimensions to conventional analysis - be it from the perspective of the social sciences or from other disciplines such as phychology and history.

Finally, many of Illich's assertions are unproven or need a great deal of qualification. Take, for example, his assertion that 'economic discrimination against women appears when development sets in. It does not go away; nothing indicates that it ever will' (p. 65). Although a great deal of his analysis refers to Europe, Illich backs up this particular assertion by referring to studies on women and development in Third World countries, such as Esther Boserup's and others, which have argued that colonialism and the economic development that followed tended to deteriorate the position of women in many Third World countries.

There are two problems with Illich's use of this type of argument. One is that colonialism and economic modernization has come to most Third World countries with a specific economic system called capitalism, with its corresponding tendency to generate class differences, inequality in the distribution of resources and income, and growing hierarchies in the labor market. There is a gender (and a racial) dimension in the formation of these hierarchical divisions, but at the root there are basic class differences and a specific organization of production based on profit and the market. Boserup in fact has been criticized for failing to see that it was not modernization per se but the system under which it was introduced - with all its economic, social and ideological complexities - that deteriorated the position of women (Benería and Sen 1982). Illich, on the other hand, fails to mention other studies which argue that capitalist economic development has often had a contradictory effect on women; it has 'freed' them from feudal institutions that, as with bonded labor, tied them to landlords and all types of oppressive patriarchal forms such as arranged marriages while, at the same time, it has placed them at the mercy of the market and the hardships of wage labor (Deere 1977; Wiegersma 1980; Heyzer 1982). The overwhelming implication of these studies is not that women should return to the past but that economic development could take different forms that would generate greater equality between the sexes.

This takes us to the second problem in Illich's argument, namely, his tendency to idealize the past as if the world of vernacular gender was one without discrimination against women. A strong anthropological response to Illich's arguments has already appeared (Scheper-Hughes 1983) and I do not want to reproduce similar arguments here. However, one does not need to dig very deep into the anthropological past to realize that what vernacular gender offered in most cases to women includes institutions such as chastity belts, foot-binding, seclusion and lack of mobility, repudiation, clitorectemy and other sorts of what anthropologist Gayle Rubin called 'fetishized indignities' which have been inflicted upon women in most societies. The trick in Illich's analysis is that these indignities are not mentioned. This not only allows him to idealize the past; it also prevents him from recognizing any progress made in women's emancipation throughout history.

DEFINING CONCEPTS

Perhaps one of the most irritating features in Illich's analysis is his tendency to define and redefine terms and concepts as it suits him while ignoring the way they have been defined before and used by a wide variety of authors. To illustrate, by defining economic discrimination as a feature pertaining only to the post-seventeenth century realm of 'economic sex', he precludes it from appearing earlier, say in the inheritance laws of primogeniture that predominated in many European societies in the past, or in women's lack of access to many levels of public life. The examples are numerous; why they are not viewed by Illich as economic discrimination while wage differentials between men and women are defined as such is an issue that he needs to explain. In the last resort, the point is not so much whether they are examples of economic discrimination; the important fact is that they represent discriminatory treatment that places women in a position of subordination, a term that is barely discussed by Illich.

Another interesting example is his definition of gender, a key conceptualization in his analysis. This is a concept that has been widely used by feminists to differentiate it from sex: while the latter has clear biological roots and expressions and might be viewed as 'natural', gender refers to the socially-constructed differences between the sexes. Gender therefore points to characteristics that have to do with culture, ideology and socialization, although it also has deep connections with the material; the importance of this differentiation rests in the need to emphasize gender as a social construct subject to change.

Illich chose to write a book on the subject of gender while reversing the feminist categories of gender and sex:

> I use gender in a new way to designate a duality that in the past was too obvious even to be named and is so far removed from us today that is often confused with sex. By sex I mean the result of a polarization in those common characteristics that, starting with the late eighteenth century, are attributed to all human beings (p. 3-4, emphasis mine).

As mentioned earlier, Illich also speaks of gender as a complementarity that is 'enigmatic' and 'asymmetrical' in a way that 'only metaphor can reach it' (p. 4). He therefore leaves us with a definition that is puzzling. To begin with, what is the difference between the duality of vernacular gender and the polarization of economic sex? The implication of course is that the first is natural and the second man made and that the first is harmonious and the second full of friction. Thus, he argues that the transformation of one into the other generated 'envy' among women:

> ...envy for the other gender's schedule and rhythm, thus appeared, an envy destined to remain as a central characteristic of modern life, an envy fully 'justified' under the assumptions of unisex work but unthinkable under the shield of gender (p. 174).

For Illich, it turns out, women's struggle towards equality is not the result of a new 'consciousness', nor part of humankind's march towards liberation; it is unadulterated envy, a negative consequence of a unisex world. There is a profound reactionary message in this vision:

> Gender implies a complementarity within the world that is
> fundamental and closes the world in on 'us', however ambiguous and
> fragile this closure might be. Sex, on the contrary, implies unlimited
> openess, a universe in which there is always more (p. 81).

For Illich, there is something pernicious in this 'unlimited openess' while the closed world of the past seems to offer a mythical ideal. On the other hand, the universe 'in which there is always more' is connected with this unlimited openess and with Illich's interest in the subject of scarcity. In fact, he sees a close connection between the 'fading of gender' and the 'growing intensity and variety of scarcities' (p. 19). It is for this reason that he views his work on gender as part of his wider interest in the subject of scarcity.

Although these unclear connections are not explored at any length in Gender, Illich raises an interesting issue, namely, to what extent what we call progress – that which makes possible 'a universe in which there is always more' – is really progress. As in his previous books, his answer is in the negative. For those of us who are critical of many of the results brought about by 'progress', there is something appealing in his message. We are aware, for example, of the problems of consumerism and its creation of ever-increasing 'wants' while basic 'needs' for a good proportion of the world population remain unmet. But we are weary of any solution based on an unfounded idealization of the past. In addition, Illich never makes any connection between the negative aspects of progress and the specific economic system(s) that generate it. As a result, he is unable to suggest a transcending alternative and, instead, opts for the return to the past. In the same way, there is something appealing in a world free of friction between the sexes. Yet Illich's reaction to women's struggle for equality is a groundless idealization of a past where he sees a harmonious cooperation between the sexes.

This is related to a key question in Illich's vision of the past – and ours – namely, what is the meaning of complementarity and asymmetry. There are two alternative meanings. One is that they imply a world of separate but equal relations. The other is one that generates relations of dominance/subordination. This fundamental distinction is not made by Illich nor is the issue central in his analysis although it is mentioned in several footnotes:

> Asymmetry implies a disproportion of size or value or power or weight ... a relative position (p. 75).

However, for Illich 'the complementarity between genders is both asymmetric and ambiguous' (p. 75) and the ambiguity seems to prevent him from dealing with the issue of power relations in a central way. In his footnotes, he implies that the complementarity and asymmetry of vernacular gender generated a balance or parallel spheres of different and non-conflicting power relations between the sexes (see footnote 84, p. 115). To substantiate his assertion, he refers to a number of studies while ignoring the great variety of authors who have emphasized the oppressive nature of vernacular gender for women (Scheper-Hughes 1982).

What is interesting is that feminists are sympathetic to the argument that once upon a time perhaps men and women were equal. Since the appearance of the new wave of feminism, anthropologists have debated Engels' thesis on the origins of women's subordination (Reiter 1977). The debate is far from conclusive. Illich ignores it and leaves us only with the impression of the rosy past. In addition, Engels' thesis was formulated very concretely around the connection between the introduction of private property in early societies and the need to control paternity and women's sexuality for inheritance purposes. It was formulated with the use of historical examples such as the transformation of the Greek Gens and the rise of the Athenian and Roman states as well as with examples from the Celts and Germans, all of which preceded, by many years, Illich's end of vernacular gender in the eleventh century. The neglect of this major issue on Illich's part is a major gap in his work.

Finally, another definition used by Illich is worth mentioning, namely that of patriarchy and sexism. As he points out, many authors use the two terms interchangeably, both indicating an institutionalized system of male dominance. However, for him, the concept of patriarchy is a 'power imbalance' limited to the reign of vernacular gender. Sexism, on the other hand, is specific to modern societies:

> Patriarchy I take to mean a power imbalance under the assumption of gender. Sexism is clearly not the continuation of patriarchal power relations into modern societies. Rather, it is a hitherto unthinkable individual degradation of one-half of humanity on socio-biological grounds... each individual woman, under the regime of sex, is forced to compete with men (p. 34, emphasis mine).

This definition gives us a new clue to Illich's negative view of industrialized society which is consistent with what we have discussed so far: the problem with sexism is centered on the fact that, under the realm of economic sex, each individual woman is forced to compete with men. Under patriarchy, as defined by Illich, men and women do not compete because they remain in their clearly defined and separated spheres.

There are two problems with this argument. One is Illich's usual assumption that the power imbalance under patriarchy is part of the rosier past. The other has to do with his identification of the roots of sexism with the need for women to compete with men, particularly in the labor market. This seems to be more a moral and paternalistic position than an analysis of the process by which the subordination of women took new forms as industrialization and capitalism developed. The gradual introduction of a wage labor system made labor market inequalities and discrimination a new expression of the asymmetry between the sexes. The shift of production away from the home also generated profound changes in the nature of the family and the role of men and women within in. This has been widely analyzed by a variety of authors who show both the continuity and the transformation of old patriarchal forms into the new (Zaretsky 1976; Tilly and Scott 1978). Both patriarchy and sexism, even as defined by Illich, imply a system of male domination; for women it makes little difference whether it comes, in Illich's terms, under the realm of gender or of economic sex.

WORK, CULTURE AND GENDER

In this section, I want to make use of Illich's notions of 'gendered' and 'unisex' tools for the purpose of returning to some of the questions posed at the beginning of the paper. For Illich, gendered tools belong to the realm of vernacular gender; they imply that 'In all pre-industrial societies, a set of gender-specific tasks is reflected in a set of gender-specific tools' (p. 90). Industrialization makes the work of men and women converge:

An industrial society cannot exist unless it imposes certain unisex assumptions: the assumptions that both sexes are made for the same work... There would be no competition for 'work' between men and women, unless 'work' had been redefined as an activity that befits humans irrespective of their sex (pp. 9-10).

The key question here is what does it mean to speak of gendered tools. Illich's implication is that they form part of a natural order of things by which human activity and the division of labor between the sexes is governed without tensions. I want to argue that the gendering of tools is a social construction that can also be found in industrialized society. Although machines can be used by men and women indiscriminately in practice gendering takes place along the lines of occupational segregation. Commodity production, far from generating 'the loss of gender', as Illich argues (p. 94), introduced new forms of using gender as a labor category in production. As we know, most jobs in the garment industry continue to be predominantly female despite all the technological changes introduced since the industrial revolution. Sewing machines are used by women while the cutting of garments is normally done by men - the use of scissors often justifying higher wages for the male workers. Women, of course, know how to use scissors and men can learn to use the sewing machines. Yet gendering has de facto taken place in this and many other cases.

I have argued elsewhere in greater detail (Benería 1984) that employers make use of 'gender traits' that workers have acquired through a given process of socialization for the purpose of placing them in specific slots in the labor process. Thus, in modern production women are found clustered in tedious assembly work that requires dexterity in manual work, discipline to work in small spaces and a low degree of mobility (as with the assembly of electric and electronic equipment and toys). These are characteristics often required in labor intensive industries where women tend to concentrate. Women are also over-represented in short-term, part-time and unstable jobs - domestic piece work being an extreme form among them. In all these cases, a connection can be traced between the specific task being performed and specific gender traits of workers. For example, manual dexterity, patience, discipline, and the ability to work in small spaces are traits that women acquire through their concentration on household-related activities. The connection between gender traits and the hiring of women in part-time and unstable work was typically expressed by a Mexican manager who said that 'young women are ideal for short term employment because they actually like to stop working, say for a week, so that they can visit their parents in the country side, go shopping, or help in the home' (Benería, 1984:17). Similarly, the high representation of women in domestic piece work is also related to their primary involvement in domestic work and the rearing of children.<4>

Gender traits are not necessarily universal and may vary widely across countries and cultures, and across ethnic and religious groups. From the large body of literature on women and development that has appeared during the past fifteen years we have learned two important points. One is that most pre-industrial societies have a clearly defined gender-related division of labor; men and women tend to perform gendered tasks along Illich's vernacular gender lines. The other is that what is considered male and female tasks varies across societies, particularly for activities performed outside of the household (Boserup, 1970). This suggests that there is little that is 'natural' in these different patterns of work even though they can be rationalized or explained through a variety of factors that range from the economic to the ideological and cultural. Numerous studies of the sexual division of labor in different societies have provided interesting illustrations of the interaction between these factors.<5> What is important here is to emphasize that there is much in common between the gender traits acquired in an industrialized society and, for example, the ideology of seclusion in Islamic societies or the taboos connected with the gendered tools of societies under vernacular gender; this commonality is that they are social constructs, therefore subject to change under the influence of economic and social factors.

We can agree with Illich in that the historical trend has been towards the breaking down of the rigidities in the division of labor in traditional societies. The gradual increase in women's participation in the paid labor force in industrialized societies has contributed to this. Despite the limits set up by occupational segregation, women have, slowly and with mixed results, been moving into what were previously viewed as male jobs. During the past fifteen years, there has been an intensification of questions regarding traditional concepts of femininity and masculinity. These economic and cultural factors are at the root of what appears to be a gradual change in the division of labor within the household, at least in some countries, towards men and women sharing the tasks associated with domestic work and child care.<6>

While for Illich the breaking down of gender rigidities is a negative development, it is likely to be viewed as a progressive step even by those of us who think that there is still a long way ahead before equality between the sexes is achieved. The fundamental difference here is that, for him, equality is not an achievable nor necessarily a desirable goal while, for feminists, it is a basic component in the construction of more egalitarian societies.

CONCLUDING COMMENTS

Rather than being part of the backlash against feminism, it seems to me that Illich's book is a profoundly reactionary message without malice. There is a naive nostalgia for the past in his message and a lack of understanding of the depths of the feminist message – combined with what seems to be a fear or perhaps a revulsion against the notion of equality between the sexes. For those of us who are concerned about the negative aspects of industrial society, there is a certain attractiveness in Illich's criticism of the evils of industrialization. Yet most of us do not want to return to the past because we agree that there is some progress in not having to get up at 5 a.m. to grind corn so that men can eat their tortillas when they get up two hours later, or in not having to wash clothes by hand, or carry water on our heads or the fire wood on our backs, or in acquiring an education without patriarchal limits to what can be learned. Being freed from physical labor or from exhaustively long hours of work is, if nothing else, a step in the right direction of creating space for individual and collective development and liberation.

A fundamental flaw in Illich's analysis is that he ignores the institutional framework under which industrialization has taken place. Historically, it was capitalism that brought us the industrial revolution; the unprecedented dynamism generated by this mode of production is based on greed, class domination and a value system saturated with the dictates of the market. The industrialization undergone by non-capitalist societies, such as in Eastern Europe, has also taken place under the framework of hierarchical productive and social structures with a gender dimension to them (Molyneux 1982). Given that gender traits can be used as a criterion to place women in the lower echelons of the labor structure, it can be argued that more egalitarian societies are likely to provide the most appropriate framework for breaking down gender inequalitites. Illich's neglect of this dimension in the analysis leads him to look at the past for solutions rather than to envisage a different future. As a result, his ideal future is tainted with his mythical vision of the past; to us the challenge is to recognize past achievements and understand the problems still facing us while searching for new models for the change ahead.

Notes

<1> In the United States, and despite the implementation of affirmative action and other policies dealing with discrimination and the wage gap, Census data show that the gap increased between 1970 and 1980. (See study by Gordon Green, The New York Times. January 16, 1984).

<2> In particular, see the articles from the symposium 'Beyond the Backlash: A Feminist Critique of Ivan Illich's Theory of Gender', Feminist Issues, Vol. 3, No. 1, Spring 1983.

<3> A summary of the literature on the domestic labor debate can be found in Himmelweit and Mohun, 1977. Theoretical discussions and empirical studies around the underestimation of women's economic activities have been numerous; they have involved academic circles as well as government and international agencies. For illustrations, see Safilios-Rothschild 1982 and Bería 1982:119-48.

<4> In a study of 140 cases of women involved in different types of domestic piece work in Mexico City during 1981-82, it was found that most reasons given by woman for working at home were related, directly or indirectly, with the 'ideology of domesticity' and with the specific forms in which it prevails in today's Mexico (Bería and Martha Roldan, work in progress).

<5> See, for example, the studies by Mies, Heyzer, Young and Croll included in Bería (ed.) 1982. For a theoretical perspective on the subject, see Barrett 1980.

<6> In the United States, a national survey carried out by CBS/New York Times in 1977, found that the notion of sharing responsibilities in marriage is becoming more acceptable: 46% of the men and 50% of the women surveyed expressed a preference for a marriage in which both husband and wife have paid jobs, both do housework and take care of children. Pleck and Rustard (1980) also report similar trends.

14 Work, needs and three cultures

JOHAN GALTUNG

Work is a central concern for all human beings, 'work' is a central concept in any social science. But there is something which is even more central and which immediately brings us closer to the other concept to be discussed here, 'culture': needs. I doubt very much that one can have any theory of work without a theory of needs, or at least a typology
of needs.

The typology I shall use is a very simple one, dividing human needs into four classes, claiming universality for the classes, but not for the concrete definition of the elements within those classes, and certainly not for the concrete way of satisfying them. The typology is as follows:

Table 1. *A typology of needs with their negations*

	actor- dependent	structure- dependent
material/ somatic	SURVIVAL (violence; death)	WELFARE (misery; death)
nonmaterial/ mental-spiritual	FREEDOM (repression)	IDENTITY (alienation)

To the left is the distinction between needs that are more material/ somatic and those that are more nonmaterial/spiritual (I do not use the expression 'psychological' needs, assuming that those would be the needs of, possibly even for, psychologists and less than universal). Like all such brutal cuts into human and social existence it is far too crude, but nevertheless useful. And then there is the distinction between actor-dependent and structure-dependent needs, needs that for their satisfaction (and particularly for their dissatisfaction) are more dependent on the concrete action of concrete actors, and needs that are more dependent on the enduring operation of social structures.

The four words in the table in capital letters can only be understood by reading the table headings. But they can also be taken in their more immediate meanings: 'survival' simply means to survive; on top of that comes 'welfare' meaning the satisfaction of all those concrete material/somatic needs for food, clothing, housing, labor-saving devices, health services, schooling, and perhaps transportation and communication. Some of these border on the mental-spiritual. Both of these classes of needs can be counteracted in well-known ways, through direct violence leading to death, quickly (for instance by standing in the way of a bullet) and by structural violence also leading to death, but more slowly (for instance by being exposed to a drought, because the water has been channelled away to greener, more income-producing pastures).

And then there are the nonmaterial needs, for freedom and identity. I do not see them as an adornment on top of the other two, something that can wait till the other two have been met, one way or the other. I see them as operating all the time, as being expressions or dreams of human beings and, for that matter, probably also of animals (a zoological garden gives some indication of what it means to an animal only to have the needs for survival and welfare met, and not those for identity and freedom. They look despondent, lackadaisical, apathetic).

Much more can be said about needs, but let us proceed immediately to work. I think it is reasonable to conceive of work as the human activity needed above all to guarantee survival and welfare, nothing less, nothing more. The quantitative level at which survival and welfare are guaranteed will differ in time and space. But the basic point here is something different: work is not merely a question of what, but also of how it is done. And to discuss this 'how', I think the other two classes of needs come into the picture, and very importantly so.

More concretely, let us try to make use of the other two classes of needs, 'freedom' and 'identity', as two dimensions to describe types of work from a more qualitative point of view:

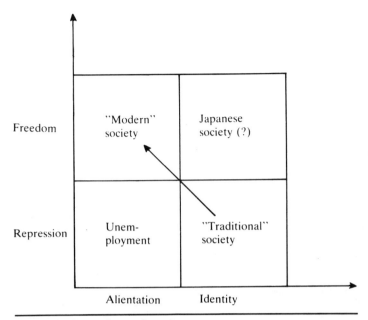

Figure 1. *A typology of work*

There is a well-known arrow in the figure, as usual pointing from 'traditional' society to 'modern' society. Nobody will deny the significance of this arrow, either in reality or in theory, although it should not be over-estimated; it does not tell the whole story. But the story is important. The point of departure is work with identity, unifying nature which delivers the raw materials, the soil and the sun, the water and the minerals, the plants and the animals; the people with whom one works, the fellow producers; and the people with whom one consumes the work products, the fellow consumers. All of these are united in an economic cycle of very limited extension. There is identity with it all, which is not the same as saying that there is harmony. There is an element of insubstitutability, it is this nature, those people - not some other nature and some other people. Precisely because of the lack of substitution possibilities, there is an element of repression. One is not 'free', or more particularly, condemned to be free: one is condemned to be exactly where one is, with rather limited opportunities for moving except, possibly, for the change of some aspects of nature if the mode of production is nomadic.

Then there is what is known as 'modern' society or mode of production: the economic cycles are quickly expanding, and, more importantly, there is a high element of substitutability. Nature can be brought from everywhere, the place of production can be changed. One can jump from one to the other, and if one does not do so oneself, others do, so that the fellow producers are changing all the time. And the same applies to the consumers: changing, shifting all the time, most of them unknown. Of course, the condition for all this substitutability

133

lies in transportation/communication and the introduction of a medium of exchange which facilitated all kinds of substitution much beyond what could be done through barter: money. Buying nature, buying labor, ultimately also buying capital; selling products; that is what 'modern' society is about, both in its private and state capitalist formations. An enormous amount of freedom is gained in the sense of substitutability, where people change their environment or parts of their environment any number of times; but, always, at the expense of a corresponding level of alienation, of loss of identity.

Thus the world is changing, history moves – we do not say forwards or backwards, history just moves. And behind those two modes are two cultures, very different and intimately related to the modes of work. Two work cultures, so to speak, linked by complex transformation processes.

The major dimensions for an analysis would be two very important aspects of any culture: the person-nature relation and the person-person relation. A traditional work culture would need as its underpinning a tight, close relationship to nature, a strong feeling of identity with exactly this part of nature, not just any. Whether society is nomadic or sedentary, nature is close. And there would be a similar closeness between people, where people are not seen as substitutable but as parts of oneself, much in the same way as nature. Traditional peoples problably used to see it that way; we are still used to thinking of Mediterranean cultures in Europe and traditional cultures in the other continents in that way. And it is probably correct, there is probably much to it.

This means that when these cultural conditions are negated then the stage is set for another type of work, 'modern' work, based on freedom rather than identity. This is impossible without two major cultural constructions: the construction of nature as inanimate, highly substitutable, one piece with a particular chemical composition is just as good as any other piece with the same chemical composition; one animal of a certain species just the same as another. Needless to say, natural sciences were the conditions for this type of construction, imposing on nature a high degree of substitutability precisely by defining equivalence classes in nature, things of the same kind, through endless typologies and generalizations based on abstractions which defined essential characteristics.

Similarly, the social sciences were called in to do the same work in order to provide the background for substitutability among people. Psychology defined equivalence classes of people according to aptitude in general and intelligence in particular; pedagogical sciences, according to educational level; the science of economics, according to their potentials in production and consumption; and sociology/politology/anthropology, according to their position in social networks and structures.

But that could only form a basis for substitutability, not for individuation. The individual had to be constructed, had to be defined as 'man alone', somebody who not only could be detached but also, on occasion, should be detached. Changes were needed in the most basic aspect of culture, the religious infrastructure. When Protestantism is seen as important in this connection, it is probably not so much in the way Weber emphasized as in a much more simple way, the contribution to the construction of the individual by relating the individual through his and her deeds and thoughts (particularly the latter) directly to God. The person became movable under the eyes of God, as an individual in his and her own right. The medium of that mobility was money, hence a strong tie between Protestantism and capitalism was only to be expected.

One may say that all of this is trivial; these or similar things have been said again and again. That, however, does not make them less important. It may also be important to point out that there is a two-way relation at work here; not only do changes in culture relate to changes in the way of organizing work, the latter will certainly also lead to the former. Or, perhaps, better expressed, a culture based on insubstitutability/collectivism will relate to traditional work in one family with a certain inner consistency, and a culture based on substitutability/individualism will relate to modern work in another family, also with a high level of consistency. In other words, they are both reflections of different social cosmologies; work is one way of articulating that cosmology, the patterns of belief are another.

However, having used a fourfold table as a point of departure, one is, of course, also led to the question of what might take place in the other cells. Moreover, is it really true that the arrow is a one-way arrow, or could it possibly function as a two-way arrow? And, in that case, could the process be from here to there and back again, or an oscillating one, possibly also touching the other two corners of the table? In short, could we not make the way of looking at work somewhat more complicated than a simple traditional/modern dichotomy, with an arrow smacking of the 1950s in US social science?

Of course we can, and one key to that would be to look at what is tentatively seen as the Japanese mode of work or Japanese mode of production, JMP. And here, one approach is to look at the words. The word for work in Japanese is hataraku, which also means 'to function'. It sounds very different from the Christian conceptualization of work as something painful, something related to sweat and hard labor, in order to earn one's bread. One may say that, in the West, this was overcome; work is certainly not very hard for very many, so much so that in 'modern' society we tend to refer to it not as work but as job (strangely enough the same word in English is used to mean exactly the opposite of what that biblical person stood for!). The question, then, is where Japan stands on this dimension between work and job.

The answer is, as is so often the case with Japan, neither with one, nor with the other, nor in-between, but in a certain sense, above, beyond. I think this can be particularly clearly seen if we make use of two other dimensions, also very frequently found in such analysis, to discuss work systems:

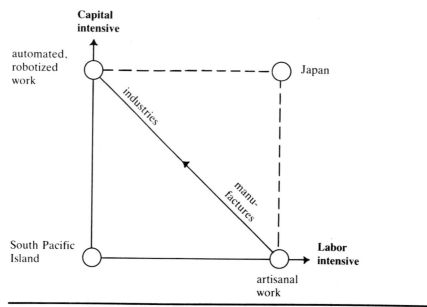

Figure 2. *Another typology of work*

Down in the right hand corner is a very labor intensive form of work with no capital, or almost none, put into the means of production. Usually such work is referred to as artisanal, and it is usually seen as traditional and as being high on identity and low on freedom, with little mobility of factors and products, and with little chance to substitute anything for anything.

Many such people can then be put together in one big room, for instance a room vacated by closing a Catholic monastery, and the result would be manufacturing, doing it by hand, but many people together in such a way that there is a certain economy of scale. Some capital is put into the setting for the production and some more complicated means of production are also acquired; but the work is still done by hand, manufacture, without inanimate sources of energy beyond water and wind.

Industry starts with the introduction of inanimate energy, and is then taken further by substituting more and more capital for labor until the ultimate form is found, automated, even robotized forms of work with almost no labor at all. Strangely enough, this particular process is also very often referred to as 'development' although it actually is a way of getting rid of people in general and the working class in particular. And this was also partly the intention – I presume.

The interesting thing in this particular figure is that there is actually no bottom left-hand corner. There has to be either labor or capital to do work; unless one introduces the South Pacific Islands with nature only, abundant, generous, making work superfluous. However, this is perhaps not so interesting from our point of view, as it is a rather extreme case. More interesting is the logical opposite of the South Pacific Island, Japan.

The basic point about Japan, the third work culture to be discussed in this connection, is the way in which that country tries to combine labor-intensive and capital-intensive production. More particularly, this is done by combining artisanry and robotization. May be one could say that the typical Japanese production process is an ARA chain, with three links in it. First comes an artisanal phase with the sub-contractors to the big corporation, very small production units, often family based, producing parts that go into the process in a rather artisanal way. The quality is very high, the capital input relatively low. One is reminded of the Swiss watch industry and how it related to Swiss farms, which were idle during the long winters and worked on parts for that industry.

The second phase is highly industrial, and not only that, it is even automated, robotized. Everything is put together, there are assembly lines and all the things associated with the most 'modern' industry.

And then there is the third phase, where the products coming off the assembly lines from the industrial phase of the total process are regarded more as raw material, to be taken apart again, revised, brought up to a higher level of quality by the proverbial Japanese super-worker, the honko. In this part of the process very high levels of quality can be attained. I would compare it to an author revising the manuscript after he has dictated it and it has come off the 'assembly line' provided by the kind services of the secretary who has to listen to all that dictation. It has nothing to do with 'quality control'; it is not a question of the author checking every five pages, revising them a little bit here and there. It is a complete re-working of the whole thing, cutting and pasting, bringing out a new product. Often, as is well known, this process also goes through several stages. The product of the assembly line is an input rather than a finished product; even raw material for this third phase.

The interesting thing about the Japanese mode of production, is, therefore, that it combines artisanal and superindustrial culture, and consequently also combines identity-oriented and freedom-oriented types of work. There is no doubt that modern natural sciences are used and that a money economy plays an important role, making it possible to substitute one piece of nature for another, one product for another, some times also one worker for another. But, at the same time, there is, unquestionably, in the Japanese factory a high level of identity. To use classic sociological terms: it is universalism combined with diffuseness. Everybody is treated according to certain common standards (including promotion according to seniority, and life-long employment), but a wide spectrum of the personality of the employees is taken into account, including what in Western culture is known as personal or private. That cuts down on alienation, creates much more identity and makes for interesting combinations.

To conclude, it is clear that we have here three different work cultures operating in the same world. And there is also a culture of unemployment, both repressed and alienated at the same time, neither in contact with others, nor possessing the means that makes for 'freedom' in a 'modern' society. So let me use that to pose a little question: could it not be interesting to think in terms of career patterns, not so much for societies as for individuals, among these four forms, from one to the other, provided society is rich enough to harbour all of them? And that, ultimately, would be a question of whether it has a culture rich enough to legitimize all four types – including a culture of unemployment, under certain assumptions.

To avoid misunderstandings, however, let me add some notes of caution. I am impressed with the Japanese art of rejecting Western contradictions, working out a both-and where we only manage to see an either-or, like our famous 'modern/traditional'. In no way, however, does that mean any applause for other aspects of the Japanese Mode of Production, such as the damage to nature; the damage to social structure when a tightly integrated state-capital complex presides over a structure where men exploit women, the young and the old are marginalized and the big corporations exploit the small; not to mention the damage to world society when dependencies abound in a highly competitive world. Seen in that perspective Japan suddenly becomes very similar, even 'more similar than most'.

Nor is it obvious that some of this cannot be learnt and imitated by others. But aspects of Oriental philosophy, particularly Daoist and Buddhist attitudes to contradictions, no doubt facilitate Japanese practices in this field. And the 'zero defects' mentality and achievement works better in a Confucian climate with well-defined rights and duties. And – the tiny indication given of some aspects of Japanese work culture by no means applies to all: life long employment, for instance, is hardly given to more than 25-30%, and then almost only to men (but many of these are working in the export sector, so the impact of the work style is felt all around the world.

But even so – once more: there are things to be learnt! The world still has surprises, fortunately.

15 Everyday life in Europe and the effect of the 'protestant work ethic'

GUSTAF WINGREN

The kind of manual labour which provides us with houses to live in and food to eat has always been going on. Mankind survives only because this work is constantly in progress. However, the valuation of this indispensable labour varies a lot in different cultures. In some places it is held in contempt, in others it is honoured and considered sacred. Europe is unique in this respect, in that through the centuries it has accommodated two completely opposite valuations of manual labour.

In this context, the 16th century Reformation is a turning-point. This is particularly the case concerning the two leading reformers: Luther in Wittenberg och Calvin in Geneva. Of these two, Luther is the pioneer. He coined the German expression 'Beruf' and gave it the meaning 'manual labour'. He did so as early as 1521-1522. The emphasis falls on manual labour, that it is good and commanded by God. It is a 'Vocation' from God, which is connected with the fact that the whole doctrine of vocation is formulated as a polemic doctrine, polemical against the celibate and monastic life. Calvin continues the polemic and formulates a strict work ethic.

The reason why the doctrine of work became of crucial importance during the Reformation era was due to attempts during the Middle Ages to combine harmoniously the two opposite valuations which Europe inherited from Greece and from Israel. In these attempts to harmonize two contradictory views, the Biblical one, with its origin in the Israelite tradition, was deprived of its content. The dichotomization of existence, which was borrowed from Greek philosophy, became dominant during the Middle Ages: matter, the body, was the inferior, the world of ideas, the invisible, was the superior. The Reformation tried to restore the Biblical view of matter as something created (Agrell 1976: 150-152).

This affects two aspects of the everyday life of most Europeans (at least in the northern part of Europe): marriage, as against celibacy, is seen as something positive, and manual labour is regarded as positive in comparison with the contemplative life in the monastery.

One sees more clearly how necessary these two 'positions' are, by clarifying what it is that characterizes Greece and Israel respectively: they represent two incompatible visions of what 'real life' is. The peculiar thing is that the two visions were at one time conjoined. The peculiar thing is, so to speak, the Middle Ages.

In Greece, heavy labour was done by slaves. The wise man, the philosopher, discussed and comtemplated but did not take part in any manual work. A Jewish Rabbi, who possessed knowledge of God's will, was also obliged to have an ordinary profession; moreover, he ought to be married. According to Greek philosophy, the true being, the idea, was characterized by unchangeability, absence of motion, absence of variation. On the other hand, the one who really exists, Jahve, was apprehended by the Israelites as being active in history. It is typical that the prophet sees God as active in the Exodus from Egypt and in the liberation from Babylonia, while no Greek philosopher sees the true Being appear at the battles of Marathon or Salamis.

The Old Testament is a collection of completely profane stories about a people on earth. The concentration on the secular and the physical continued in the New Testament where the description of God's relevation is focused on the vision of a man who heals bodies – blind, paralysed and deaf bodies – often without a 'spiritual' sequel of any kind. The parables are even more remarkable. Not in any parable does Jesus talk about someone doing 'religion'. On the contrary, only motives from everyday life are consistently used: farmers who plant their seed, shepherds who seek lost sheep, women who bake bread. It is impossible to imagine Plato or Aristotle using such examples in teaching of the true Being.

However, in Europe these two world views have been fused into one unity. The great and ingenious fusion was carried out during the high tide of the Middle Ages, the thirteenth century. The contradictory valuations were distributed amongst different individuals. Marriage was maintained in accordance with good Israelite tradition and became one of seven sacraments of the Church. At the same time, it became possible for anyone who abstained from marriage to enter a monastery. In the world one should work and make money. The monk abstained from possessing material goods and chose a life of poverty, prayer and complete devotion to God. The difference in level between spiritual and wordly is prominent but at the same time the inner community and solidarity between the different parts of the Church emerges distinctly (Vontobel 1946:3-5).

LUTHER'S CONTRIBUTION

Luther came from a family who worked with their hands. His father worked in mining and gradually gained an independent position as a miner. The family continued in these and similar ways of life; the son, Martin, was the only one who got the opportunity to study. He became a monk while still young, belonged to a rigorous order and severely subdued his body in a celibate life, in constant agony of God's last judgement. By profession he became professor in Biblical exegesis, 'doctor biblicus'. In his work he discovered the enormous impoverishment of the content of the Bible, the loss of Biblical substance which medieval scholasticism had brought with it.

On the basis of many years of Biblical studies he launched a frontal attack against the monastic life, carried through, theoretically, in the great treatise of 1521 on the monastic vows, and, practically, through marriage and the establishment of a family in 1525. The woman he married was a former nun; both of them broke their monastic vows.

Two theological components are combined in the formation of Luther's doctrine on worldly labour as a vocation from God (Beruf, vocatio). The first component is the famous, now almost incomprehensible doctrine on 'justification by faith alone', which means that the Christian, in his relationship to God, builds his assurance of justification solely on faith, trust and confidence. Not one single act that I perform has the object of 'making me a Christian'. God tells me in the word of the Gospel that I am justified before him. When I have faith in this word, I am a Christian. 'Deeds', that is, activity on my part, can only be motivated on the basis of the external needs, the 'poverty' that surrounds me on earth. Deeds must therefore be worldly - this is the second component.

The monastic institution implies a double disobedience against God's will. In the first place, the monk enters into a spiritual activity, a 'deed', an 'achievement', with the purpose of gaining God's approval. In so doing he destroys faith which is pure confidence in God's Gospel without 'deeds'. Secondly, he leaves the world where the earthly needs are to be found. And in so doing he destroys the love for his neighbour. The man who loves his fellow-being, loves to be in the world. He enjoys himself and is pleased with the opportunity of daily carrying out manual labour and accomplishing things beneficial to his fellow-beings: sowing and harvesting, building houses, producing shoes and clothes etc.

That this love for one's neighbour can make use of ordinary professional work in order to reach one's fellow-beings with needed external gifts, has to do with the construction of everyday life at the time of Luther. What did manual labour consist of in the 16th century? There was, as yet, no industrialization. 'Work' with the hands was farming, stock-raising, craftmanship. The working man formed a product with his hands and saw in his immediate surroundings the consumer who received the product and used it. The work from the worker's hand implied that 'the neighbour' (=the one who lived in the neighbourhood, the one who was near) received something good and useful in his hand. If the worker loves his neighbour he wants to produce a good product. There are no 'Christian' shoes, but a Christian makes good shoes for his neighbour. That which is good and full of love is embedded in worldliness.

As a critique against the form of piety in which Luther had participated during his time in the monastery, it is now emphasized in the reformational writings that true holiness is in the world, it is concealed, hidden. 'Hidden are the saints, hidden is' the Church.' Every attempt to separate the sacred from the profane, every endeavour to make the sacred visible in an isolated place, every such attempt was rejected (Wingren 1957:182-184).

To the hidden, that which should not be separated from the profane and become visible as something singularly sacred, also belongs what Luther calls 'the cross'. In the monastery one practised 'mortifications', voluntary suffering which one performed in order to resemble Jesus; shirts of hair, lashings with a scourge, etc. This is child's play, says Luther. The craftsman will carry his true suffering in the world, in his work. And here, in his work, he goes through a suffering that is beneficial to someone else. The childish forms of pain that one goes through in the monastery are not beneficial to anyone: I remain in the centre all the time, in an egocentric way. What one vainly tried to achieve in the monastery happens spontaneously when a person carries out his ordinary profession. The worldly life is, in itself, full of 'Christ-conformity'.

This doctrine of 'the cross' in everyday life was part of a very comprehensive interpretation of human existence in general as a life in two different 'kingdoms', the earthly kingdom and the heavenly kingdom. Both are divine, both are governed by God, but they are governed differently. God governs the earthly kingdom, where deeds are performed at many places of work, 'with his left hand' through the Law. And God governs the heavenly kingdom, which human beings already participate in through faith, with 'his right hand' through the Gospel. The heavenly kingdom will appear in its full strength at the resurrection from the dead. Here on 'the earth of the cross' we now taste death, while in faith and confidence we walk towards eternal life in heaven.

This point has very dangerous political consequences within the doctrine of labour, dangerous in particular for those who have little-valued professions. The Law and the Gospel have, namely, been put into the hands of human beings in certain particular offices. The Gospel has been entrusted to 'the ministry of the Word', i.e. to the parish pastor. The Law is administered by the authorities, the prince, the city council and the judge. The minister preaches the Gospel and the authorities make sure that people obey the laws. The ordinary people work under these two divine 'hands'. Everyone serves the other. The service is performed by everyone attending to his own business. No one tries to interfere with anyone else's assignment. 'If you mind you business and I mind mine, whatever happens will turn out just fine'.

Originally, this whole interpretation of life was construed as a protest against a tyrannical church. The Reformation aimed at liberating elementary human life, a declaration of the majority against the attempts to trample on the bodily and subordinate it to a centrally governed church with its pope, hierarchy, celibacy and monasteries. But the assumption behind all this was: the human life that shall be liberated is found in farming and craftmanship and all the thousands of activities necessary for the maintenance of life that are carried out by different members of the family in the household. Every well-organized household at this time functioned as a residence, restaurant, school, hospital, home for old people, workshop, all at the same time.

It is within this local structure that the fatal changes occur. At the time of Luther, 'my neighbour' lived quite close to me, in my immediate vicinity, while I was working. Both in farming and in craftmanship at that time, both in the country and in the city, work formed a human community: what was produced was consumed by the worker's neighbour – and was consumed as something necessary for the maintenance of life. It appeared meaningful to produce the product through work and to see it in function in a life-building manner in the human community.

If one looks at the community-shaping factors, incipient industrialization implies, in the first place, that the relation between the owner of the factory and the employees is cut off. During the time of the guilds, the journeymen lived their everyday life close to the master; they often had their meals at the master's table, in his household. In this environment the apprentices were trained to become journeymen. Correspondingly, the farms functioned in a community-building way through the work with animals and in the fields. With the success of industry's new type of production, the workers, however, came to live by themselves as did the owner of the factory and his family. They do not meet each other outside the working-place. The community between them is broken (Wingren 1980:665-669).

142

Secondly, the relation between the breadwinner's work and the community of the family is broken. The man leaves the home in the morning and returns back tired in the evening. With the exception of short breaks for meals, the growing children do not see their father during the day - they have no experience of seeing their father at work. Work is something distant, it brings in the money the family needs, but it lacks human features. Nevertheless, according to the Lutheran doctrine, this inhuman process, void of community, ought to be the ideal image of 'love for one's neighbour'. The love that Jesus talks about in the New Testament, is realized by the father over there in the factory!

The third loss of community is in the long run even more fatal: the distance between the worker and the consumer who uses his product becomes greater and greater. Here was the crucial argument at the start of the 16th century why a Christian ought to choose manual labour in the world instead of spiritual exercises in the monastery. What the monk does benefits no one, what the manual labourer produces meets a real need among his fellow-beings. The more industrialization advances, the less important become the questions concerning the real needs of one's fellow-beings. A completely different question dominates the planning: which products can sell?

The increase in production as such becomes the main purpose. Through advertisements and publicity campaigns it is possible to create needs that do not exist. Since service to one's neighbour was the most important part of the original argumentation for a purely worldly work, and since this aspect receives less and less emphasis the closer we get to present times, the Protestant work ethic of today ought to evolve into a critique of the production system. But this practically never happens. On the whole, most Christians accept the current development of society. The protests from the churches have mainly concerned private moral questions (sexuality, abortion etc.). There are explanations for this which will be discussed later on.

Hence the idea of work as a 'vocation' was formed within a social structure dominated by craftmanship and farming, while those human beings who should practise their Lutheran faith in their everyday life were forced to live in a totally different structure, formed during the progress of industrialization. Craftmanship was most severely affected. Farming and stock-raising were for a long time carried out in more or less the same way as they had been during the 16th century. Consequently, it was easier for Lutheran piety to survive in the country than in the big cities where, instead, new kinds of religiosity prevailed.

The change from city to country reflects the new situation in a conspicuous way. As a matter of fact, the Lutheran Reformation in Scandinavia started its triumphal procession as a typical urban phenomenon. In Sweden the Reformation started in the Great Church in Stockholm; in Denmark St. Peter's Church in Malmö early became of crucial importance. Gustav Vasa met the greatest opposition from people living in the country, Dalarna and Småland. Three centuries later these same provinces were the stronghold of Lutheranism.

Here, we can see a repetition of what happened with Christianity's first contacts with Europe. The word for 'pagan' was then the Latin word paganus, 'one who lives in the country'. Without exception Paul sends his letters to the big cities where the first Christian congregations were founded. Later on, the division of the European countryside into different parishes, the parochial system, became the firm backbone of the Church. The farmers, who had earlier been pagans and unwilling to accept the Gospel of the Early Church, gradually became the advocates of a Catholic piety loyal to the Pope and antagonistic towards the Lutheran novelties that were preached in the cities, and in the end the only group where the idea of work as a vocation could really stay alive.

What Lutheranism would have needed in order to master the new situation of industrialization morally was, most of all, a completely different doctrine of the law than the one Martin Luther represented in the 16th century. From the 18th century on, Neo-Calvinism shows a much greater constructive power than does Lutheranism. The reason for this is that, right from the beginning, Calvin had a different doctrine of the law than Luther. Calvinism provided more opportunities for an independent Christian interpretation of the law which deviated from the authorities' patterns of action and made it possible to tolerate criticism from below against unrighteous goverment.

Through this Calvinistic move the original Protestant work ethic formulated by Luther is modified. The movements in the Lutheran Churches which are called 'revivals', have nearly always Neo-Calvinistic elements (Troeltsch 1923:794-964).

CALVIN'S OPINION OF THE LAW

According to Calvin, the law is, in a way, the most central part of salvation. It is true that, like Luther, he says that God out of pure grace declares man to be righteous, a righteousness that is freely given to us through the Gospel. But, for Calvin, God's aim in freely offering salvation is different from the aim Luther talks about. The final aim for Luther is freedom from the law and resurrection from the dead. Calvin underlines with force and constantly repeats that the effect of salvation is the heart's new willingness to obey God's eternal law. For those who have faith the law is a friend.

This difference between Luther and Calvin appears insignificant but it implies great and revolutionary consequences for everyday life. The following three implications are of particular importance.

In the first place, the Christian congregation – and not 'the world' – becomes the arena for exemplary obedience to the law. Calvin also has a doctrine of 'two kingdoms' in his system, the kingdom of earth and the kingdom of heaven, and, like Luther, he is of the opinion that God has put his law into the hands of the worldly authorities. But he does not mean that the Church should preach an exclusive Gospel. The Church also preaches God's eternal law: its members have, from a purely moral point of view, a deeper understanding of what the law demands than does the world (Wolf 1958:38-57).

Secondly, this implies a kind of political preaching relatively unknown to Lutheranism. When the Calvinistic parish pastor Reinhold Niebuhr got an assignment in Detroit where the Ford factories are located, he dealt, in his sermons of around 1917, with problems that the newly introduced 'assembly line' created for the workers. This led to a direct dialogue between Henry Ford and Niebuhr concerning concrete working

144

conditions. Such confrontations are common in countries where Calvinism is strong, and more unusual where the traditional type of Lutheranism dominates (cf. Niebuhr 1932).

More important for the modern formation of the Protestant work ethic is, however, the third aspect: the tendency to make the group of the faithful visible, those who conform to God's law, really honest Christians. Luther considered every such division of human beings as a manifestation of repugnant self-righteousness. He repeats: 'Hidden are the saints, hidden is the Church.' To make the truly faithful into a limited group within the population appeared to him as a detestable reintroduction of monastery life. At the sight of ordinary simple human life, seemingly irreligious and totally worldly, Luther was inclined to conceive - precisely here - real and pure love for his neighbour. The opposite tendency became dominant in Calvinistic Geneva, the desire to discover who were the blameless (Krusche 1957:184-190).

In countries like Holland, Scotland and Switzerland, where for a long period Calvinism permeated the whole population, this moralistic spirit became part of the generally accepted social pattern. The same is also true for great parts of the United States, the culture of which today appears as a secularized form of Neo-Calvinism. It is an historical fact that the most effective examples of modern capitalism have occurred in this part of the West, which explains why Max Weber and his pupil Ernst Troeltsch, in their analyses of the origin of capitalism, have shown a greater interest in Calvin than in Luther.

Through the development of the revival movements which usually included minorities in the population, the Calvinistic understanding of the law has, however, been very influential outside those countries where the Calvinistic creed had the chance of influencing the State Churches - and consequently, whole countries. What has survived today of regular Christian worship in Norway, Finland and Sweden rests to a large extent on remnants of old revival movements with obvious elements of a Calvinistic understanding of the law and Christian morality. If he returned to these Scandinavian Churches which call themselves 'Lutheran', Martin Luther would probably be surprised by many religious phenomena in their present life. He would think that he had once again entered a 'monastery'.

But this is a different kind of monastery. One does not live in celibacy, but in marriage. The family plays a dominant part. On the whole, 'moral questions' are now equivalent to questions concerning sexuality and the family. One does not live without money, 'in poverty', like the former monks and nuns had to do. On the contrary, one saves and takes good care of the savings. But one emphasizes the distance to 'the world': no extravagances, no expensive pleasures. This asceticism is also an element of 'monastery' in professional life. And - a fact of no little importance - one advances socially through the generations.

Children reach higher on the social ladder than did their parents. Important scientists were earlier often the sons of ministers. The cultural columns in the daily press are today written by 'God's grand-children', born and raised in pietistic family environments.

It is characteristic of Calvinistic piety that success in business, in social mobility and in the general improvement of standard, is often seen as a sign of 'God's blessing' (zur Mühlen 1978:638). It is typical of this

Protestant way of life to accept success thankfully and at the same time remain faithful to a rather puritan life style of hard and conscientious work. In this lies the essential reason why the normal form of Protestant piety rarely creates any critical ideas concerning the means of production in society, regardless of how destructively this apparatus functions. God obviously shows his good will and grants his blessings through the lasting results offered to me and my family by the factual existing conditions of production.

It is up to other groups to criticize the direction of production, groups usually not committed to any Christian faith in any denominational form. Their valuations are, strangely enough, however, related to such ideas that, in earlier times, used to emerge out of the arena of the Christian faith. For example: our work ought to aim at meeting real needs that people today spontaneously see but which do not appear to be profitable enough to pay any attention to. Or: Swedish export ought not to take advantage of the poverty of the underdeveloped countries but instead endeavour to give them in time the same opportunities that we have.

Such arguments are of little importance for the adherents of the Protestant work ethic, who would rather first invest in an increase in personal income and, secondly – on this basis – spend money on philanthropy, collections, aid to the underdeveloped countries, support and gifts. This is what, in the history of the Church, has earlier been called 'charity'. Luther's break with the monastery institution and his new conscious worldliness in the identification of 'love for one's neighbour' on the one hand and ordinary contributions to society on the professional level on the other, implies, on the contrary, a departure from 'charitable' solutions. For Luther, love is material work that changes the conditions of life without resorting to philanthropy.

RETROSPECTION

If we now look back upon the history of the Protestant work ethic from Luther's break-through until now, almost half a millenium, we arrive at a surprising conclusion. The real Luther has been practically swept away by developments. And further – if any of Protestantism's contributions in the area of working-life ought to be of current interest at all, it is precisely Luther's original intention, that which is now forgotten.

When law and morality, which, in Christian vocabulary, is usually called 'personal sanctification', becomes central, it usually implies – with a certain deterministic inner necessity – that I, myself, become central. The self can be extended a little and become 'I and my family', but it is seldom more than that. This is what has happened with the Protestant work ethic. The most fundamental reason for this suppression is a purely theoretical element in the train of thought, namely Calvin's characteristic conception of the law. This theoretical element cannot be found in Luther.

During a long period of time Luther had been occupied daily and constantly with his own personal sanctification. It was in his inner being, in his 'spiritual' life, that holiness should reveal itself. In his judgement, however, it never revealed itself; quite the contrary. After his years in the monastery he considers the preoccupation of trying to

146

achieve holiness as a disease: it is as being 'one's own prisoner'. This disposition is fatal to faith in God and to love for one's neighbour.

A consequence of this is his frenetic emphasis on the good in worldliness. The more our behaviour is liberated from 'religion' the purer and healthier it becomes. The subtle finesse of life in vocational work is precisely that I do not become Christian through work! Work has no other object than to support fellow human beings. It is not through this support that I become Christian. I am 'righteous before God' through faith, confidence and trust in God, 'faith alone'.

During the 20th century we have gained a Protestant work ethic in totally conformity with social life in general which subordinates itself without friction to the prevailing means of production. The groups which today criticize this pattern speak of the needs of fellow human beings, as did Luther; they expose the egocentricity in our behaviour just as Luther did. But they are not carriers of the Protestant work ethic. On the contrary, they believe that the Protestant work ethic is incorporated in the core of society from which it reinforces the distortion of all production.

In this they are correct, which is paradoxical. Martin Luther wanted to perpetuate conduct which was worldly. He seems to have got what he wanted but in a strange and roundabout way. Those who today carry forth his protest are children of the world, devoid of religion.

Part IV
Work and Education

16 Discussant's paper on work and education

DONALD BROADY

I would like to open this discussion with some remarks on the concept of qualification as used in research on work and education and then present a diagram of different types of qualification research. This will enable me to comment on the papers written for this session.

The word 'qualification' comes from medieval Latin qualificere, 'to shape quality, to give quality to something, to condition something' (qualis, 'of what kind, such as', and facere, 'to make'). In research on work and education, qualification can be used as a concept to designate the conditioning of (e.g., by education) or the characteristics given to the labour force or the prospective labour force.

In other words, qualifications may be understood as qualities or properties given to man in one context - e.g., in educational institutions - and used in other spheres of life, especially in working life. This is what I suggest. Otherwise the concept of qualification will be blurred and confused with all kinds of socialisation, learning, influence. Used in educational research 'qualifications' are thus not just knowledge and skills as measured in the educational institutions by points or test scores. The word 'qualification' rather signals a relation to the future use of this knowledge and these skills; a relation between education and work.

Now, as you understand, I am trying to keep to the theme of our session: work and education. Most of the qualification research, though, concerns work without education. In the sociology of work, or in labour market research, 'qualification' usually means properties of the labour force without too much concern about how these properties are acquired. This is true, too, of Martin Carnoy's paper for this session, though his ambition is to understand changes in schooling. In Sweden, on the other hand, it is mainly educationalists who are interested in the relation between work and education. There seems, therefore, to be little genuine research on work and education.

At this point, I would like to present my diagram for distinguishing the various approaches to empirical qualification research which are necessary in order to deal with the different aspects of this work-education relationship.

```
┌─────────────────────────────────────┐
│                                     │
│   1. Development in technology      │
│      and work organization          │
│                                     │
└─────────────────────────────────────┘

┌─────────────────────────────────────┐
│   2. Qualification demands          │
│      2a At the work place           │
│      2b On the labour market        │
│                                     │
└─────────────────────────────────────┘

┌─────────────────────────────────────┐
│                                     │
│   3. Qualifications of the          │
│      labour force                   │
│                                     │
└─────────────────────────────────────┘

┌─────────────────────────────────────┐
│                                     │
│   4. Acquisition of quali-          │
│      fications                      │
│                                     │
└─────────────────────────────────────┘
```

Figure 1. *Types of research on the relation work - education*

1. Most studies which are labelled qualification research, e.g. in the sociology of work, concern level 1.

2. There is no automatic link between changes in technology on the one hand and changed qualification demands on the other. There is no simple way of deducing the latter from the former. New technology might imply an intensification of the work process without altered qualification demands, or new uses of the qualifications which the labour force already has.

2a.2b. It is important not to confuse the demands you meet on the labour market – that is, on the market where you offer your labour for sale and where it is bought – with the demands raised by the actual tasks to be accomplished at the work place. On the labour market the exchange value of your labour is what counts, at the workplace the use value.

Both Judith Háber and Martin Carnoy discuss the devaluation of or the inflation in exams and certificates which has taken place in many countries in connection with the educational explosion of the last few decades. They point to the tensions which follow: too many people with higher education for the positions available in working life, causing frustration and perhaps political unrest (there is a saying that unemployed academics are the most unreliable citizens). In the terms of the proposed distinction between the demands raised by the labour market and the qualification demands raised by the work places, the devaluation of exams and certificates can be described as raised labour market demands without corresponding workplace demands. You need more education to get the same job.

Here I would like to present an alternative to Háber's and Carnoy's explanations of this phenomenon. Háber looks first at the economic development: society can afford to keep young people in education and can dispense with their labour. Secondly, she points to the changing character of the higher educational institutions, today no longer institutions for the elite but open to everybody. To me this explanation seems somewhat circular. Carnoy's explanation is more complex. His focus is on state interventionism, when it comes to explaining both the educational explosion and the undertakings of the state today to absorb the mass of 'overeducated' people into the public sector. Further Carnoy makes a forecast: business interests will try to change education in order to expand the vocational character of higher education and to reduce the students' expectations of a remunerative and creative job.

It seems to me that Carnoy sees the state and capital, or the managers too much as homogeneous and monolithic entities or central subjects in the historical process. Therefore I would like to hear Carnoy, and Judith Háber, comment on an alternative, more sociological type of explanation put forward by Pierre Bourdieu and his colleagues at the Centre de sociologie européenne, Paris. In short, the impetus for the so-called educational explosion in France was that one section of the bourgeoisie, well equipped with capital, changed their social reproduction strategies. During the last few decades, instead of primarily letting their sons inherit the money and the enterprises, they have made more extensive use of elite schools - and even created a couple of new elite schools. The advantage they get from this arrangement is that the succession can take place inside the family (or, at least, inside the group) in a less obvious way - by means of their sons' educational merits rather than just capital - and they can reduce the risk of having to compete with well educated challengers from lower class groups. The disadvantage from an individual point of view is that the reproduction of the economic elite via the educational system only functions in a 'statistical' manner. There is no guarantee that the sons in a specific family will be successful.

According to Bourdieu and his collaborators, this changed reproduction strategy among the economically dominating groups resulted in an inflation in titles and exams, a process which accelerates the more the value of educational titles was derogated. Even if the process was started by groups who were more dependent (than others) on education for their reproduction, and for their struggles with other groups, it was thereafter imposed on all classes and class groupings, who have been forced to accept a more extensive and long term use of the educational institutions.

Without going into detail (see for example Bourdieu 1979: Chap. 2) I just want to hint at this type of empirical research which makes it possible to study the state not as an intervening actor but as a point of intersection for the struggle between social classes and fractions. I know that Carnoy is, in principle, sympathetic to such an ambition, but I am not sure how far from treating the state, or capital, as a central subject he is willing to go.

To return to my diagram:

3. The third level, the qualifications of the labour force, corresponds in general to what Frigga Haug and others in Berlin call 'Handlungs-fähigkeit', capacity to act.

4. The fourth level concerns the acquisition of qualifications, for example, in educational institutions. This is the terrain of socialisation research, etc. Jan Holmer's paper for this session belongs on this level, as do the main points in the paper by Anders Mathiesen. The latter also makes a methodologically interesting attempt to use data from level 4 to draw conclusions regarding developments on level 3.

(My diagram, I must add, is most valid for the relation between work and institutionalized public education. It applies less to in-job training, to the companies' own internal labour markets, or to a highly segmented labour market. And we should keep in mind that, according to OECD-economists, and others, the boom in education in the West during the 80's will take place under the auspices of companies.)

It is important to indicate the levels referred to in different qualification investigations. Suggesting, for example, dequalification on one level does not necessarily mean dequalification on another level. Take for example Franz (or with the Hungarian form Ferenc) Jánossy's classic study from 1966, to which Háber refers and which has been most influential for qualification research in the German language area. Jánossy's focus of interest was on the tensions between levels 2 and 3, namely between the qualification demands of the work places, on the one hand, and the actual qualifications with which the labour force was equipped, on the other. The mismatch between these two levels is, according to Jánossy, the main explanation for the economic difficulties at the end of a typical reconstruction period such as the German or Japanese 'economic miracle'. He used the metaphor of the relation between the shoes in a family's wardrobe and the feet of the family members. He was also interested, in other respects, in the tensions and contradictions between different levels.

This focus on tensions and contradictions is also an important part of Martin Carnoy's paper. For most of us, the most wellknown segmentation model in labour market theory is that of Michael Piore. Let me use a diagram (figure 2) to pinpoint the differences between Carnoy's model and Piore's:

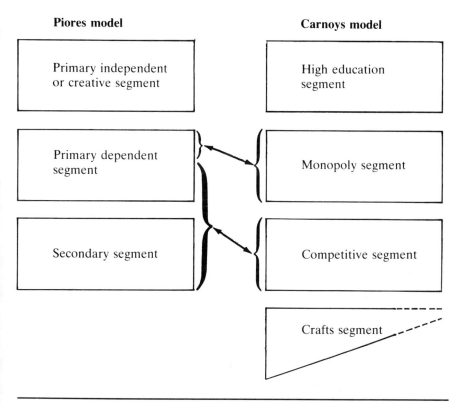

Piores model

| Primary independent or creative segment |
| Primary dependent segment |
| Secondary segment |

Carnoys model

| High education segment |
| Monopoly segment |
| Competitive segment |
| Crafts segment |

Figure 2. *Models of labour market segmentation, Piores model versus Carnoys*

To a large extent, Carnoy's model mirrors American conditions; for example, the third box, where most workers are not members of unions, and the general distinction between unionized and non-unionized segments. This does not apply to the conditions in Sweden and many other European countries.

In our discussion it would be interesting to confront the positions of Martin Carnoy and Anders Mathiesen with that of Frigga Haug. Carnoy observes quite a lot of dequalification tendencies, at least at the first level in my diagram, i.e. the level of changes in technology and organization. Anders Mathiesen argues that a massive polarization or bifurcation has taken place at the fourth level, more exactly in Danish vocational education since 1960. In contrast, Frigga Haug and Projekt-gruppe Automation und Qualifikation have for more than a decade advocated the possibility of a massive rise in qualifications as a result of automatization.

As a background, we should remember that Frigga Haug and her colleagues in their positive evaluation of the emancipatory potentials linked to automatization have met with hard resistance from the dominating qualification research traditions in West Germany based on Horst Kern and Michael Schumann's classic Industriearbeit und Arbeiter-bewusstsein (1970). Kern and Schumann argued that the technological changes in the sixties meant dequalification for the majority of workers in industrial manufacturing industry, and, for an albeit growing but still rather small minority, higher qualification demands, which altogether means polarisation or bifurcation, the term most often used in the Anglo-Saxon world).

So, in general terms, Carnoy's and Mathiesen's empirical conclusions are compatible with this dequalification/polarization thesis advocated by Kern, Schumann, Baethge and the Soziologisches Forschungsinstitut (SOFI) in Göttingen, i.e., Frigga Haug's main antagonists in the West German debate. With Kern and Schumann's new book (1984) there might be a new turn in this debate, at least when it comes to perspectives on the most recent developments. There might be a more general consensus that the number of dequalified jobs is radically decreasing.

Frigga Haug made an interesting remark on this subject.<1> She found the whole discussion on dequalification v.higher qualification v. polarization rather fruitless. Instead, she argued, we ought to define qualifications as the specific form of capacity to act (Handlungsfähigkeit) in a capitalist society, including all the social and other conditions imposed on this capacity. The new technology has created disorder in it, and this leads to problems - even as regards thinking about qualification!

As to Anders Mathiesen's paper, we should bear in mind how he reached his conclusion regarding a polarisation in Danish vocational training (cf. A. Mathiesen 1979). Since the fifties there has been a sharp quantitative decline in traditional apprentice training combined with rapid growth especially in extremely short term job-training courses, often no more than a few weeks in length. This means that every year a considerable number of qualified skilled workers leave their jobs, retiring or, most often, getting less qualified jobs in another sector, and at the same time. young unskilled workers enter the labour market - this is indeed derogation of living labour! Parallel with and in contrast to this, some vocational training, namely in the engineering, machine, construction sectors, etc, has became more specialized and commercial school education has, in general, become more elitist. All this means polarization - at the first level in my diagram, nota bene! At the end of his paper Mathiesen raises the question whether this supposedly fragmentized and polarized labour force corresponds to changes in work, but he does not answer the question.

Finally, a comment on Jan Holmer's paper, which is of quite another character. It is a presentation of what in reports from the project 'Fack i företagskris' (Gothenburg University) is often referred to as action research. When the ship building industry in Gothenburg was in severe crisis (during the late seventies) and thousands of employees risked losing their jobs, researchers and unionists initiated a joint project which resulted in investigations, study circles and interdisciplinary university courses for workers, followed by another university course for blue and white collar workers from Volvo.

Here I think, the questions handed over to us by Christian Berggren and Åke Sandberg are relevant.<1> They pointed to the problem of white and blue collar workers fighting each other (when faced with the new technology), and leaving the managers to take the initiative in developing the long term plans for the use of this new technology. Blue collar workers are usually convinced that, as white collar workers become more numerous, they will somehow always keep the in-jobs anyway while the blue collar workers risk getting fired. Therefore, the strategy of the latter and their unions is to make themselves indispensible to the company, and demand more education.

There is one final point I wish to take up in connection with Holmer's theoretical point of departure, Oskar Negt's ideas of worker education.

In 1969 Negt carried out a famous educational experiment with workers from IG Metall and IG Chemie, the two largest blue collar trade unions in West Germany. Earlier he had written a booklet on this subject (Negt 1968), to which Holmer refers. (I think that Holmer's critique of this early and rather occasional booklet is perhaps to overdo things a little.) He is right that, at that time, Negt, like all of his discussion partners, was of the opinion that such worker education ought to take place under the auspices of the established labour unions (an amusing detail is that this standpoint was inspired by André Gorz' book on unions - times are changing). But for many years, one of the most central arguments in Negt's work is what he and Alexander Kluge (1981:1262) say in connection with a discussion of the Mitbestimmungsgesetz ('the co-determination act', an earlier and somewhat softer version of the Swedish medbestämmandelagen, 'Joint Regulation Act').

This Mitbestimmungsgesetz can be exercised only by representatives, which means the transformation of worker politics into representative or delegate politics. This transfer of proletarian needs into the forms of the representative public sphere is the kernel intrusion of workers politics.

Whatever Holmer thinks of Negt's position, he has, nevertheless, to face the risk to which Negt and Kluge are pointing. In his paper he raises the question of the significance of the fact that, as a result of the courses, the participants gain upward moblility, for example inside the union organization. In 1969 Negt tried to deal with this problem by directing his courses primarily to Bildungsobleute, i.e., to workers who themselves were to lead study circles and the like. It would be interesting to hear Holmer's own answer to the question he raises. In his paper he mentions that a couple of the participants did in fact qualify for posts in the unions as a direct result of the courses. Is this a hindrance to the ambition of contributing to 'equality of participation' - to use the concept which the chairman of our session, Kjell Härnqvist, introduced in the educational debate fifteen years ago?

Notes

<1> In the discussion on work and technology.

17 Education and the changing American workplace

MARTIN CARNOY

Schooling is shaped by work, and for more than a century in the United States the nature of work has been defined by the development of industrial capitalism. This relationship between schooling and work is not direct, however. It is transmitted through the prism of the State. Formal education, as a major source of social mobility, greater knowledge and skills, and, for some, even self-respect. American schools play contradictory roles, but what goes on in them is still rooted in an inherently unequal production process and a hierarchical workplace. One of the schools' chief functions is to reproduce work divisions and work relations. Schooling is more democratic than the workplace, and, as part of the State, it is susceptible to political demands. But these demands for a more democratic education – usually expressed as a demand for more and better schooling – are also closely related to work and the division of knowledge associated with different jobs.

Education plays a contradictory role in reproducing relations of production, but analyzing that role requires examining the characteristics of the changing nature of work. This context shapes the schooling process at several levels. First, work in a capitalist society conditions the fundamental relations in schools – of teachers to school administrators, students to teachers, and students to students. Second, who gets how much schooling is related to the division of labor in the production process. This division, in turn, is the product of conflicts in production and the way those conflicts have been resolved historically. The workplace changes as workers contest the conditions of work and attempt to increase the rewards they get for their labor, and as employers adopt new technology to increase output per worker. Third, what is taught at different levels of schooling is influenced by the skills and attitudes required by jobs in the labor force.

Understanding the changing nature of work provides a background for analyzing the kinds of reforms that those forces supporting the reproductive dynamic may try to introduce in schools in the future. The changing workplace also gives us insights into the changing nature of social movements and the kinds of reforms they may push for in schools.

What are the underlying relations in the American workplace? What is the present division of labor and how is it changing? We can only give brief answers to these questions, for our goal is limited to developing guidelines for understanding changes in schooling.

159

WHAT IS THE NATURE OF CAPITALIST PRODUCTION IN THE UNITED STATES?

The changes in the American workplace are many and various, but will not be presented in detail. In general, the changes are the same as in other high-technological, capitalist, industrial countries.

Self employment has shifted to wage employment, mostly in large enterprises. The organization of work is complex, but has remained hierarchical and fragmented and most workers perform repetitive and routinized activities.

Thus, the internal discipline and control of the workplace by the few at the top of the organization are cemented by both hierarchy and the division of labor. <1>

THE LEGITIMIZATION OF LABOR ORGANIZATIONS

The workplace, then, is organized to reproduce capitalist relations of production and the concentration within a small segment of the population of capital accumulation and ownership. But characteristics of the workplace have been and continue to be shaped by conflicts between employers and labor. In the United States, the workplace is healthier today than it was fifty years ago, and workers have more rights, primarily because labor organizations have struggled for greater protection on the job and for increased job security. Much of this struggle has come to be directed through the state.

Employers, by contrast, have sought throughout the industrialization process to find new ways to increase the difference between labor's productivity and wages. Labor's response to these efforts has been to organize to resist and, in some cases, to oppose the capitalist system. With the advent of the Depression, the threat of labor militancy reached such proportions that employers reluctantly accepted the recognition of labor organizations as legal entities. These organizations indirectly became associated with apparatuses of the State, joining schools and other State institutions as arenas of conflict between the democratic and reproductive dynamics of capitalist society.

The history of the trade union mevement in America since the turn of the century is not only a history of worker struggle for higher wages and better working conditions in the place of production, but also a history of struggle for increasing worker influence over the State in order to raise the possibilities for economic gains and protection against employer antilabor practices. In the context of that latter struggle, choices were made both by the State and by labor organizations around the issue of the kind of labor organizations that would represent workers in America and the role of labor in the production system.

In an effort to mediate the capital-labor conflict of the post-1890 period (a conflict characterized by frequent violence and the potential for a widespread labor revolt) in favor of a peaceful continuation of capitalist development, the State gradually recognized the need for organized labor to have an effective role in the capitalist production system. Labor gained recognition and influence in wage and production policy because of its willingness to engage in political and economic conflict with the owners and managers of capital. Recognition was certainly a labor victory yet not all worker organizations were recognized by the State. As recognition and inclusion were being extended to the American Federation of Labor (AFL), the State was simultaneously destroying the International Workers of the World (IWW), which opposed many of the employer's prerogatives associated with property ownership. The state chose to include those labor leaders who were willing to help preserve capitalist social relations of production and to participate 'constructively' in the preservation of a State that fostered such production. Thus the AFL (and later the CIO) agreed that the role of labor unions in the production sector should be limited to bargaining with employers over clearly defined issues of wages and working conditions, not over control of production or the relationship between employers and employees. These State-sanctioned bargaining units took on the function of enforcing the division of labor worked out by the corporations and of channeling worker militancy into legal activities. Collective bargaining under the National Labor Relations Act (NLRA) and the Wagner Act regularized the interaction between labor and business, particularly the large corporations.

The State-recognized union is bound by collective bargaining agreements to make workers adhere to contracts negotiated with management. This is part of the regularization of the labor process. American labor unions not only are limited to confronting the system of production through collective bargaining, they are part of the labor-market control mechanism for the corporate hierarchy (Aronowitz 1973). Whereas small competitive firms face difficulties in dealing with labor unions because they usually cannot pass on wage increases to consumers in the form of higher prices, large corporations, dominating a high fraction of the market for their products, can pass on a large part of those negotiated wage increases to consumers. Although large domestic firms may face competition from abroad, even there extensive foreign investment covers their interests in foreign markets and in the importation of American-manufactured goods using foreign labor. Thus, the State's recognition of unions as bargaining units, though often fatal to small firms, provides the large firm with stability in the supply of labor and control over the labor force through worker organizations themselves.

Most important, since the unions have a stake in corporate capitalism, they serve as a buffer against the rise of worker groups hostile to corporations. The union hierarchies that emerged in the 1930's have monitored radical challenges to corporate control of the production system. They have 'educated' their workers to limit their demands to collective bargaining and to channel their grievances through the conventional arbitration machinery rather than taking direct action. They have ostracized radicals who question the system. And they have strengthened the segmented labor markets that separate unskilled from skilled work, and unionized from nonunionized labor. Yet such unions, as organizations of workers, are always in a certain amount of conflict with management over the distribution of revenue - favoring higher wages and benefits rather than management's desired higher profits and capital expansion. Unions have, for example, consistently backed higher minimum wages and, more recently, the Equal Rights Amendment (equal pay for women). Unions have also lobbied for greater State-financed benefits, such as social security, unemployment compensation, and welfare assistence. These increases in the social wage may have also cut into the share of capital controlled by the private sector (Rowles & Gintis 1982).

These activities pose contradictions for capitalist reproduction. They illustrate how even corporate worker organizations are inherently in conflict with corporate management. The two may share an interest in smooth capital accumulation, but they also represent different interests: higher wages and better working conditions versus control of profits and returns to stockholders. This explains why, in the early 1980's, management – with the cooperation of a pro-business regime in Washington – has attempted to dismantle the power of American labor unions, and new firms have fought to keep unions out.

THE STATE AS EMPLOYER

As the union movements grew under State recognition, the State greatly expanded its own role as employer. Indeed, both legally sanctioned collective bargaining and public employment were a response to the threat of massive labor unrest during the Great Depression. In 1920, the State employed 9 percent of the labor force; in 1930, 10 percent; in 1940, 13 percent; in 1970, 18 percent; and in 1980, 16 percent (Carnoy, Shearer & Rumberger 1983: Chap. 6).

The growth of government employment took place largely at the state and local levels. Growth of the school system was a particularly important factor in increased public employment. Since the Second World War, government has also tended to employ an increasing fraction of college graduates, minority males, and women – especially college-educated minorities and women – and pays blacks and women more than the private sector does for similar jobs (Carnoy, Shearer & Rumberger 1983: Chap. 6). When differences in education, age, and work experience are accounted for, blacks and women receive more in the public than in the private sector while white males receive less than in the private sector (Carnoy, Shearer & Rumberger 1983: Chap. 6).

The State sector, therefore, provides opportunities for minorities and women that the private sector is apparently not willing or able to provide. The State does this in response to pressures on the public sector to fulfill the mobility aspirations created by the American ideology of a classless society characterized by equal opportunity for all. Women's employment in education, social welfare, and other public-sector service jobs results also in part from a historical and cultural process of using educated women to deal with children and indigents. The State's willingness to respond to the failure of the market system to provide equal employment opportunities for less advantaged groups seems to reinforce the unequal relations of production in the private sector. But it also undermines those relations by providing and legitimating alternative employment based upon more egalitarian criteria.

This direct intervention into labor markets creates contradictions in the public sector. Since unemployment has been a continuing American economic problem, as minorities and women become better educated the public sector must absorb increasing numbers of marginalized workers. Rising costs have created increasing resistance to maintaining this role. Furthermore, public employees' unions, once organized, have attempted to raise wages, thus increasing public employment costs even more. The State is in a dilemma of having to employ more and more highly educated workers who cannot find jobs elsewhere but of being unable to raise taxes to cover the cost of that employment, particularly given demands by monopoly capital interests for a strong U.S. military posture (O'Connor 1973).

The most important characteristic of recent government expansion is the increasing role the State has played in the economy. Whereas in 1980 16 percent of Americans were directly employed by the government sector, it was estimated in 1979 that another 7-8 percent were employed in quasi-private firms that depended on government contracts (National Journal, May 5, 1979:730). Thus, one in four members of the labor force is directly or indirectly a government employee. Furthermore, another one-half percent of the labor force is in prison, at an annual cost of approximately $13.000 per prisoner in 1978 (U.S. Dept. of Commerce 1981, Tables 313 and 333), and (in 1979) the government paid out $1.120 per capita in social insurance and welfare (social security, federal retirement, disability benefits, unemployment compensation, Medicare and Medicaid, and veterans benefits (see Carnoy & Shearer 1980:340).

THE PRESENT STRUCTURE OF THE LABOR MARKET AND ITS CONTRADICTIONS

The same processes of capitalist development that have characterized the United States since the early eighteenth century – the increasing division of labor and the attempt to lower labor costs – provide the basis for continuing contradictions. For the most part, both minorities and women have been relegated to low-paying, low-status jobs, with little prospect of upward mobility in the private sector.

Nonetheless, the relatively high wages of even women and minorities in the United States compared to those abroad are driving many competitive industries to relocate production in low-wage countries for export back to the United States. In effect, this reduces the employment possibilities for the marginal groups here, increasing the reserve army of the unemployed despite the restriction on immigration. Furthermore, monopoly industries have shifted from exporting their goods to foreign countries to producing them there for sale in the local market. Transnational monopolies have extended the division of labor in the firm to the international level. Workers are separated not only by departmental ladders, but by national boundaries, language differences, and long distances.

Changes in the technical and social organization of production in the last century have therefore divided the job structure into segments or clusters. Each segment has different wage levels, entrance requirements, and promotion patterns, and each is predominatly staffed by workers from particular backgrounds (see Carnoy 1980; Gordon, Edwards & Reich 1982). The great majority of workers are divided not only into job segments, but also into different types of firms. In the private sector, one group of firms is marked by capital-intensive technology and long-term planning horizons (monopoly firms), whereas the other group is marked by relatively low capital per worker, short planning horizons, and even a short firm life (competitive firms).

These segments are overlaid by the discriminatory character of present-day capitalist production. Considerable evidence supports the view that women and blacks (as well as Spanish-speaking minorities) are discriminated against in the labor market on the basis not of their skills but of their gender, race, or ethnic background. There is a close

163

relationship between race or ethnic group and class.<2> But discrimination against women cuts across social classes and is rooted in another historical phenomenon – patriarchy – that preceded capitalism but now under capitalism appears in new forms (for examples, see Hartmann 1976). Even so, women and minorities (especially blacks) are concentrated in competitive industries and the public sector, which gives a particular character to those industry segments.

For analytical purposes, today's work structure can be divided into three segments, each typified by different work conditions and required worker characteristics. The first is a well-paid segment of jobs requiring high levels of general education that cuts across both competitive and monopoly sectors of the economy (this is the 'high-education' segment). Technical change constantly creates new jobs within this segment, but it eliminates many jobs formerly requiring high education. There is job competition on an individual basis within this segment, but the high education requirement has, until recently, restricted access to males from middle- och upper-class backgrounds.

Employees in this segment have the most autonomy, the highest pay, and the most job security of any group of workers in the economy. Although there are substantial individual differences in income and power within this segment – and considerable competition among workers for the most important and best-paid jobs – the relatively privileged position of the group as a whole contributes to a strong sense of identification with the profitability goals of the employer, and with the general principles of division of labor, hierarchical control of production, and private property. Currently, however, circumstances that have bolstered the privileges and job autonomy of the high-education segment are dissolving. The separation of planning from execution is increasingly applied to mental as well as manual work. Intellectual work itself is increasingly subdivided into relatively routinized tasks that require a high level of education but little job-specific experience, and that involve only minor or moderate individual responsibility for capital value.

Furthermore, the traditional role that the public sector has played in absorbing highly educated minority and women workers is also being attacked. The fiscal crisis of the State has stimulated attempts to reduce public-sector employment at both the federal and the local levels. This means, in effect, that women and minority professionals (as well as lower-segment public workers) will be thrown into the private labor market, where relative wages for those groups are lower and the number of professional jobs fewer. The data we have cited showing the imnportance of the public sector in enabling more highly educated minority and women workers to move up occupationally and receive higher salaries also suggest that the cuts in public-sector employment for those groups will produce a large surplus of labor for the more highly educated segment of the private sector. Whether public-sector workers forced to take lower income jobs in the private sector will do so smoothly is another question.

Second, there is a 'unionized' segment characterized by unionization, internal hierarchies, and relative job security for employees with seniority. Although the jobs in this segment do not necessarily require more experience or education than jobs in the competitive sector, they are more highly paid than those jobs. Workers in this segment have historically been able to capture some of the gains from the increased labor productivity brought by mechanization and have been able to maintain higher wages through nonmarket mechanisms that have restricted the entry of lower wage labor. A central unifying feature of jobs in the unionized sector is that their content can be more or less routinized and codified in a set of rules and standard operating procedures. Jobs in this sector are finely subdivided components of larger processes. Though there are some jobs that involve individual operation of large machinery and thus retain some scope for individual feelings of mastery and accomplishment, many more are repetitive assembly-line tasks. By their very nature, these jobs afford the worker little intrinsic satisfaction, so that the motivation to perform them must come from outside the job – from its circumstances rather than from its content. The major circumstance rendering work in this sector tolerable is, of course, the relatively high salary level. On the average, salaries are still below those of the high-education sector; but for levels of education through junior college, jobs in the monopolized union sector pay relatively better and afford more stable employment than jobs in the competitive sector. There are also established standards of productivity and working conditions on unionized jobs to protect against arbitrary dismissal or speedup.

Education can become a liability in the unionized sector. A highly educated employee is likely to view routinized jobs as even more stultifying and boring than otherwise, and is likely to be more ambitious for upward mobility and new experiences than the fixed seniority systems in this sector can accomodate. What is required on these jobs is a willingness to relinquish meaningful work experiences to obtain income and job security. Fulfilling activity will only be sought outside the workplace.

Third, there is a 'competitive' segment characterized by the lowest wages, least steady employment, and poorest working conditions and advancement opportunities. This segment includes not only jobs in competitive firms, but also clerical jobs in monopoly firms. The latter have developed only with the growth of monopoly and mass production itself. From the outset they were separated from production jobs in the monopoly segment and were never the locus of struggle by a previously entrenched group of workers. Hence, employers were able immediately to recruit low wage labor for them. Jobs in the competitive segment are overwhelmingly staffed by women, minority group members, and other relative newcomers to wage labor.

The overwhelming majority of workers in the competitive segment of the labor market are those who have not obtained or cannot obtain jobs in higher segments. These categories include workers without at least a high school diploma, workers with a high school diploma who have been denied entry into the unionized sector by discriminatory regulations and practices, young workers waiting for an 'opening' into the monopolized, unionized sector, or workers who either desire or are constrained to work less than full time. Workers who fall into one of these categories are not just a random sample of the labor force. Women, blacks, Chicanos, Puerto Ricans, illegal aliens, recent immigrants, and workers from impoverished rural backgrounds contribute a disproportionate percentage of adult labor in the competitive-segment. Teenagers who work are almost exclusively confined to competitive segment employment, regardless of race, sex, or socioeconomic background; teenagers from minority groups are frequently unable to find employment at all.

The competitive segment, then, is a low-skill, generally low-education market. Although dependability and discipline are desirable and may command a slight wage premium even in this market, employers must take what they can get and depend on tight supervision and the threat of dismissal to extract labor from their workers. Submissiveness and passivity are the traits most characteristically required by such jobs.

Finally, there is a dwindling crafts segment, jobs requiring traditional manual skills that can only be learned through lengthy practical experience. Craft workers are largely organized in craft unions, which through licensing and certification procedures attempt to restrict competition for members' jobs. They are located in both the monopoly and competitive spheres, and many craft workers are self-employed. Craft workers are relatively well paid and exercise more autonomy over their work activities than any workers except those in the high-education segment, but technological advances constantly undermine the need for craft skills.

These differences in social relations imply that different sets of skills, values, and attitudes are relevant to productivity in the different segments. Neoclassical models of labor markets generally assume that wages are closely related to productivity; therefore, the relationship of worker characteristics such as education and age to earnings represents a relation between worker attributes and worker productivity. The level of wages and the return for additional education and experience in work are assumed to reflect the contribution to output of more schooling and more experience. The firm pays workers in accordance with their marginal product because of competition in the job market for workers by employers and for jobs by workers.

This notion is a theoretical, rather than an empirical, construct. There is no convincing way to verify that wages equal productivity across jobs or firms producing different products. Since people with higher education and experience do tend to receive higher wages, we can infer that, unless employers are completely irrational or maximizing something other than output, there is some correlation between productivity, education, and experience. Yet, this relation can only be assumed to meet the productivity claim of neoclassical economics under conditions of perfect market competition and full employment. No one argues that such conditions are an accurate picture of reality. We already know from numerous studies that the relation of education and experience to earnings is different for different sexes, races, and occupational groups.

THE CONTRADICTIONS IN LABOR MARKET SEGMENTATION

The expansion of the labor force in the 1970's has taken place under particular economic conditions. Absolute employment grew rapidly (2.5 percent annually) between 1970 and 1980, but real weekly wages declined 16 percent over the decade (Carnoy, Shearer & Rumberger 1983: Chap. 3). The spread between productivity increases and real wage increases grew even though productivity growth slowed down. Yet profits did not rise significantly, probably because the costs of nonlabor inputs - particularly energy - increased rapidly, and demand decreased.

However, there has been a trend toward maintaining or raising profits in the 1980's by holding down wages, even to the point of absolute wage reduction. Part of this strategy is reflected in the union-busting policies of the Reagan Administration. More generally, the increase of women in production work, the incorporation of illegal aliens into the competitive segment, runaway shops, and the rapid incorporation of highly educated workers into the labor force are all facets of the reaction on the part of capitalists to the need to maintain or increase the profitability of capital. But all also create contradictions in the production process.

THE CHANGING NATURE OF SOCIAL CONFLICT

Our analysis suggests that as private employers attempt to hold down pay in the face of labor pressure for higher wages, conditions in the labor market change in ways that have significant implications for social conflict in general and for the educational system in particular. Some of the changes of the last fifteen years include a continued increase in the percentage of women in the labor force, high rates of youth unemployment (especially minority youth unemployment), and increasing average education both of the unemployed and of those workers employed in menial, repetitive jobs. Associated with all these factors is continued government social-welfare spending to soften unemployment, and private-sector inability or unwillingness to absorb more highly educated minorities and women at wages approximating those of white men. Government social-welfare spending and direct employment have changed the labor conflict in recent years and distinguish the economic crisis of the 1970's and early 1980's from previous crises. We have suggested that the social crisis of the 1930's changed the conditions of capitalist production, involving the State in mediation and allocation of its increasing share of total national resources. As the American labor movement continued to confine itself to traditional wage-bargaining struggles, refusing to raise the labor-corporate conflict into the political arena except by backing particular candidates, organized labor as such gradually lost its vanguard position in social movements. The legitimization of unions within the State shifted the dynamic of conflict away from private production and the traditional wage struggle. The new social movements – the civil rights movement in the 1950's and 1960's, the antiwar movement in the 1960's, the women's movement in the 1970's and 1980's, the environmental and consumer movements in the 1970's, the anti-nuclear movement in the 1980's – all focused directly on the State. These movements affirmed more than ever before the direct interventionist role of the State.

But the State collects its revenue mainly from individual income, property, and sales taxes. Under the New Deal accords, labor and employers could both gain from economic growth. Employers' profits remained high and permitted capital investment that raised worker productivity to offset increasing real wages. And as long as the economy grew steadily with real wages, increasing at about the same rate as productivity, prices remained relatively stable and tax revenues also increased. Labor and capital did not resist higher taxes as long as wages and profits were increasing.

In the late 1960's, this delicate arrangement began to break up. Government spending increased rapidly to pay for an unpopular war in Southeast Asia. At the same time, massive domestic spending on programs for inner cities was used to head off urban unrest. In an already tight labor market, profit rates fell and wages as a percentage of gross national product (GNP) rose significantly. The wage bargains achieved by many unions were lucrative. Employment increased at record rates. All this, combined with the rights in the ghettos of major cities in 1964-68, and the antiwar movement in 1967-71, changed the way business viewed the future of the New Deal accords (Carnoy, Shearer & Rumberger 1983). Not only did growth slow in the United States after 1972, but there was a shift of private investment from productivity-increasing to wage-reducing investment. The oil crisis reinforced the trend. The primary concern of business is profits. Unlike the postwar period when profits were rising even with increased real wages, the 1970's saw employers essentially abandon the old accord in favor of reducing real wages (hence increasing profits) through political struggle.

Labor, in turn, attempted to hold its position by pushing up the State's social welfare spending. But now increases in such spending had to be eked out of a declining growth rate. Social spending did rise in the mid-1970's, yet the rise was not great enough to offset falling wages (Bowles & Gintis 1982). The mass of Americans translated their frustrations with falling purchasing power into anger against the State, particularly against inflationary spending and rising tax rates. In James O'Connor's terms (1973), the need for the State to expand government spending for defense and as a response to falling real wages flew in the face of voter resistance to increased taxes, leading to the 'fiscal crisis of the State'. Voters saw inflation as a government spending problem rather than the result of a labor-capital conflict that labor was losing.

The backlash was first manifested in tax resistance - for example, the passage of Proposition 13 in California - which resulted in a severe slowing in the growth of real public spending on education and other locally provided services. Then the Reagan Administration came into office promising to cut government spending and taxes as a means of stimulating general economic recovery. Social-welfare spending and taxes were cut, but military spending was increased substantially. The State had also become unabashedly anti-union and the unemployment rate had increased to almost 11 percent by the end of 1982. In addition, the tax and spending cuts together changed U.S. income distribution in favor of the rich.

The tax revolt and voter support of conservative economic policies have had an impact on education. As the generation of postwar babies began to leave schools, the middle class showed itself less and less willing to pay for more education through taxation. Proposition 13 in California lowered property taxes, which in turn resulted in less real spending per capita in California schools and a sharp slowdown in per pupil real spending, even though the number of pupils in California public primary and secondary schools dropped from 5 to 4 million between 1976 and 1981 (California Dept. of Finance 1982, Table F-8). Spending per pupil (in 1976 dollars) rose from $1,546 to $1,767 between 1976 and 1981; spending per capita fell from $357 to $299. Class size has increased and the number of class periods in each day has decreased. Federal aid to education - which had been central to expanding education since the early 1960's - has been cut sharply. Reductions in student loan programs and in funding for social science research have hurt colleges and universities. There have been moves to 'privatize' education through legislation that provides tax credits for tuition paid to private schools (James & Levin 1983). Simultaneously, the Reagan economic package cut other social welfare spending and federal employment. These cuts have indirectly and directly reduced government employment outside education, so that social mobility for women and minority groups through such employment has been reduced drastically (in 1980, about 50 percent of college-educated women and minorities were working in the public sector - see Carnoy, Shearer & Rumberger 1983: Chap. 6).

This assault on public education and State employment is a direct attack on the New Deal interpretation of capitalist ideology - an interpretation in which the State both provides the educational means to social mobility and underwrites the American dream through its employment and income policies. The assault also represents an attempt to restrict the democratic aspects of schooling and expand schooling's skill production in a more strictly class reproductive structure. In that structure, parents with enough income would have many options about where to send their children to private school, whereas public schools would become - even more than they are now - holding operations for less employable minorities, with correspondingly lower expenditures per pupil.

The conflict over public spending and taxation is an expression of a social conflict that is being carried on largely in the political arena of the State. Corporate leaders themselves are divided over the extent to which a conservative policy on such spending should carry the day. Many are concerned that high rates of unemployment and a sharp redistribution of income could lead to a popular attack on corporations and then to structural change. Also, employers in such education-intensive sectors as research and development and the high-technology industries worry that eroded educational expenditures will reduce America's comparative advantage in technology and world commerce. Most employers, however, continue to focus on reducing labor's bargaining power and on increasing the proportion of State resources going to capital rather than labor to raise profits and expand corporate control of economic development. This strategy has worked in the early 1980's because labor has been divided on the issues of taxation, social-welfare spending, and the fiscal crisis of the State. But the result has been to make employment and education major issues and points of conflict.

In their role as taxpayers, voters charged with paying for the fiscal crisis of the State have turned against the State. The social movements of the 1960's failed to impose themselves politically and produce alternative solutions to the crisis that would preserve and extend the democratic gains of the postwar period. With that failure, corporate economic power reasserted itself in an assault on those gains.

Part of that assault, with direct assistance from a frustrated workingclass, was on the educational system. As funds were cut from education, the groups that hoped for improved access to better jobs were increasingly cut off from those jobs. At the same time, the availability of any kind of work for minorities was reduced by a traditional conservative economic strategy of disciplining the labor force through higher unemployment rates and anti-union policies. The effect on the schools of educational spending reductions, increased unemployment, and falling real wages has been to reduce their 'democratic' side and make them increasingly oriented toward reproducing the relations of capitalist production and its class division of labor.

Notes

⟨1⟩ This section is a summary of a longer chapter. The editors would like to thank Mats Eriksson, University of Karlstad, for his contribution.

⟨2⟩ Much more than sex and class, race and class have become entwined in American social life. Nevertheless, the fact that racial discrimination has been shaped historically by particular institutions such as slavery does make it different from a 'pure' class issue. The best recent analysis of race in the American economy is Reich 1981.

18 What are we trained for?

JUDIT HÁBER

INTRODUCTION

It has by now become a commonplace that the breaking up of the traditional family (functioning also as a production unit) has entailed far-reaching consequences for the transformation of the entire way of life. It is the breaking up of this form of existence and activity structure that started the process in which activities are pursued increasingly outside the family, that is, the 'small world', and what is more, in which the knowledge required to solve the tasks facing man in the different spheres of life is obtained increasingly within the framework of various institutions. That this process of 'specialisation' and division of labour has gone a long way is demonstrated by the fact that not only are the years of elementary education spent at school, and not only are the various special qualifications obtained in schools, but the societies of the developed world also offer school training in several fields of everyday knowledge, such as cooking or driving – to mention only two of the long list.

I do not wish to evaluate these changes, but only to put them down as facts. The processes in question signify, on the other hand, that the life of 20th-century man has become, on the whole, largely institutionalised and, specifically, in regard to the ways and means of acquiring knowledge, it has grown to be 'schoolish'. In other words, the role of school as an institution has increased in the life of the individual. As a matter of fact, this is also expressed in the ever higher level of education extending to an ever wider circle. To use the fashionable term of the past decade, an 'educational explosion' has taken place.<1>

ECONOMY AND EDUCATION

What has made way (the question is not concerned with Hungary only, but with the entire developed world) for this kind of explosion? Very schematically: economic development, that is to say, the growing richness characteristic of society on the whole has enabled society to keep young generations for increasingly long periods at a so-called child's status, and to dispense with young people entering service at an early age and, instead, have them trained at schools of some kind for a longer time. The process has been expressive of the interests of individuals as well as of those of society. The various movements of radical or progressive ideologies have also acted towards educational perspectives becoming available to increasingly larger groups of the population; and it has been with the same aim that modern societies did

171

not wish large social groups (such as the young, if they are outside the work organisation) to live outside any social organisation, and thus beyond any social control.

Economic development and the rising of educational standards have taken place simultaneously. The attention of economic developers has increasingly turned to education, and education as a growing sector has started to effectuate changes within its own system: improving it, or enlarging it, or both. Education was now faced with a dual task: to provide for general education, and cover the economy's need of specialists.

In Hungary, this problem did not give rise to keen debates until the 1970s, posing questions, about the demands made by society and the economy on the educational system, and the tasks to be fulfilled by the school reform emerging at the time. It was suggested that one of the most important tasks of school was the satisfaction of the need for specialists, more exactly, that school education should provide for a due balance of labour demand and supply in economy. Even though this has not always been put so strongly, the thought was lurking (and in some cases still is) in the debates about so-called 'over-training', in which the educational system was blamed for producing too much highly qualified labour in comparison with the number of existing jobs. Of the numerous questions raised in the course of such debates (I shall return to several others later on) it is necessary to say a few words in general about the connexion between education and the economy considered as ideal in a certain sense.

The educational system serves the economy if it trains specialists of an adequate number and qualification with respect to the given economic standards and does its best to satisfy such needs. However, any efforts to satisfy needs estimated only in a 'daily' (that is, 10 to 15 years) perspective can and do lead only to incomplete solutions. This is not to say that education should not take into consideration economic needs in the long run. From the aspect of satisfying economic needs, the school functions well if it 'runs forward' in comparison with the needs of the day, for in this way it also serves economic interests. This seems to be confirmed by historical experience. In his book The Trend of Economic Development and Periods of Restitution Ferenc Jánossy (1966) writes:

> The multitude of giant machines cast a shadow on human knowledge and activity, though, in the final account, they are what determine the abundance flow of goods... The fact seems to be forgotten that it is man himself, that is, human development, on which economy is in fact dependent, and it often seems as if the rate of progress were basically determined by the spread of machines of an ever higher perfection.

It is the basic idea of the book that education does not serve economic development solely by satisfying momentary economic needs, but much rather by providing for a continuously rising level of qualification of the labour force and, instead of a narrow specialisation, by giving people a wide general training. (In this context, it makes sense to raise the question of over-training from one aspect: in the case where it is an unhealthy phenomenon, that is, where over-training means over-specialised training.) According to this view, it is not profitable for the economy to eliminate over-training with respect to the available jobs, for the educational system has to take into consideration a certain amount of potential labour force demand of the future. Therefore, the educational system has not to train the labour force in the limited sense of the word but, high-sounding as it may be, to release people with the highest possible level of general knowledge (which would also provide for more convertible positions in the labour market).

From one point of view, these principles are not to be considered farfetched, since the correlation between the development ability of the economy and the qualification standards of the labour force has been well tested in several countries already (one of the most illustrative examples was the West German 'economic miracle' after World War II). All the same, the holders of this view cannot close their eyes to the problems of reality that have appeared in the past decade.

THE PLACE OF EDUCATION IN THE SYSTEM OF THE DIVISION OF LABOUR - ON THE BASIS OF HUNGARIAN EXPERIENCE

Modern societies - among them the society of Hungary - are based on a division of labour. The division of labour valid for big social units just as for small groups is, as is well known, not only rational and thus promoting a better function of life (or of some of its spheres), but, at the same time, it establishes a hierarchy of the positions taken within the division of labour. It is, further, a fact that the various posts in the division of labour are tied to various educational levels. Thus, in accordance with the character of society determined by the division of labour, the qualification acquired is, or has grown to be, a part of the hierarchical structure present in the whole society.

The grading of qualifications comes about, strangely enough, somewhat 'unnoticed'. That is to say, the various school qualifications are not appreciated only according to the field and contents of the knowledge determining their special line (for example, general and technical fields, arts, natural sciences), but the school system itself classifies the qualifications (and the qualified?) acquired at its various levels. For example, if someone has made the eighth grade of the general school, he is no only talked of as having completed the eighth grade but as having complied with the compulsory education requirements and completed his primary studies. The vocational school, the specialised school and the grammar school are parts of secondary education - though with differences in rank. The vocational-school leaving certificate, the holder of which is a skilled worker, is not adequate for admission to a college or university. First a secondary-school leaving certificate has to be gained, which the other two types of secondary schools, the specialised school and the grammar school (both middle schools) give their students who have passed their examination. The institutions of higher education, colleges and universities give diplomas, testifying to the acquirement of a qualification ranked at the top level.

In recent decades, certain types of school certificates have been devalued. To what extent this process of devaluation has been due to the devaluation of certain types of knowledge is too complex a question for the scope of this paper. It seems, however, quite clear that this fall in value is connected with the ceasing of the earlier élite (or comparatively élite) character of the types of school in question, and the now mass attendance at these schools. A good example of this is the spectacular change in the status of the grammar-school leaving certificate, which has been manifest, among other things, in the strong 'feminisation' of the grammar school studentship. The same phenomenon is apparent, though to a lesser extent, with respect to the diplomas of higher education, at least inasmuch as these qualifications have lost their 'rarity' value. At the same time, it is found that the educational system reacts to these facts and, which is interesting, with the result that the training period is extended, or the institutional status of the type of school in question is raised. This was the case for example, in the training of teachers and kindergarten teachers when, in contrast to earlier practice, this training was raised to the level of higher education (not on the university but on the college level.) This, I think, was to make up for a lowered status. Nevertheless, in spite of the devaluation processes affecting the various levels of school qualification, different values are attributed to the different forms of education obtained on the different levels of the educational system. This means that the holders of the various certificates or diplomas 'expect' something of their qualifications, partly owing to tradition i.e. to the prestige (even though falling) of the given type of school, and partly because different statuses 'belong' to the different school qualifications (they expect more of a higher qualification); that is, they are not just pleased with their additional knowledge, but expect higher positions within the hierarchy of the division of labour. Thus, for example, when someone enrols at a university, he expects (if not everybody, but the vast majority) that he will find a job corresponding to his qualification (in our case, an intellectual one), even though the university does not guarantee to offer such a job. If this does not follow - and not because the individual in question did not want to take the job 'due' to him, but because he could not find such a job - it is not certain that he will think: well, never mind, in any case I have 'additional knowledge' since I am highly qualified. And this is not limited to the intellectual sphere. It is not certain, either, that the holders of skilled worker certificates employed as semi-skilled or unskilled workers are not frustrated, that they feel good and are glad about having 'over-trained' - to refer to what has been said earlier - and that, as such, they are the hidden reserves of economic development.<2> At the same time, it is quite obvious that, looking at it from the human aspect, it would cause problems if the school channels were narrowed.

That people do not only expect higher qualification to give knowledge essential for their intellectual development, but also something directly to improve their status in life (more interesting work, a preferred activity, higher prestige) is partly due to the fact that since the 1960s promotion in the hierarchy of the division of labour has been possible through acquiring a higher qualification. (This holds even if some people have gained the qualification demanded for their post subsequently.) The matter in question is what sociology expressed, in its own terms, years ago, in the following: school has grown to be the primary channel of mobility. That the school can fulfil this function has not been brought about solely by the enlarged capacity of daytime courses, but also the introduction and spreading of evening and correspondence courses have served the same purpose, allowing a correction of career in the adult age.

School qualification plays a very important role, sometimes even apart from the special line, in the situation of people in general - now centring our attention on the young - from the aspect of starting a career (and even from the aspect of later times). This is demonstrated by the data in the following table:

174

Table 1. *Entering a career as unskilled workers, having dropped out of school at some level of the educational system, by type of school (Source: Szénai 1983:37)*

Type of school abandoned	Number of those dropped out	Division
General school	308	67,4
Vocational school	89	19,5
Specialised secondary school	30	6,5
Grammer school	25	5,5
Secondary educational institution	144	31,5
Higher educational institution	5	1,1
Total	457	100,0

It is to be seen that the drop-out from school, or failure to perform for some reason (the reasons are not shown by the data) offers the unskilled worker some kind of status with a high probability, even if not for good in every case. It is clear that the changing of this status is in some way dependent on the type of school from which someone has dropped out.

A few correcting remarks, or such as can render the picture somewhat more complicated, must be made. I share the opinion of many that a great number of those who work in lower positions than those they are qualified for feel their career to be a forced path and their studies fruitless.<3> Members of this group certainly feel bad. The above-mentioned devaluation process does not take place only in institutions: it may be that the qualification someone has acquired is of no such value for him that it seems worth making every effort to obtain a job in his special line, it may be that better working conditions (this is not always better work, but can be, for example, a cleaner job or a workplace nearer to one's home), or higher earnings are more important to him, even if available through less qualified work, than pursuing activities corresponding to his qualification. And, one more remark, statistical data only show whether someone holding a skilled-worker certificate is employed as a skilled worker, a semi-skilled worker or an unskilled worker, or someone holding a diploma in engineering is employed as an engineer or not; in other words, whether these qualifications and activities are in harmony with respect to rather formal categorisation criteria. However, the same statistical data do not say anything (for they cannot) of the work itself the individual in question does in one or another position - what kind of work it is in fact. In my opinion, two things follow from this. On the one hand, we must be careful in evaluating incongruences, since not only the above-mentioned phenomenon causes tension but, on the other hand, looking at it from the human aspect, work and qualification may formally correspond, and yet the proper task may not require the qualification obtained, which can present a situation just as frustrating or alienating as the exactly measured incongruence. This case being immeasurable, we cannot get an exact idea of its dimensions, yet everyday experience indicates that it is not a easily negligible phenomenon, for it does create tension.

Speaking about the connexion between work and education, a final point of view must be considered. The educational system is necessarily stable, which means, in this case, that the structure of the school system and of the various types of schools, and partly the curricula are not to be changed too often. This kind of stability is, however, necessarily concomitant with a certain degree of rigidity. As opposed to this, the economy is by all means more mobile, if not as a whole, at least in its sections: work processes appear and disappear, new technologies are introduced while old ones are abandoned; the structural changes of the economy lead to a restructuring of jobs and perspectives. That is why the educational system cannot be expected to provide even for a comparatively balanced labour market, or why a discrepancy between the structure of the school system and the job structure will come about in any case. The various special courses serve to lessen or to bridge over this discrepancy. I do not see it as a sign of certificate-hunting (even if such motives do exist) that these courses are attended. For example, in 1981-1982, of 5 million working people 180,000 attended courses training for manual trades, and 140,000 attended courses training for non-manual occupations.

This is to say that the various courses are attended by a very high number of people and thus they cannot be neglected, though they are not integral parts of the general educational system, but have a role in the training of labour. Some of those attending courses training for manual or non-manual jobs improve knowledge acquired earlier, others acquire their qualifications in this way. An investigation made by the Institute of Sociology reveals two main strategies of gaining a qualification (of course, non-intellectual careers are meant): first, to acquire or to further develop a qualification within the general educational system (either attending daily courses all along, or at evening and correspondence courses), second, to learn a trade at the courses offered by enterprises and factories. The existence of courses bringing up-to-date, enlarging, or specialising qualifications shows that the economy tries to adjust its actors to the changing circumstances in this way.

REFLECTIONS

To finish my paper, I wish to say something very personal. I am an intellectual and have started work as such. Although I know that, as an intellectual, I live under much better circumstances than people with much lower qualifications, I have no permanently guilty conscience because of this. Also, I do not hold myself to be a realist in the sense of someone interested only in practical things, for whom humanitarian values are not too important. All considered, the question discussed by the symposium, that is, whether in 1984 work is 'emancipation or derogation' seems to me a question to be addressed mainly to intellectuals. I do not deny that for many people work is an activity of vital importance and therefore valuable, not only because it is a source of livelihood. I do not deny that many wish to do 'self-accomplishing' work – even if not expressed in this term – and do their best to find such a field of activity for themselves. Nevertheless, for the great majority of people (taking into consideration the entire advanced world) the question does not arise at all, because it cannot arise. There are too many kinds of hard, physically exhausting work (or even causing a disease), dirty work, or routine work (the latter often being what is 'only' uninteresting, but less exhausting and therefore better). Under such circumstances work itself cannot be emancipating for the vast majority of people. And yet, the many kinds of unpleasant work mentioned above notwithstanding, I would not say that work is derogating for most people, for I think that whether one experiences either of those two categories depends on whether the question exists for him at all. People work because their livelihood depends on it, and also, they work for work itself – a regular activity providing a connexion between man and world. From this latter point of view, work is also of vital importance. This statement is borne out by a lot of experience gained with respect to how pensioners feel about life when they have left the world of work. If this function of work is also considered when judging its emanicipating effect, a faint yes may be voiced. I would stress, all the same, that this is due more to the situation of life created by work than to the actual character of the activity performed. This status of work in today's world is, in my opinion, a firm truth of which we must be aware. And I think that this awareness must include the fact that we intellectuals are in a privileged position also on account of being able to do such work with respect to which a positive answer can be given to the question raised by the symposium – if not for each intellectual, at least for intellectuals as an occupational group. However, I repeat, the question concerns only this group.

Notes

<1>   *Percentage of the population having completed certain education*

	% of the population over 15 years of age having at least completed eight grades			% of the population over 18 years of age having at least completed secondary education		
Year	Men	Women	Total	Men	Women	Total
1941	16.1	14.1	15.1	7.8	2.6	5.1
1949	21.9	19.5	20.6	8.6	3.6	5.9
1960	34.5	31.3	32.8	12.0	6.6	9.1
1970	55.1	48.0	51.4	18.2	13.9	15.9
1980	71.2	61.7	66.2	24.2	22.4	23.3

Percentage of the population over 25 years of age having received higher education

Year	Men	Women	Total
1941	3.4	0.4	1.8
1949	3.5	0.6	1.9
1960	4.7	1.2	2.8
1970	6.5	2.4	4.3
1980	8.6	4.8	6.6

(Source: 1980 Census. Budapest. 1980:30)

<2> Julia Szalai's computations based on census data show the following
in regard to the 1980 situation:

Percentage of "over-trained" workers

	Active earners		
	Men	Women	Total
Holders of skilled worker certificate employed as semi-skilled or unskilled workers in percentage of the total number of the so qualified	11.8	18.5	13.3
Holders of secondary-school leaving certificates or diplomas of higher education employed as semi-skilled or unskilled workers in percentage of the total number of the so qualified	6.9	5.5	6.2
Together: percentage of semi-skilled and unskilled workers having completed more than the eight grades of the general school in the total number of the so qualified	9.2	8.3	8.8

(Source: Antal and Szalai, 1982-83:20)

<3> There may be innumerable reasons for landing on a forced path.
Jobs may be available in the given line, but not in the settlement
where the person concerned lives or wishes to live. Perhaps he
could find a job in his special line only at a place where he does
not wish to live (for example, a small village), or where he cannot
find a dwelling. Perhaps he is compelled by family circumstances to
work at a place where only an unskilled job is available; etc.

19 The Swedish university providing corporate further education for blue and white collar industrial workers

JAN HOLMER

INTRODUCTION

As was stated in the invitation to this conference, the theme, work and education, is meant to

> deal with the role of education in relation to the demands and requirements of working life and with the principles for co-ordinating education and working life.

I would like to begin by relating what I have to say about the role of education and the demands of working life to two contributions made at a seminar held a few years ago on the subject of empirical qualification research. Thus, my intention in this paper is to treat the issue of qualifications for working life (primarily the place of work) in normative rather than functionalistic terms:

> What is the work situation today and what should it ideally be? Given various alternative pictures of working life... what do we find to be missing in education today which makes it impossible to achieve the necessary qualifications for the ideal state we have drawn up? (Abrahamsson 1981:13).

However, my subject is based more on socialization research than on qualification research (Broady 1981:42), which means that my focus is on the problems and needs of the individual - 'psychological acquisition of social conditions' - rather than 'objective societal demands' (Broady 1978:192). As regards 'the principles for coordinating education and working life', I will be basing my statements on examples taken from higher education/university education and co-operation between the representatives of higher education and employees of the shipbuilding and automotive industries with limited educational backgrounds. The following is a brief history of that co-operation.

Between 1977 and 1981 a number of university teachers and researchers held courses, which took various forms, including the study circle, with shipyard workers from Götaverken in Gothenburg. These courses came into being because of the structural crisis in the shipbuilding industry. Götaverken was the only shipbuilding industry in Gothenburg which was still operating, and it was only able to do so because it had received large government subsidies. These subsidies had been the subject of a great deal of political criticism. The local trade union leaders began trying to obtain information about the problems they were facing, including strategies for the survival of their company in the face of immediate mass redundancies. This type of concrete problem became the focus of our co-operation which took the form of study circles, empirical studies, theoretical analyses, a course, and the formulation of various proposals. After some time, this co-operation took the final shape of an interdisciplinary university course worth twenty credit points (one semester of full-time study) for workers in this situation. A similar course began in the autumn of 1983 for blue and white collar workers at Gothenburg's automotive industry (Volvo). This course, too, was the result of prior co-operation.

This paper is a report on some of our experiences and the thoughts which have been provoked by this co-operation, particularly the study circles and the university course. As regards the "shipyard crisis circles" I will discuss the prerequisities for the courses and their results, using as my point of departure some of the theories of class-specified socialization and the anchoring of the circles in the trade unions. Then I will go on to discuss the university course and issues related to the role of the university in this type of context.

THE SHIPYARD CRISIS CIRCLES

The relationship between the demands of the individual and those of society and the conscious process of influence with regard to social customs has been the subject of many analyses and schools of thought including, over the last century, names such as Spencer, Ellen Key, Freud och Dewey (Sjöstrand 1968:111-116). This process and the theories surrounding it are 'among the central issues of education' (ibid.). Particularly 'primary socialization' is considered to have a major effect on human socialization, language development, level of ambition and interest in education, etc.

In an educational situation, there are many factors apart from the teaching itself which affect what and how we learn. The experience the participants bring into the classroom, from home, school and work, is also decisive. Socialization at home and at school can, in turn, be seen as dependent on the production process, where demands are made on the labor force in terms of characteristics and skills.

Generally speaking, primary socialization is taken to mean the incorporation of norms and values which takes place in the home, while secondary socialization is taken to mean the corresponding process att school and elsewhere. Certain schools of thought consider what takes place in the production process to be primary socialization and the adaptation of the production process in the home and school etc., as secondary socialization. The concept of qualification generally refers to this adaptation to the production process (the labor market and places of work) and is then used synonymously with the concept of socialization (particularly) secondary socialization). Axelsson (1982:16), for example, writes that the concept of qualification:

> originally relates to the question of the knowledge and skills of the individual. Its meaning is similar to that of the terms secondary socialization...The terms can also correspond to primary social-ization...

According to Broady (1981:46)

there is good reason to maintain that the core of the theory of qualification is qualifications acquired in some context (such as through education) and used in another context (such as in the sale of manpower on the labor market or at places of work).

In his discussion of the theories of socialization and qualification, Broady (1978) proposes a distinction made by Illeris et al which implies that the processes of socialization and qualification are actually one and the same process. On the other hand, the theory of socialization deals with the psychological acquisition of social conditions, while the theory of qualification deals with the objective societal demands on this process and the societal institutions which mediate these demands.

Particularly in adult/tertiary education previously-acquired habits, etc. may be expected to affect the course of education to a considerable extent. These habits are generally considered to be socially marked, that is to say there are certain given traits which are considered to distinguish certain categories of individuals because of the similarities in their socialization conditions both in childhood and in adult working life.

The demands for experienced-based learning that have been put forward may be seen in the light of this way of thinking. In brief, these demands are based on the implication that education based on the experience of the participants is the most likely to succeed. The greater the extent to which the education integrates the various experiences of the participants from their homes, their leisure time and their working lives, the greater the possibility that the course they are taking will affect them.

The shipyard crisis circles we held were based on these ideas, rooted in the ways of thinking mentioned above, which in their turn, were based on the sociology of knowledge taken from Berger and Luckman (1966), and the theories primarily of Negt, but also of Freire. I will now discuss some of the points in and points of departure of Negt's theory, since I will be discussing some of his assumptions which I find fruitful, though not unquestionable, both in practice and in theory. Negt's way of thinking implies special class-specific ideas and perspectives which are presumed to be based on the socialization process the individual in question has undergone. Lorenzer (1976), for example, describes (with reference to Negt and Popitz (see below)) how it begins as a dialectical process between the instinctual needs of the individual and the social customs passed down to him by his parents. Other German studies indicate that workers have a 'social topik' - a common conceptual outlook - rooted in their common social-historical experience (Popitz et al 1957). This 'social topik' is presumed to be a suitable point of departure for worker education.

> Use of these 'topoi' in the social contexts in question should result in special interest and readiness to learn. In the long run this should be able to lead to liberating alterations of consciousness (Huch 1977).

And Negt (1977:79) states - in a discussion of Bernstein's terms formal and public language - that this use could take place 'in the medium of formal language and empirical science'. Thus, in Lorenzer's (1976:120) words, it can serve to eradicate worn-out patterns of action and interaction and to break down ideological barriers and defects builts in via socialization. Negt formulates his demands on worker education under the headings of the exemplary principle and sociological imagination. The term 'exemplary principle' means that the individual item of specialization should be a reflection of the whole, and it should be possible to place it in a broader social perspective, while 'sociological imagination' means the development of the ability to move from one point of view to another, for example, to see structural contexts in individual life histories. Using these terms, the following didactic principles may be formulated:

1. Education shall take its point of departure in the individual experience of work and of everyday life.
2. This experience is to be used as an example or expression of social conditions
3. It is to be related to the educational subject at hand.

It should be emphasized that this didactic model requires that the context of the educational process at hand be included in the model. As Hultengren writes (1978:99):

It is related to the political situation with which the education is affiliated and that institutions's relation to the total situation of the participants. Knowledge of the total situation of the participants and of the trade union also means knowledge of the specific historical and economic conditions.

When Negt states that he bases his theories on the interests, experience and problems of the participants, he does not mean 'industrial-sociological' experience. Rather, he has a Marxist view of work and capital as his point of departure. The objectives of this education, based on social theory, are that it should be possible to point out obvious contradictions and conflicts in society and use them as material for study, the extent of the process depending on the socio-psychological prerequisites of the participants (Negt 1978). By indicating contradictions in society, exemplary learning aims to clarify rational-izations and repressions. Thus it works by destroying defense mechanisms which exist as stereotypes and prejudices and which hold back conscious observation of contradictions and conflicts in society. With the necessary alterations, the exemplary principle is also applicable to other categories with their own special sets of experience.

I will now report on some of our experience from the study circles at the shipyards, which were based on the principles formulated by Negt, after which I will present some questions for discussion and further study.

1.

Neither the work of Negt and Hultengren nor the study circles at the shipyard took their point of departure in empirical studies of the ideas and experience of the participants. Our project and our study circle work - including lectures, group discussions, participant reports, etc - were based on the assumption that they would be important to the analysis of and effect on the ideas and experience of the workers who participated in them. There is nothing in the course of our work or our results (described in detail below) which indicates that this was not the case. But we have not solved the basic problem of discovering what those ideas, etc. are.

That is to say, Negt's model lacks, in practical application, the fundamental fact on which it is based. I think this is a common flaw in the type of 'liberating education' for which Negt (and Freire) are known. Thus one question which arises is whether these class-specific ideas do exist and, if so, what they consist of (after which the didactic question of how they are to be incorporated into the educational process remains). In the studies cited below, the power structure of society is the focal point, Negt's methods are meant to indicate opportunities for altering this power structure.

Popitz et al (whose research results are based on interviews with 600 mill workers in the Ruhr valley in the mid-1950s) find certain common ideas as to the nature of society and the situation of the worker in that society. Negt bases his work on Popitz' interpretation of reality.

Popitz and his co-workers indicate both a collective awareness (a common social destiny) and a productive awareness (the value of productive labor). The industrial worker's view of society (as opposed to that of the white collar worker) is dichotomic. It can be classified by type, depending on how the dichotomy is viewed (as unchangeable, etc). Huch (1977:90) states that:

> ...Popitz and his co-workers noticed a 'similarity' in statements made by the interviewed workers which 'went as far as formulations. It indicates a general, relatively fixed, limited fund of ideas, opinions and theses...'. The authors refer this 'social topik' to common social-historical experience.

More recent German studies have both confirmed Popitz' results regarding the different views of society held by workers and by higher social classes, and revised some of his assumptions (see Grimm, below, regarding different aspirations in different subcategories, etc).

Popitz' results have also been compared with the situation in England. In Bulmer (1975) a number of English sociologists have made a critical examination of Lockwood's assumptions (and thus also those of Popitz) on various types of workers and their impressions of the class structure of society, etc. At least one clear fact emerges from the enormous quantity of research results they present: among English workers there is considerable differentiation both among and within various occupations as regards understanding of the power structure of society, etc. For example, according to Lockwood, the typical shipyard worker, like the typical miner, is a traditional proletarian worker. In Lockwood's typology, such an individual has expectations basically limited to his own way of life, a strong sense of solidarity with a work-dominated collective spirit and a consciousness of 'us' as opposed to 'them' (they have the power). His sense of solidarity also takes expression in his trade union work, which is based more on a sense of class solidarity than of private gain. However, studies of English shipyard workers (ibid.:79) show that:

> 'images of society' of shipbuilding workers have been characterised more by paradox - or perhaps confusion - than pattern... there is considerable diversity of social perspectives among shipbuilding workers...

Another English study (made among 951 workers in various trades) indicates that (ibid.:156) 'coherent consistent ideologies in the conventional sense do not exist'.

The authors propose that future work use other methods (than attitude surveys):

> We need to know not simply the final result of whether workers are able to synthesize ideological contradictions, but also the process by which they attempt to do so. One method would be an <u>intensive though structured set of discussions</u> with individual <u>workers, actually challenging them about contradictory lines of thought.</u> (My emphasis)

On the whole, there is no basis for an unambiguous interpretation or point of departure for a didactic process except in terms of very general conditions (such as the type of result reported, for example, in Korpi's (1978) study of Swedish metal workers). In her criticism of Negt, Marianne Gronemeyer (Negt 1978:81) states that goals deduced from social theory need not necessarily be important to the learner. Instead, she pleads for a considerably greater differentiation by social-psychological type. Thus it is clearly difficult - irrespective of the terms on which education takes place - to base that education on the participants' images of society, etc. to more than a very basic extent. But, taking my examples from the shipyard crisis circles, I would assert that what is possible is to let the knowledge developed from prior studies (for example, the relationship between a company and the trade union, etc.) establish the point of departure in the classroom for discussions of vision versus reality, allowing the experience of the participants to affect these discussions, etc. However, this does not mean that the teaching is based on this experience. Rather, it is the lack of knowledge about these ideas which makes it necessary to have a working form in which the experience and problems of the participants can be analyzed, and where the contents of the teaching comprises increased skills, factual knowledge and insights, and perspectives.

Thus, two primary questions are:

a) Are there class-specific or other collectively analysable ideas - and, if so, what is their nature - among, for example, the group of workers in question here?
b) How can these ideas be used as a point of departure for the teaching process or somehow be given consideration in this process?

2.

I would now like to bring up a number of problems related to a summary of the results and effects of our work in the shipyard crisis circles.

> The participants were supposed to study...what social conditions 'generate contemporary threats and problems'. They were to make a critical examination of the perspectives which were being asserted and to study the potential for change and gradually develop an alternative view of reality. This alternative view would lead to a joint action program and to actions to affect the course of events. (Eriksson and Holmer, 1978:97).

The study circles at the shipyard took the form of co-operation between two parties: the trade union clubs and the researchers. What was specific to these activities was that they took place under uncommonly tangibly expressed economic-political conditions. The crisis in the shipbuilding industry was in an acute phase, one expression of which was a merger between the two large shipbuilding industries Eriksberg and Götaverken as a result of which thousands of people lost or risked losing their jobs. It is important to keep these events in mind when discussing trade union involvement in the study circles.

During and immediately after our work in the study circles, individual results could be seen: skills - for example, in the collection and analysis of material; factual knowledge - for example, as regarded certain aspects of the economic situation; insights and perspectives - for example, as regarded decison-making processes in society and the ability of the individual to affect them, and the fact that individual worries can also be seen as collective problems. Taken as a whole, this led to increased self-confidence and affected the abilities of the participants to contribute competently both in discussions with their fellow workers on the shop floor, in their study group and in the extended study circle activities, and in their contacts with representatives of the company, politicians and the mass media. On the other hand, we know very little about the political, social and cultural resources which participation in the circles led to in the longer run. Their studies made it possible for these workers to examine some of the problems in their working and everyday life analytically. But what we know too little about is whether the perspective they developed on their everyday experience of the production process etc., led to their subsequently being able to understand and influence their situation as producers and consumers. Borgström and Olofsson (1983) have attempted to illuminate this type of issue as well as the effects of participation in the circles. This is an 'ex post facto' study which makes use of the standard of living studies carried out by the Swedish Central Bureau of Statistics. The authors indicate relationships which may be presumed to confirm the supposition that participation in the study circles contributed to an increase in political-cultural and social resources. 'Resources' is then taken to mean not only knowledge which leads to action but also real participation in various activities. This, in turn, can lead to what Bengtsson and Härnqvist (1972:210) call 'equality of participation' in their discussion of various types of educational equality - i.e. education as a means of making the individual participate actively in and influence the development of society.

Some of the tangible results of our study circles were considered valuable by the study and follow-up committeee of the local union club. In publications written by individuals closely affiliated with the local union club, the shipyard crisis circles are mentioned as emulatable examples of how the trade union can work in terms of studies, follow-up, and research and development. In one report (Stange and Ivarsson 1981:54-55, and 67) the emphasis is placed on the forms of work and co-operation. In others what is emphasized is the fact that the participants learned to make demands based on what they had learned through this co-operation (see, i.a., LOFO 1 1980:28-30, and 50), and in yet another it is the content of the demands which is stressed (Beckholmen 1979:173). A report written by the shipyard crisis circle participants (The Union in a Corporate Crisis 1978) was distributed in an abridged version and quickly attracted the attention of a couple of thousand members. It was used as course material in new study circles with between two and three hundred participants, after a study guide had been prepared.

In these new study circles, a working form was used which was new to this local union club and which meant that the participants were allowed to evaluate and analyze more themselves, as less centrally-produced material was used. Circles for committee chairmen and follow-up groups also developed as a result of the shipyard crisis circles. With the encouragement of the club board, the participants continued with the analyses and follow-ups they had begun.

Another way in which follow-up work in the local club was encouraged was through the appointment of two follow-up secretaries (who had participated in the shipyard crisis circles). Thus the courses also qualified the participants for posts in the trade union organization.

According to Negt, worker education programs should come under the auspices of the official trade union (Hultengren 1977:23)

> both because of the potential they represent in terms of money and equipment and because the trade unions are sure eventually to discover that they cannot satisfactorily fulfill their function, and because the majority of workers are loyal to the union... we must build our work on contradictions and conflicts, even those among union leaders.

Resources, vested interests and loyalty are, thus, the primary reasons. But Negt makes no distinction between the interests the individual may have in terms of working to increase his knowledge and the interests his trade union may have in that development. In the complicated economic-political context surrounding the shipyard crisis circles, the strategy of the trade union leadership indicated that they preferred (Boglind 1981:217-218)

> to build up mutual understanding of the necessity to cut down the labor force and increase its effectivity in order to ensure the future existence of the place of work in accordance with the conformist strategy

rather than to develop their own alternatives.

Thus the formal organization did not function as the 'bearer of the reformist, system-altering interests of the employees' (ibid.:214), nor did it function as the bearer of the interests of the individual employee in terms of the law on employment security. Yet in some of the study circles and among individual members insights about alternatives and perspectives on opportunities did develop.

Negt may be right in seeing the desirability of a collective agent, and in wanting the trade union to fulfill this function in the development and exploitation of alternatives. In a survey of higher education courses for active trade union members within the Swedish Trade Union Confederation we write (Eriksson and Holmer 1981:25):

> The academic knowledge and competence which is now being disseminated among and used by professional groups in the upper corporate echelons may be questioned and supplemented in terms of

knowledge acquired and made available through the trade union representatives...

But it is conceivable that the trade union perspective may become problematical when the focus is on studies for the individual worker. Conert (1978:126) also says that the most important criticism which can be levelled against Negt is that the Negtian type of worker education is not clearly anchored in trade union practice. According to Conert, there are educational barriers which should lead to the modification of objectives, particularly as regards making the methods of guidance and the structuring of the processes of experience and mediation of information more concrete and detailed. In this context, Conert mentions three complex factors which must be taken into consideration:

A. The current superficial structure of courses offered through the trade unions (such as time limits and the heterogeneity of the participants.)

B. Subjective barriers to the process of exemplary learning caused by restrictive forms of acquisition and preparation of social reality (such as fixation with what is close at hand, concrete, 'realistic', and fixation with the ideological formulas of the trade union). These factors, and others, lead in one direction, and that is toward confirmation of present circumstances. Conert questions whether these processes, which result from society, can be 'corrected' by cognitive means without changes in society.

C. The difference between trade union courses and policies of practical action. This is a question of whether the course can be followed up in terms of practical actions, in the trade union and elsewhere.

This leads to the following questions:

a) Do clichés and ideological bonds prevent the development of knowledge which might have been useful in the long run?

b) Isling (1980:222ff) deals with opinions (in the 1930s and 40s) which held that gifted students from the lower social classes should take the alternative educational route via study circles and folk high schools instead of studying at upper class schools, because this would make them better able to serve the interests of the workers' movement. The current situation could remain as it was, since it served as 'useful injustice'. Similar thoughts can also be found in Johansson (1970:39-40). Are courses like the one in this project 'useless justice', in that they rob groups which have few enough inherent resources, of individuals who could represent their cause? If the course leads to a qualified position in the union, does it, by increasing the career status of the participants, fail to satisfy the interests of those for whom it was intended?

c) To what extent have the participants been able to find satisfaction in and understand or affect their working situation, home lives and social lives, seen in a more long-term perspective (political, cultural social resources).

THE UNIVERSITY COURSE

In the previous section (the shipyard crisis circles), I took up some of the questions which may be asked in conjunction with the prerequisites – individual and organizational – for studies, and the results and effects to which such studies may lead. In this section, I will discuss the contribution of the university, beginning with the question of recruitment.

1.

Research results indicate that there are still great class differences with regard to recruitment and degree completion at Swedish universities (Svensson 1980). More than one-third of the children of the upper classes continue studying until they obtain a higher degree, as compared with only 4% of the children of the working class.

A similar disproportion is reported for non-matriculated university students. A study at Lund University indicates, for example, that very few people (<5%) taking the courses which were reported on, had occupations which come under the heading 'working class' (Nelsson 1982).

In an assessment report on work experience and higher education it was found that (Abrahamsson et al 1980:124):'higher education has become increasingly important in terms of further education and professional training. However, today as previously, those who take advantage of the new opportunities are the already well-educated.'

A similar tendency has recently been reported with regard to the importance of student grants (Reuterberg and Svensson 1983).

On the international level as well, research results indicate the difficulty of attempting to reach groups other than the traditional university students. In a review article including a discussion of external studies and experience of such studies in most industrial countries, Willén (1981:249) states that: 'It is still difficult to find a university which is satisfied with its efforts in this direction.'

As exemplified above, many studies indicate the lack of 'equality of opportunity' which affects both young people and adults from the social classes with the least resources. But there is only a little research which points out the obstacles and motivation problems upon which this uneven recruitment is based.

Children who grow up in working class homes generally tend to develop less interest in education than children from the middle class. No expectations are placed on the metalworker or his children by his fellow workers or the trade union as to his pursuing university studies.

Johansson and Ekerwald (1976) examine the question of why some adults pursue studies while others do not, using factors touching on attitude and motivation, among some twenty adult students in comparison with a 'twin group' of non-students. In their summary they write (ibid.:183): 'The fact that there are not more (adult students) is due to complacency, lack of energy, time and financial means or to a lack of self-confidence.'

Grimm (1967) has made a detailed study of German textile and metal-workers and their 'educational abstinence'. She describes the workers' notions of social reality, distinguishing three groups with varying levels of aspiration and consequently with varying notions of society, educational opportunities, etc. In her opinion, lack of financial means is secondary to what she refers to as insufficient information (lack of facts about what the educational system has to offer). This lack of information is due to affective distance (a lack of emotional closeness or community of values in relation to other individuals based on prestige, income and education). According to Grimm, the lack of long-term planning is also secondary to this informative and affective distance. Grimm states educational distance to be the cause (i.e. the cause attributed by the worker himself to this lack of status) of this affective distance. By educational distance she means the distance individuals find between themselves and others based on their differences in educational status, which gives them different social ranks. The educational distance felt by the worker is expressed in insecurity with relation not only to education but also to making suggestions at his place of work, or trying to affect things there. Education is associated with differences in vocabulary, language level and thought expression, and the insecurity with which it is related is also projected onto the child, and takes expression, for example, in a lack of confidence in the child's achievement potential.

Grimm's findings may be compared with the findings reported by Bengtsson and Härnqvist (1972:220) with regard to the tendency to proceed to upper secondary education among various social groups:

> If we select the educational level of the parents instead of social class affiliation for our expression of differences in family background, we find that the inequality continues and is sometimes even reinforced... The educational level of the parents is not a single, simple piece of information, but contains components such as information about education, the value placed on education, the possibility of helping children with their school work, and the general level of language and culture in the home.

We have made no systematic analysis of our experience from the university course and prior education as regards informational and affective distance. Discussion with our course participants indicated that they had very little knowledge of higher education, its organization and what opportunities were available. Their affective distance to their studies was found to be extensive, and it was not found to be considerably reduced by their university experience. Although the participants saw their course as a positive experience, none of them indicated an interest in going on to non-matriculated studies in any subject the course touched on. However, there was a great deal of interest expressed in a 'continuation course' to be held in the same form as the course they had finished (see details below).

Therefore I would like to ask the following questions:

a) Is informative and affective distance to (higher) education as great as our experience suggests?
b) What explanation of this distance can we find in the participants' notions of society and in the structural reality behind these notions?
c) How can this distance be altered, either through co-operative projects of the type we participated in or in other ways?

Now I would like to describe the contents of this course and the question of what contribution the university can make to increasing the knowlege of the group in question.

The course - 'The shipyard crisis, employment and industrial policy' - was a twenty credit point course offered over one year (corresponding to half-time studies). The classes were held every Friday in course facilities at the Eriksberg shipyard (which has now been closed down). The funding for salaries and administration was made available by the Gothenburg Regional Board for Higher Education.

The participants' studies were financed – in terms of compensation for working time lost – in the form of grants to the participants from the local trade union branch. This financing was made possible because the president of the branch was also an officer in both the division and the confederation. According to the syllabus, the course was meant to be a contribution toward the development of knowledge on regional industrial problems, using the participants' knowledge of the shipbuilding industry and the crisis in that industry as the point of departure. The course was meant to further, among other things, the participants' trade union work and to lead to concrete proposals.

The course was divided into three subunits - historical description, consequences, future assessments - in which teachers from approximately ten subjects plus a number of representatives of public agencies and organizations worked with the course participants. These various subunits were tied together in terms of a group project which took its final shape as a report (Andersson et al 1981) containing papers on the Swedish economy, industrial policies, trade union strategies and the shipbuilding branch.

Pursuant to §2 of the Higher Education Act, higher education should be based on scientific principles. Higher education is also required to focus these scientific principles and methods on problems in working life and society. This may mean that the university has to integrate information from various disciplines, and enable the students to integrate this information with practical experience and their own opinions.

As discussed above, in a university-level course intended for workers, one can expect that the experience, opinions and problems brought to the course by the participants may differ in some respects from those brought by the more traditional groups in higher education - with respect to language, political position, general notion of society, etc. This type of course is, for both parties, an unusual encounter between formal language and the scientific method of analysis on the one hand and public/everyday language and practical awareness based on category-specific factors on the other.

What, then, does the special competence of the university and its teachers and researchers consist of? How can they contribute to increasing the knowledge of the participants in the type of course described here? We found that the most useful knowledge and skills the university could provide were related to the necessary methodology and perspectives for carrying out investigations and writing reports. This relates back to the above mentioned requirement that university level education should be based on scientific principles and focus on the form and content of undergraduate education: the students are to be provided with factual knowledge and with knowledge that will equip them to go on learning on their own. This knowledge is to be based on research results, and their studies are to give the students practice in the application of research methods and the ability to make independent critical analyses, etc. Our experiment indicates that the group project is central to the course, not only because it provides a framework and is a tangible goal for the learning process, but also because it gives the university teachers a good opportunity to contribute their special skills and for the participants to evaluate and absorb what they have learned.

As a complement to the questions I have posed above regarding qualification within the union, political, social and cultural resources, recruitment, etc.,I would like to conclude by relating to my initial question '... what do we find to be missing in education today...?' (Abrahamsson 1981:13). To what extent can we expect our universities and other institutions of higher education to offer the type of course I have sketched in order to contribute to the development of alternative, 'ideal places of work' in terms of 'high participation figures, good personal and social development, knowledge of the means of production and the condition of production' (ibid.) etc? And what possible consequences could education, as part of the social and factual aspects of working life, have for the leisure time of the employee, and vice versa – what are the scattering effects? What could the universities and institutions of higher education contribute to what is known as 'equality of participation'.

We are now carrying out a study which will give us material, through interviews and participant observation, on which to test some of the above-mentioned hypotheses and results. We hope that this will give us greater knowledge of the prerequisites and methods for the type of tailor-made further education for industrial workers and white collar workers discussed above.

20 Wage-labour and polarization within vocational education in Denmark 1960-1980

ANDERS MATHIESEN

Work must always be understood historically. The concrete social forms of work are conditioned by the specific historical, social organization of production. And this paper will briefly outline how work and especially vocational education has changed as part of the development of industrial capitalism in Denmark since the 1950s. In capitalist production the form of work is wage-labour (Lohnarbeit). Consequently, the individual employers decide how to organize the labour process and which kind or 'quality' of labour power they want to use.

These few words indicate the theoretical point of departure for the following contribution to the discussion on work and education.

As a whole this paper is primarily based on a research project financed by a state commission on low income.[1]

VOCATIONAL EDUCATION AND THE CAPITALIST STATE

The problems dealt with in this article must be seen in the light of some more general and fundamental trends in government education policy, and indeed in new functions of the capitalist state that have emerged since World War II. In the course of the 1950's, education policy in Denmark became increasingly connected with and conditioned by state economic policy - and with state planning in general - to a hitherto unknown extent.

Developments in the last twenty years, especially within the planning of vocational education, have proved how the interests of various fractions of capital are met by the state apparatus, in cooperation with the political as well as trade union representatives of the working class. It is, however, the power of monopoly capital in particular (the Federation of Danish Industries and the Danish Employers' Association) that is increasingly interwoven with the power of the capitalist state.

More and more educational tasks and institutions have been placed under the education ministry's jurisdiction, and have thus become involved in central educational planning. At the same time, representatives of employers' associations have controlled the planning of (especially) vocational education, through an increased involvement in governmental committees and in the controlling bodies of state vocational educational planning. In this way vocational education has been changed in accordance with the short-term and current requirements of various groups of employers during most of the post-war period.

In principle, employers' associations and labour unions are equal, but in reality, they are not.

POLARIZATION WITHIN VOCATIONAL EDUCATION

Concerning the terminology, individuals in the labour force who have no vocational training beyond the obligatory school are considered as a special qualification category. It will be referred to as the 'residual group', and is primarily characterized by 'negative' qualifications. That is to say, persons who are willing to endure monotony, to resign to totally externally determined work processes, and who will adjust to physically unpleasant and socially detrimental work (see Lutz 1969:227ff).

Detailed analyses of the development of vocational education in Denmark since the 1950's show that traditional apprentice training has partly been replaced by some new 'basic vocational courses' (EFG) and a number of shorter theoretical courses at vocational schools (1-3 years) and especially by a great number of extremely short job-training courses (about 3 weeks).

Fig. A gives a more subtle outline of the past twenty years' polarization within vocational education. The outline is based on statistics concerning the absolute number of persons who, in any given year, have taken some form of vocational education. Fig. A is divided between the commercial and clerical area and, on the other hand, all education in trade and industry. In the commercial and clerical area one can immediately see the development and trend in the composition of the new intake of trained labour power (apprentices, Hx, HHx, etc.). In the area of trade and industry, however, one can only talk of an outline of the main tendency, since the composition of qualifications varies from one branch of industry to another.

However, analyses of individual qualification categories within the area of trade and industry have shown that, in the course of the past twenty years, there has been increased curriculum specialization in the major areas (for example, engineering, construction, etc.). This specialization was made possible through centralization of vocational schools, etc. In addition, especially for commercial school education, each category in Fig. A covers a great number of subjects and courses, varied in level and duration, which are not specifically named in the statistics (Mathiesen 1979: Chap. V).

The outline in Fig. A shows that the yearly number of apprenticeships was reduced by almost half in the period 1965-1975, despite the fact that, in the same period, there was an increase in general employment - with variations for individual industries. Since 1975 there has been a moderate increase of apprenticeship.<2> Furthermore, the rapid increase in various very short job-training courses should be noticed. The corresponding examinations in single-subject courses at commercial schools increased quite drastically, too. In 1975 almost half the participants in courses for semi-skilled workers were under 25 years old. These very narrowly limited job-training courses have gradually grown to include just as many young people - about 15,000 a year - as the number of young people who got an apprentice education in trade and industry in 1980. In addition to this, there is the 'residual group' who do not get any sort of vocational preparation at all (about 30,000 a year).

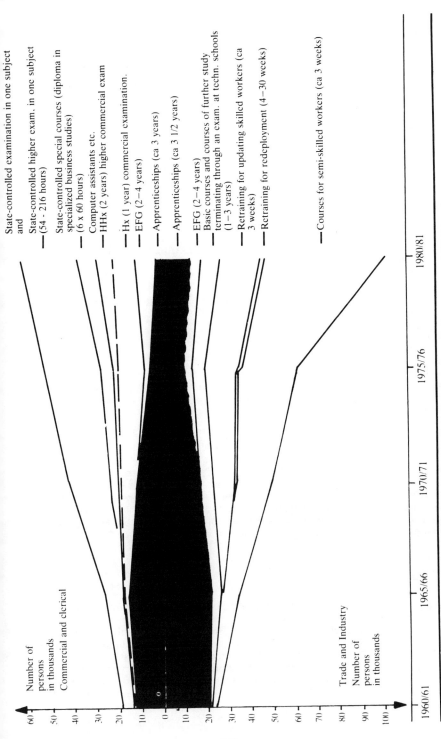

Figure A. *Schematic outline of development in the number of persons (CPR-nr.) who began a non-academic, vocational education in each year from 1960–1980*

State-controlled examination in one subject and

State-controlled higher exam. in one subject (54 - 216 hours)

State-controlled special courses (diploma in specialized business studies) (6 x 60 hours)

Computer assistants etc.

HHx (2 years) higher commercial exam

Hx (1 year) commercial examination.

EFG (2–4 years)

Apprenticeships (ca 3 years)

Apprenticeships (ca 3 1/2 years)

EFG (2–4 years)

Basic courses and courses of further study terminating through an exam. at techn. schools (1–3 years)

Retraining for updating skilled workers (ca 3 weeks)

Retraining for redeployment (4–30 weeks)

Courses for semi-skilled workers (ca 3 weeks)

Number of persons in thousands
Commercial and clerical

60
50
40
30
20
10
0
10
20
30
40
50
60
70
80
90
100

Trade and Industry
Number of persons in thousands

1960/61   1965/66   1970/71   1975/76   1980/81

195

This development, illustrated in Fig. A, is what is meant by polarization within vocational education. The main tendencies have been confirmed by more elaborated, separate analyses for each branch of industry. Structurally it is the combined effect of developments in basic school education and curriculum specialization, and structural differentiation in vocational education. Vocational schools have gradually taken over an increasing part of institutionalized vocational preparation, which is thus increasingly placed under the direct control of industry (vocational schools are private institutions, publicly financed). This happens at the cost of more or less common basic education in school.

Precisely the branch specialization in large industries (engineering, construction, etc.) and a more elitist orientation in commercial school education are at the core of the polarization that Fig. A illustrates. Compared with apprenticeships, the new, more theoretical education at vocational schools, and the short labour market courses can both be seen as 'split-offs' caused by the altered division of labour in individual workplaces and industries as well as the shift in functions between basic school education and vocational schools. In this way the educational system has been changed in accordance with short-term profitability or private industry during the past twenty years.

To sum up: The changes in vocational education during the past twenty years have been

- specialization of the curriculum,
- structural differentiation, and
- polarization of student inflow going, on the one hand, to a quickly growing number of short, specific job-training courses and, on the other, to some more theoretical vocational school education, which requires a longer theoretical schooling (in secondary school), both at the cost of a longer and more coherent apprentice training.

This is what has happened and what is actually being intensified on the level of education and vocational training.

One of the most important facts is that, every year, a still greater number of skilled workers must give up their skilled jobs and qualifications in favour of unskilled jobs and short, specific jobtraining mostly within another branch of industry. Consequently - in the long run - the stock of skilled workers in the labour force as a whole is undermined.

THE POLARIZED QUALIFICATION STRUCTURE WITHIN THE LABOUR FORCE OF THE PUBLIC SECTOR

Corresponding developments can be observed within higher technical and higher commercial education for the private sector. Education for the public sector is recorded in less detail for the first half of the period since 1960. About one third - 33% - of the total Danish labour force was employed in the public sector in 1980 (i.e. about 900,000), but in 1960 the public sector only employed 15% (about 300,000) many of whom were persons with higher education. During the 1960s and 70's the total labour force has grown from about 2 to 2.7 million. (These and the following figures are based on Mathiesen 1980:370-373).

There has not been the same tradition of apprentice training in the public sector – as for trade and industry. Consequently, the explosive growth in the public sector since the 1950's has led to a fairly rigorously polarized employment-structure as regards vocational qualifications – especially within the social sector and the health sector. In 1980 the social and health sectors employed about 400,000 persons – of whom 85% were women, and 33% of these had no vocational education or training at all; more than half of those employed within these sectors had less than full time work.

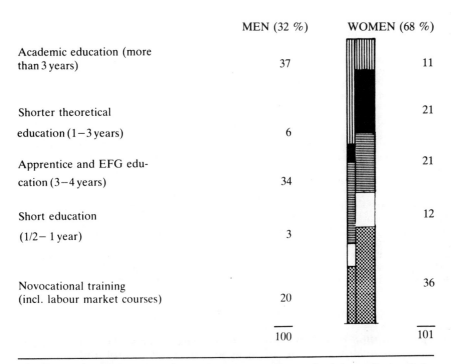

	MEN (32 %)	WOMEN (68 %)
Academic education (more than 3 years)	37	11
Shorter theoretical education (1–3 years)	6	21
Apprentice and EFG education (3–4 years)	34	21
Short education (1/2– 1 year)	3	12
Novocational training (incl. labour market courses)	20	36
	100	101

Figure B. *Relative qualification composition (%) in the labour force of the public sector in Denmark 1976 – men and women separately*

The relative composition of qualifications (1976) for the public sector as a whole is shown in Fig. B, based on the Low Income Report (Mathiesen 1979: Chap. IX). The figures in Figure B indicate many factors. Only one factor is pointed out here. Compared with the large and central areas in the private sector – e.g. engineering and construction, where more than 60% of the labour force has an apprentice education and about 30% no vocational education at all – most of the public sector has quite another composition. This is what is meant by polarized employment-structure (i.e. relative composition of qualifications in the employed labour force).

POLARIZATION OF THE QUALIFICATION STRUCTURE OF THE TOTAL LABOUR FORCE

The combined effects stemming from curriculum differentiation in basic school education and structural differentiation combined with curriculum specialization in vocational education have made a growing polarization of the qualification structure look like a 'natural' and 'free' development. But these structural changes within the educational system as a whole were brought about by political decisions on different levels.

The polarization that took place within the total Danish education system in the course of the 1960's is a combined effect of two trends. On the one hand, there was vigorous growth within academic preparatory (theoretical) education, and in higher education. On the other hand, vocational education showed a concurrent shift towards shorter job training, a job training that barely covered restricted job demands. And that took place at the cost of apprenticeships. The 'residual group' continues to comprise one third of each year group of young people leaving primary and lower secondary school, and for this category of labour power the only vocational preparation consists of compulsory basic school education. More detailed analyses of the development in the qualification structure of the labour force show that inequality in educational distribution among the Danish labour force has been intensified in the course of the past twenty years (see Table 1 and Fig. C).

Table 1: Outline of relative qualification compositions (%) in the renewal of qualifications in total labour force 1960, 1970 and 1980.

	1960	1970	1980
Academic and longer theoretical education (3- years)	10	11	9
Shorter theoretical education (1-3 years)	4	11	12
Apprentice and EFG education<3>	37	20	14
Short education ($\frac{1}{2}$-1 year)	6	18	16
Semi-skilled courses, etc. (up to $\frac{1}{2}$ year)	2	19	32
No vocational education (i.e. the 'residual group')	41	21	17
Total	100	100	100

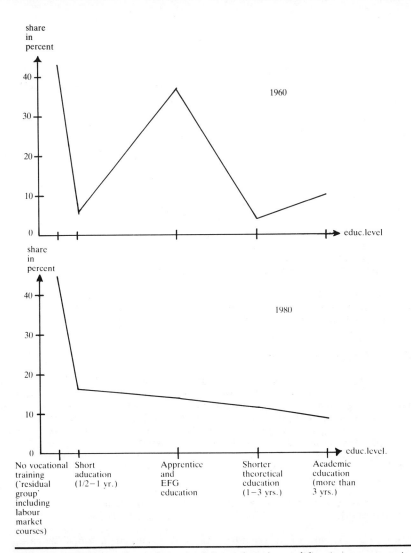

Figure C. *Outline of trends in the labour force's qualification structure in the period 1960–1980*

Table 1 and Fig. C give an approximate estimation of the yearly renewal of qualifications in the labour force in 1960, 1970 and 1980 – including new intake of young workers (see Lavindkomstkommissionen: Table IV 30). It should be noted that the short job-training courses for semi-skilled workers comprise a government financed job training (approximately three weeks) that completely corresponds to the training that unskilled workers previously got on the job, and that was previously paid for by individual employers. Accordingly, these job training courses do not mean any change as regards the qualification structure. That is why the 'residual group' and these 'courses for semi-skilled workers' merge into one category of qualification level in the survey of the labour force's qualification structure in Fig. C.

199

The polarization in the total education system has meant that a few more people get a longer and more theoretical education; however, the many subordinate workers' vocational preparation (i.e. schooling and training) has been shortened. The 'residual group's' more or less unchanged share of renewal of qualifications every year in the total labour force - about 40% - means that, over time, still more workers in the labour force had only a short, specific job training as their vocational education. If this tendency continues unchanged, an increasingly larger part of the total labour force's qualifications will gradually be reduced to narrowly defined job skills.

Over a period of time, developments within the educational system have led to a constantly stronger fragmentation of the qualifications of labour power - i.e. labour's educationally conditioned skills etc. That is what has happened on the level of qualification structure of the labour force as a whole. The question is to what degree and how such a - with regard to skills etc. - fragmentized and polarized labour power corresponds to changes in work (technologies used, its organization, and qualifications required) - i.e. workplace structure.

Finally, I shall briefly outline, what this polarization means with regard to qualifications, what it means to labour power and unions, and how this development has been decided.

CONCEPT OF QUALIFICATION

1. Polarization in the qualification structure of the labour force as a whole can be characterized - with regard to skills - as a constantly stronger separation and specialization of what is mostly called intellectual work (vertical division of labour) and, at the same time, a very strong division and specialization of simple operations in work (horizontal division of labour). That is what is called fragmentized job-qualifications, and in so far as this development in vocational education reflects demands from the workplace structure, it must mean derogating work.

   But at the same time other dimensions of qualifications have been strengthened.

2. If one can speak of a parallel strengthening of a work morale, it seems primarily to be a result of the progressive dissolution of the 'material' relations in the programs of vocational education - i.e. the fact that the educational process as a whole omits to point out and make understandable the cohesion among the many simple tasks and operations which comprise a total work process. At any rate, there does not seem to be a basis for speaking of explicit efforts to intensify discipline in the educational programs. But to many individual workers the need for 'a meaning in/with life' makes even meaningless concrete work appear to be a possibility for structuring life. Consequently, abstract educational programs without 'material' cohesion create a need for 'concrete meaning' - i.e. strengthening a will to work.

3. Against the background of the structure and content of educational programs as well as the subjective need for social identity, any and all concrete work 'gives meaning' to the individual worker, and that means a strong motivation to accept the conditions accompanying

wage labour and the hierarchical structure of the workplace, etc. But acceptance of a subordinate position on the job is perhaps also to some degree the result of becoming used to educational situations which are controlled externally.

One can not speak of explicit efforts to increase discipline in the primary schools and vocational education programs in Denmark in the period after World War II, the period in which industrialization in Denmark actually took place - especially in the course of the 60's. This industrialization process caused a dissolution of work. But the fragmentation of work was accompanied by a constantly more active and outspoken, state-supported ideological integration (i.e. 'Social Studies' and 'Contemporary Studies' at the beginning of the 1970's directly presented as conflict preventive, ideological education) in lower secondary and basic vocational education. Here too there is perhaps primarily talk of not only a 'crumbling' but a breaking down of traditional conceptions - parallel to the dissolution of work.

EMPLOYER CONTROLLED PLANNING OF (STATE) VOCATIONAL EDUCATION

1. When one is to describe what the implications of polarization of vocational education are for different categories of labour power in the labour market, one can perhaps speak of a shift from one situation where the major portion of programs of vocational education were aimed at the labour market (i.e., the traditional apprenticeship programs) to another situation where a constantly increasing proportion of the labour force is trained (through short job-training courses) in the skills required to perform jobs with particular machines in the production of particular products in particular firms and workplaces. This shift implies that the market value of labour power is reduced, since the transfer of such very narrowly qualified labour power to other jobs requires retraining or requalifying.

2. The tendency for an increased portion of the labour force to be specifically trained for tasks in particular firms means in some states with large firms or corporations and with limited state operated activities in the form of short job-training and retraining programs - that an increasing part of the labour force becomes dependent on particular firms or cooperations as a result of their 'private' internal training courses. In Denmark a widespread state operated system of very short and job specific courses has been built up since the 60's, which can be crucial for regulating the labour market. In principle, dependence here is related to the state.

3. Meanwhile, the 'state operated system of vocational training' in Denmark is not an independent bureaucracy of civil servants; on the contrary, it is a strongly differentiated corporative system which, despite public financing, is controlled by representatives of both employers and trade unions within each of the particular sub-areas (regionally/geographically; branch-wise; size of firms/business; etc.) This system of vocational training - controlled by labour market interest groups, - in fact, representatives of employers' associations - has thus polarized the Danish vocational education system and the qualification structure of the total labour force - including the growing specialization among firms. In this connection, it is important to differentiate between the qualifications required as they

are formulated by the dominant groups in the labour market – representatives of monopoly capital in particular – and the potential requirements for qualifications of work itself.

VOCATIONAL EDUCATION AND THE CONCEPT OF WORK

An extreme degree of differentiation of programs of vocational training has consequences for what kind of learning and development processes can be established. And that again has decisive implications for the participants' conceptions of work. This point, among others, can be illuminated from some of the main findings of a recently completed Danish research project on vocational training – particularly, a part that deals with socialization in vocational education. The PUNKS-investigation (Sørensen 1983) reveals something about the significance of continuous educational processes. But it also shows that young people's experiences on the job play a decisive part in their interpretation of the teaching they receive at vocational schools. Teaching at vocational schools – including workshop teaching – can give some conceptions of relevant and 'emancipating' qualities attached to productive work. If these conceptions – completely uninterpreted and without pedagogical support (i.e. without interpretation from the teaching staff) – are confronted with typical norms and demands found in job situations for wage-labour, the result is usually defeatism or the wish for 'individual upward mobility' by means of further education. That is the political problem of vocational education in 1984. Who is going to control the workers' interpretation and understanding of their experiences at the workplace? That means control the workers' concept of work.

Notes

<1> A more comprehensive report on this project was published in the final report (see Mathiesen 1979).

<2> The increase in apprentice intake in the years up to 1980 must be seen in relation to the following background: first, 11,975 employers have been exempt from paying vocational schools for apprentices, and second, the new law of 1976 removed grants for students during the EFG basic vocational courses. The current increase in apprentice intake must furthermore be seen as a part of the measures to combat youth unemployment. In 1978 these measures led to the opening of more than 7,000 extraordinary apprentice and trainee jobs (of which 5,737 were in private employment, with up till 15,000 kr. paid in employer's grants per apprentice). Of these jobs, not all provided the chance for an up-to-date training. (Indsatsen... 1978:Tab. 35). The number of extraordinary trainee jobs and the amount of employer's grants has been doubled since 1980, but the total number of apprenticeships (included EFG) has remained at the 1980 level (Indsatsen... 1982:Chap. 4).

<3> EFG education (basic vocational courses) started in 1972 and is run parallel with the traditional training of apprentices for skilled work. EFG education is primarily schooling with practical training as part of the course.

Part V
Work and Power

21 Discussant's paper on work and power

GÖRAN LANTZ [1]

DEFINITIONS

The two concepts of work and power are notoriously difficult to define. Macpherson starts out with a 'narrow' definition of work. It goes without saying that a broader definition, e.g. a definition including some human characteristics of an essentialistic kind (the social nature of man, human self-realization etc) would entail, or at least easily lend itself to, asking some of the standard questions within the Marxist theory of alienation (Entfremdung). It should be noted that this 'narrow' definition of work denotes a great variety of human activities. Notice this random sample of activities which could be included in the 'narrow' concept of work: the professional activities of a professor, a journalist, a judge, an estate agent, a priest, a prostitute, and an under-secretary of state. Still most discussions about work deal with one very specific activity, i.e. manual work within industrial production. Admittedly Macpherson recognizes one important distinction, that between so-called white collar work and blue collar work.

I would like to differentiate between a broad and a narrow definition of 'power over one's own work' and 'power over one's own political government' respectively.

The statement 'P has power over his/her own work' may be interpreted as follows:[2]

1. P controls his/her work environment
2. P determines what will be produced
3. P controls the marketing of the product of the work
4. P controls the investments in the producing organisation
5. P controls the profit of the work
6. P controls the whole human edifice that is produced by work

Let us call 1 the most narrow interpretation, and 1-6 the broadest. Interpretations which include combinations of 1-6 are consequently narrower or broader to a varying extent. The broadest definition is implied in the theory of alienation of the young Marx. The narrowest is often presupposed in non-socialist thinking about the spread of power in work life.

Accordingly, the statment 'P has power over his/her own political government' may be interpreted, as regards the range of control implied (the domain of control), on a scale ranging from wide power to narrow power as follows:

1. P has control over his/her own political government equivalent to the political power of a member of a minimal 'night-watch-state'
2. P has control over his/her own political government equivalent to the political power of a member of a maximal welfare-state

Other aspects of the degree of political control might be combined with this; above all, the aspects of the extent of control. In this respect we can draw a scale ranging from formal (or institutionalized) to real (or effective) power:

1. P is allowed to elect parliamentary representatives
2. P controls those decisions within his/her society which affect himself/herself.

In this context, however, I will concentrate on the range of control.

1. PW   PP   W-Power is a special case of P-power

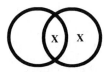

2. PW   PP   W-power and P-power have common elements

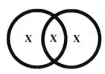

3. PW   PP   P-power is a special case of W-power

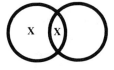

4. PW   PP   W-power and P-power are identical

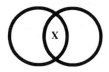

5. PW   PP   W-power and P-power are entirely distinct

Figure 1. *Relations between the two concepts of power*

206

The two concepts, power over one's own work (W-power or WP) and power over one's own political government (P-power or PP), can be related to each other in terms of simple set theory, as in Figure 1.

In classical conservatism (social conservatism and Catholic social doctrine) a narrow definition of W-power is typically combined with a broad definition of P-power (great extent of state control), with the stress laid on formal political power. There is an overlapping of W-power and P-power, but both have their separate domain too.

In liberalism a narrow definition of W-power is usually combined with a narrow definition of P-power; here, too, formal political power is accentuated. W-power and P-power are seen as distinct from each other.

In socialism both W-power and P-power are typically given a broad definition. According to an extreme interpretation of alienation theory, they tend to be identified with one another. According to a less extreme interpretation, P-power is granted its own sphere.

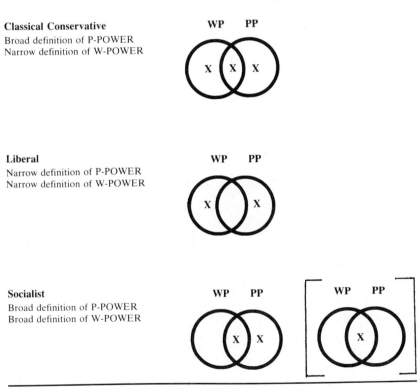

Figure 2. *Ideological views on power*

Which definitions of the two concepts are best is a very interesting question but unfortunately in this context too far-reaching. I think it should be discussed on the basis of a set of criteria of adequacy including for instance (a) linguistic, (b) theoretical, and (c) normative adequacy.

It is evident that both the liberal and the socialist view are represented among the papers for this section of our symposium.

DIFFERENT SOCIAL THEORIES

In short, Horvat assumes that the (manual) worker lacks power over his own work; Macpherson is of the opinion that today the manual worker has no power over his own work while the white collar worker has some.

All four authors seem to look upon an equal distribution of power over work as something valuable.

They differ in their opinion about the legitimate means for realizing such an equal distribution of power. For Horvat (and Macpherson?), the solution is workers' self-management; a prerequisite for this is a change in the property structure. For Eidem the solution is an increased commitment on the part of the worker to the firm; this should be promoted by supporting individual shares and by information and education aimed at giving equal opportunity as regards choice of job.

For Eidem the overall aim is an efficient distribution of power and for Horvat, Macpherson and Gustavsen it is a just distribution of power.<4>

The identification of the problem and the identification of the solution to it are for the four authors explicitly or implicitly based upon different social theories. A social theory could be described as a complex consisting of three kinds of elements: 1. factual, 2. evaluative and 3. ideological. The explicit social theory in Eidem's paper is the 'cathedral', the neo-classical market theory. The implicit social theory in Horvat's paper is another 'cathedral' - the Marxist one, that is to say, the Marxian theory of alienation and disalienation of work. Implicit in Gustavsen's paper we find a reformist social democratic theory.

Factual elements

On the factual level we find descriptions of what Gustavsen calls 'capital in its concrete form', i.e. the material basis of production. Assumptions on this level are part of what sociology and organisation theory take an interest in. Since factual statements are, at least in principle, verifiable or falsifiable there should be no inherent controversy on this level between different branches of science; as far as theories on this level are concerned there should be no conflict between sociology and economics, the difference between sociological and economic research being merely a matter of a pragmatic division of labour.

One specific question on the factual level with special reference to the problem of the distribution of power over one's own work, is whether an increase of some kind of W-power increases or decreases productive efficiency. Horvat defends the strong hypothesis that power over one's own work is a necessary condition for productive efficiency, while Macpherson vindicates the more modest assertion that there is no inherent conflict between W-power and efficiency in a capitalistic economic system. Empirical studies of workers' self-management have come to different conclusions. According to Oakshott (1978) most experiments in self-management have failed in productive efficiency, while Blumberg (1968) and Espinosa & Zimbalist (1978) have found evidence for an increase in productivity. So far there is no certain answer to the problem partly because only few and isolated investigations are available, and partly because of the problem of keeping a great number of conditions constant when comparing self-managing and other industries.

Another problem of a factual kind is the question whether actual technological development is promoting a spread of W-power or not. Horvat holds that the decentralization of work which is made possible in modern information society also leads to a decentralization or spread of power over one's own work. I think this could be questioned. Isn't it just as likely that the decentralization of work that information by computers has made possible, might cause a centralization of power? Firstly, because the organization of the workers will be more difficult, and secondly, because computerization renders centralized control more easy.

Evaluative elements

For the analysis of the evaluative elements some standard distinctions from moral philosophy might be helpful. Basic ethical principles are usually described as either teleological or deontological.

A teleological principle tells us that good consequences make an act morally right. And a deontological principle supposes that other characteristics of the act than its consequences make it morally right. A teleological ethical theory can be either want-related or ideal-related. A want-related theory – such as preference utilitarianism – considers people's actual explicit wants, irrespective of their worth or 'valuableness'. An ideal-related theory, on the other hand, such as classical utilitarianism presupposes some ranking of values; within this theory it is possible to distinguish between wants and (real) need. A teleological theory can be egoistic, particularistic, or universalistic depending on whether the consequences for myself, for a certain group, or for everybody, constitute morally right action. Utilitarianism is, consequently, a universalistic kind of teleological theory.

Principles of distributive justice are usually regarded as deontological principles. There are three standard principles for what constitutes a just distribution: 1) equal distribution, 2) distribution according to some merit, and 3) distribution according to need. All three are examples of material justice, in contrast to principles of procedural justice which tell us how a change or distribution should come about – not which distribution is right.

According to Marxist theory, moral arguments are in general looked upon as idealistic or unnecessary. But that means that they are seen as ineffective, not that they should be invalid in their own right.

Even neoclassical economic theory – which is part of the liberal tradition – often pretends to be normatively and morally neutral. Classical liberalism (Bentham) is closely affiliated to utilitarian ethics – the greatest good for the greatest number being the justificatory characteristic of all social action. Social liberalism (J.S. Mill) included a principle of distributive justice (distribution according to need up to a certain minimal standard). But also the most hardboiled new liberalism and neoclassical economic theory ('the cathedral') incorporate certain moral elements: property rights ought to be respected and procedural justice (free and voluntary transactions on the market are morally valid) is recognised. In my opinion, Robert Nozick articulates the minimum of necessary moral justification for extreme new liberalism, i.e. the above-mentioned principle of procedural justice plus the existence of property rights. He carefully avoids making moral assumptions about human needs and ends (he is strictly want-related, not ideal-related in his social philosophy), and about material justice (no redistribution according to any conceivable principle of material justice is recognized). But he cannot give up procedural justice. If Nozick represents a possible deontological justification for extreme liberalism, preference utilitarianism represents a possible teleological justification for it. According to this moral theory, maximal preference-satisfaction is what gives moral justification; and the presumption of both rights and essential human needs can be avoided.

In both Marxist and liberal attitudes to power over work (questions of minority board representation, self-management, state ownership etc) deontological arguments (rights, distributive justice) as well as teleological ones (efficiency, self-realisation etc) play a considerable role. Eidem's paper on the one hand and Macpherson's and Horvat's on the other confirm my hypothesis that, in the liberal view, teleological reasoning sets the aims and deontological reasoning sets the restrictions, whereas for the socialist, deontological arguments give the aims and teleological ones set the restrictions.

Table 1. *Liberal and socialist attitudes to power over work*

	AIMS	RESTRICTIONS
LIBERALISM	Utility (teleological)	Just distribution (deontological)
SOCIALISM	Just distribution (deontological)	Utility (teleological)

For Eidem efficient production is the overall aim. Just – i.e. equal – distribution of power is looked upon as a means of promoting efficient production. Individual property rights are restrictions on possible ways of changing the actual distribution of power over one's own work. Equal distribution of power favours rational allocation of work and efficient production. But unequal distribution is justified by the principle of distribution according to merit. Individuals have different earning capacities; the individual worker can become an entrepreneur and accumulate wealth and power; his wealth is dependent on his individual capacity for saving money. That is to say, the free market promotes a just distribution of power (according to merit). The main problem, according to Eidem, is the unequal initial distribution caused by lack of initiative (reflected in the traditional choice of unqualified jobs) among young people from the working class. This could be overcome by information and education and by giving incentives for commitment to the firm by promoting minority shareholding.

The idea of distributive justice in Eidem's paper is this: equal distribution of power from the start and then distribution according to merit. A critical question here is the following: where are we to draw the base-line for equal distribution? Why exactly at the moment when young people choose their job? Their power and their opportunities are unequal right from birth. And why not give equal opportunity even after the choice of job? A re-distribution is admittedly needed, but why only at the moment they choose a job?

For the Marxist, the worker's right to power over the product of his own work (or better: the right of the working class to power over its own work) is the aim. At least for philosophers in the Marxist tradition like Horvat or Macpherson, the requirement of efficient production is a restriction. For an orthodox Marxist it should be no restriction. Paradoxically as it may seem, property rights (in the sense of exclusive right to one's own product) are the core of the Marxist view of power over work. Lack of power over one's own work is what brings about alienation. This is also a central idea for one of the precursors of liberalism: John Locke; but Locke's perspective is entirely individualistic; individual labour gives rise to individual property. For liberals in the Locke-Nozick-tradition, as for the orthodox Marxist, property rights need not be justified by efficient production; an absolute right to the product arises when a person 'mixes his labour' (Locke) with some raw material. The extreme rights-aspect in older Marxism and in this kind of liberalism is modified in democratic socialism and in social liberalism. Here the aims of efficient production and of different welfare values infringe on the absolute right to the product of the work.

In social democracy ('The Swedish Model') as well as in classical Catholic social doctrine the main ethical interest is teleological: the realization of certain individual and social values is what morally justifies social action. Both social democracy and Catholic social theory are ideal-related: the individual and the social values that are to be realized are based on a normative theory of essential human characteristics and needs such as freedom, solidarity, the fostering of an all-round harmonious personality, (although I don't want to deny that actual Christian Democrat policy has developed in a brutally capitalistic and liberal direction.)

The main ethical interest in social theory (and consequently in relation to the problem of the power over work) can, with some simplification, be summarized in the following way:

Table 2. *Summary of main ethical interest in social theory*

	WANT-RELATED	IDEAL-RELATED
DEONTOLOGICAL (rights)	Rights-liberalism (Locke, Nozick)	Marxism
TELEOLOGICAL (utility)	Utility-liberalism (preference-utilitarianism, neo-classical economic theory)	Social democracy, Social conservatism, Catholic social doctrine

On the evaluative level there is a basic conflict between social theories about what constitutes a just distribution of social goods. For our specific purpose, let us take a look at some available principles for the distribution of power over one's own work and for the distribution of power over one's own political government. I suggest the following moral principles of distribution:

A: A meritocratic principle. Power is then to be distributed according to some merit. There might be different kinds of merit, so we can specify the principle in at least two directions.
    A1: Power should be distributed according to one's contribution to the desired results (in work or in society in general), i.e. according to objective merit.
    A2: Power should be distributed according to the amount of the labour one has expended (in work or in society in general), i.e. according to subjective merit.

B: A democratic principle. This principle too might be specified in at least two ways.
    B1: Power should be distributed equally (among all citizens).
    B2: Power should be distributed to those affected by the activity (in the work organisation or in society in general).

For the sake of completeness we may add the following non-moral principles:

C: A rationality principle. Power should be distributed in the most rational, efficient way. Some specifications of rationality may involve a moral principle.

D: No principle. Power is not to be distributed according to any principle. Distribution comes about by way of chance, or by competition or fighting between individuals, organisations, social classes etc.

Let us relate these principles of distribution to the three standard principles for distributive justice, i.e. a) equal distribution, b) distribution according to merit, and c) distribution according to need.

Evidently, the meritocratic principles (A) correspond to the principle of merit, the democratic principle (B1) corresponds to the principle of equality, and the democratic principle (B2) corresponds to the principle of need.

As I have said before, both orthodox Marxism and liberalism often pretend to be normatively neutral and they could thus both be supposed to advocate a no-principle line of thought (D). That is to say, class struggle in Marxism and the free market in liberalism determine the distribution of power. But, as I see it, they are both rather connected with the meritocratic principle (A1), although they hold very different views about what constitutes contribution to the desired result – direct work or the investment of productive capital, i.e. in practice, ownership.

Within the Swedish social democratic party there has been a controversy about whether the workers' unions or all citizens should control the wage earner funds. This controversy could be seen as mirroring a conflict between a meritocratic and a democratic principle for distributing power over work.

Should the same principle be applied for justifying W-power as for justifying P-power? It has often been taken for granted that a democratic principle is appropriate for the distribution of P-power, while a meritocratic one is adequate for the distribution of W-power.

Ideological elements

'Ideological' is here taken in a very specific and restricted sense. It stands for assumptions which are dependent on one's perspective and which are not readily interpreted as either evaluative or factual. Their verification and falsification are uncertain.

The category of ideological statements is not intended to be any kind of 'theoretical garbage bag'. Every statement should prima facie be interpreted as either evaluative or factual. If these interpretations turn out to be unlikely, one may try to interpret the statement as ideological, 'perspectivistic'. In my opinion, many disagreements about the nature of man and society are due to differences of an ideological kind.

Eidem's assertion that changing the actual distribution of power in firms might cause effects that are unforeseeable and which, therefore, should be avoided, could be interpreted as a view based on ideological assumptions about stability in the system. The actual system of power distribution is the outcome of an intricate interplay of all the individual preferences and it is, therefore, prima facie justified. On a free market a 'hidden hand' guarantees the optimal allocation of power. The classical conservative Hegelian 'hidden hand' functions in a way that is, in fact, not much different. The actual state of affairs with its institutions and distribution of power is the outcome of a historical process, where historically given institutions like the family, property rights, the state etc in their interplay are gradually adapted to each other and to natural conditions, and the outcome of this process is optimal and should not be manipulated or altered by individual persons, single groups or organisations.

Social liberalism and social democracy do not make this ideological assumption of an existing balance and are, consequently, more inclined to different kinds of social engineering.

A fundamental problem on this ideological level is the question of identifying the essential agents in society. In Eidem's paper individuals are seen as these essential acting subjects. All social action can be explained in terms of individual action. This idea could be labelled 'methodological individualism'. It is inherent in all liberal thinking. The opposite view holds that there are groups (social classes, organisations, the state itself etc.) and actions that cannot be reduced to or explained in terms of individuals and their actions. This view could conveniently be called 'methodological collectivism' or 'methodological holism'. It can be found in Marxism and in classical conservatism.

In the Swedish debate about wage earner funds there has been a notorious conflict between liberals and social democrats on the question of whether these funds should distribute power and capital to individuals or to organisations. Eidem is evidently to be found on the liberal side in this conflict.

Another question on the ideological level concerns the existence of a fundamental conflict of interests between social classes or between the parties on the labour market. Methodological individualism excludes the possibility of the existence of such a fundamental conflict of interests. Eidem asserts that the assumption of an interest conflict of this kind is a non-scientific assumption. In my opinion, all statements of what I have called an ideological kind are non-scientific. Accordingly, both the idea of fundamental conflict and the opposite view are non-scientific; both the balance theory and the instability theory, both methodological individualism and methodological collectivism are non-scientific hypotheses.

May I briefly sketch my own opinion about the relation between W-power and P-power.

I prefer relatively broad definitions of the two concepts, first and foremost because I find them theoretically adequate. In our western 'post-liberal' welfare society private enterprise is increasingly dependent on state investment and state regulation, and, at the same time, government branches are often engaged in semi-private industrial activities; the border-line between civil law and constitutional law is becoming more and more blurred. In my opinion, W-power and P-power to a great extent overlap.

My view is that W-power and P-power ought to be distributed in accordance with the same democratic principle (power ought to be distributed to those who are affected by the work and the government respectively). I agree with Charles E. Lindblom's (1977:356) assertion that 'the large private corporation fits oddly into democratic theory and vision', and with the Swedish social philosopher Elias Berg, who in a brilliant essay argues that the same democratic principle (B2 in my typology) should be applied to both W-power and P-power.

I am not quite as convinced as Eidem that moral argument (argument about the just distribution of power) and efficiency argument result in the same conclusion. I am very much inclined to agree with Robert Paul Wolff (1968:46) when he asserts that in capitalist society there is a 'divergence of the market mechanism from the demands of social utility. Over a broad and growing range of cases, effective market demand bears no relation to manifest social need.'

Notes

1) During the preparation of this paper I have profited from useful comments by my colleagues Göran Collste, Algot Gölstam, and Göran Möller in the seminar for Social Ethics of the Faculty of Theology at Uppsala University.

2) 'P controls' and 'P determines' are, in the following, to be understood as short for 'P individually or as a member of a group or organisation to some degree controls (or determines)...' etc.

3) I am quite aware of the possible objection that the choice between the above-mentioned relations between W-power and P-power could be said to be a matter of political-normative choice rather than of definition. But, as I see it, the decision – though it is a normative one – must at the same time consider both empirical social facts and linguistic conventions.

4) All of them assume that there is no conflict between the demands for efficiency and for justice.

22 The power of economics and the economics of power

ROLF EIDEM

It is common to see the firm characterized by the power to settle
issues by fiat, by authority, or by disciplinary action superior to
that available in the conventional market. This is delusion. The firm
does not own all its inputs. It has no power of fiat, no authority,
no disciplinary action any different in the slightest degree from
ordinary market contracting between any two people... What then is
the content of the presumed power to manage and assign workers to
various tasks? Exactly the same as one little consumer's power to
manage and assign his grocer to various tasks... To speak of
managing, directing or assigning workers to various tasks is a
deceptive way of noting that the employer continually is involved in
renegotiation of contracts that must be acceptable to both parties
(Alchian & Demsetz 1972:777).

These introductory lines by Alchian and Demsetz in their celebrated
article on 'Production, Information Costs and Economic Organization'
provide an excellent illustration of how the vast majority of economists,
trained in neoclassical economic theory, perceive the issue of power in
economics; their belief is, roughly, that in economic theory as such the
concept of power cannot be given any analytically meaningful
interpretation or generally acceptable definition and so should, if
anything, be left to other scientific fields of study. True, there are
some instances where economists, trained just as stated above, speak of
power, namely when firms have monopoly or oligopoly power in a goods
market, or trade unions have similar positions in a labour market. Here
the pejorative sense of the concept is invoked to condemn certain pricing
practices (firms against other firms, producers against consumers) that
are readily seen as inconsistent with the basic conditions that define an
optimum allocation in received general equlibrium theory. Also, in the
theory of games, which has developed substantially in economics (and
elsewhere) over the last two decades, the concept of power has taken on
a new, empirically more relevant meaning. However, this development is,
so far, best interpreted as a testing place for certain new ideas, the
impact of which on economists' thinking in general should not be
overrated.

But let us return now to the monopoly case, which is a good example
of the economists' attitude to power (or power relations or whatever) as
an object of scientific study within economics. Why is it that nearly all
academic economists in the world are as unanimously positive when it
comes to defining and condemning power in the shape of a monopoly as
they are negative when it comes to introducing other aspects of power,
e.g. as between the employer and the employee? To answer – or, at
least, try to answer – this question it will be necessary to present at

217

some length the basic features of the intellectual heritage – sometimes referred to as the 'Cathedral' (Hernes 1978:201; Calabresi & Melamed 1972) – common to all economists.

By definition, the notion of scarcity is really the starting point of all economic analysis. In neoclassical economics it is subsumed that scarcity – as perceived subjectively by the individual – is universal, and so provides everybody with an incentive to act, i.e. to reduce this scarcity. It is in the interest of the individual that he – or she – is able to satisfy any particular (scarcity-derived) need through as little effort as possible – by supplying labour, capital or other resources. However, since his effort-minimizing or cost-minimizing – or, more generally, utility-maximizing – behaviour is equally universal, individuals' interests will be in conflict or competition. To organize this competition people's activities as demanders and suppliers are coordinated through a system of prices whose relative values reflect the 'competitive scarcities' of different goods and services. It is then assumed that this coordination is effected in a decentralized way through a practical arrangement called markets, where prices are quoted against which all interested buyers and sellers may at any time weigh their own preferences and make any consequent, scarcity-reducing dispositions they wish.

If it is now further assumed that consumers' preference sets and producers' production functions have certain properties (that make individual choices consistent or 'rational') and that the intersections of these sets and functions are a perfectly flexible system of relative prices (which precludes monopoly tampering with prices in certain markets), then it can be proven that this coordination system has a solution which is stable, efficient in allocation and, indeed, even in distribution if only we accept or disregard the initial distribution of wealth. The merits of this proof are certainly not diminished by the fact that this concept of a general equilibrium of markets happens to be in harmony with the old notion of an invisible hand which coordinates individual decision-makers into a most-preferred division of labour. This, of course, is no coincidence; it has been suggested, that the Cathedral of general equilibrium analysis has been built precisely in the search for a 'proof' for Adam Smith's original ideas (Hahn 1981:123).

The impact of this rather simplistic model system of decentralized coordination on the world outlook and on the general thinking of the typical economist has been tremendous. Here is an intelligible, coherent statement of the basic problem of coordination and allocation, whose fundamental solution-variable – non-monopolistic relative prices – is applicable in the study of any allocation system. What more might a social scientist wish for? Few, if any, other social sciences have had anything similar, as regards generality, simplicity and rigour, to the general equilibrium analysis platform that economics is built on. It is not surprising that sociologists and others have always jealously attacked economists, pinpointing the weak descriptive qualities of the general equilibrium approach, but never – to my knowledge – its logical inconsistencies. Neither is it surprising that the economists have found it to be in their common interest to join forces to defend 'their' basic coordination model and have the whole discipline organized around it.

This brings us back to our starting point – and the monopoly case. Why are economists so reluctant to look into the causes and consequences of power in some cases but not in others? I submit that the answer has to do with the extent to which a concept of power can be interpreted and analyzed in terms of the basic (general equilibrium) market coordination model without complicating it unduly. It is as if the power of economics as a body of widely acceptable (positive and normative) theory were almost inversely related to the introduction of aspects like the economics of power. There is a general presumption that when any two people enter into an exchange relation - and agree on an exchange of some kind - it is because it benefits both. So the exchange is economical to both parties. Whether it is 'more economical' to one party than to the other is another issue. This is costly to establish and it is equally difficult to determine if this is tantamount to a difference in 'economic power' or if it depends in any way on such a difference. And so economics has, by and large, left out the aspect of power from its field of study.

Thus, to put it somewhat differently, in the division of labour among the social sciences, economics has chosen to concentrate on the (general) problem of efficiency of allocation. The 'problem of power' has been treated instead within sociology and political science (and, from somewhat different viewpoints, philosophy). This disciplinary specialization has certainly contributed to our understanding of both 'efficiency' and 'power', but it is only natural that many people should be curious to see if some cross-fertilization between the two might not extend our understanding further. Imagine the economist asking questions about how the possibility of an economy moving from a given pattern of allocation to an efficient allocation is related to a certain, given distribution of power among the economic agents; or, he might ask, how efficiency considerations have been active in bringing about a certain distribution of power among people. Similarly the sociologist might introduce efficiency aspects in his description and analyses of power.

In the following, I shall present some ideas on the long-standing issue of how 'an economics of power' might possibly be conceived of. I shall start in traditional, neo-classical economics, then gradually introduce certain specific inequalities ('power situations') and discuss how the established model would respond to these and finally ask if another, more interesting, response might not be derived from a carefully modified model. In this context the 'power situations' chosen will eventually be related to work-place conditions.

The basic properties of the neo-classical, competitive general equilibrium model have already been presented. The introductory quotation is clearly part of that heritage; the manager's power relative to the worker is said to be equal to the consumer's power relative to the grocer - because, in principle, both contracts have to be renegotiated every day. Again, if the contract finally concluded is accepted by both parties, there seems to be no 'problem of power' - at least not to the economist. Yet most non-economists (read: sociologists) find the parallel unacceptable as a description of real life (Abrahamsson 1982). Attention is called to the fact that the worker's negotiating costs - in terms of wages lost in a potential strike or when changing jobs (with removal and training costs etc) - are normally so much higher, compared with the employer's situation, when related to their respective personal wealth positions, that the game cannot reasonably be described as 'fair'. Many, also, find the analogy between the consumer's power vis-a-vis the grocer and the employer's power vis-a-vis the worker grossly misleading; the grocer's opportunity costs when withholding delivery are said to affect his personal wealth situation to a much lesser degree (because of divisibilities) than those of the worker when he refuses to work; therefore, the consumer is not nearly as powerful as the employer in their respective battlefields.

I think it is important to repeat that the introductory 'powerless quotation' refers primarily to a world of equals, each of whom has reached his or her position through fair contracting in the market. Now if it were assumed, instead, that the world was populated by unequals, whose earning capacities (in terms of revealed remuneration through the market) differed considerably - how would this affect the nature of contracting? The Marxist-type conclusion is, of course, that differences in earning capacities are carried over into differences in wealth, which, in turn, are magnified through the roles of employers and employees into which the rich and the poor are observed to group themselves; this grouping is said to introduce an asymmetry of power in contracting between employers and employees in that the greater wealth of the employers allows them to hold out longer in the event of a confrontation and so to 'win' the better part of the contract. This is believed to be unjust and calls for measures to equalize power relations.

Neo-classical economics has a number of objections to this interpretation. One is that differences in earning capacities only reflect differences in the contributions to the total income by different people, which is both informative and legitimate and has nothing to do with 'power'. A second objection is that the extent to which such differences in income are translated into differences in wealth depends largely on the propensity to save, which is a personal characteristic with little relation to 'power'; this argument may be extended to include the personal propensity to become an entrepreneur (or employer). A third objection, finally, is that the nature of the contracting situation is more dependent on the number of agents (employees and employers) in the market and on the size of the contractors' opportunity costs (e.g. the chance of winning - or the risk of not winning - a similar contract elsewhere), than on the relative sizes of their personal wealth; clearly, such opportunity costs will be higher the more specialized employees (and employers!) are; this means that when employees find themselves in a weak contracting position because their opportunity costs are high relative to those of the employer, this may be because they have deliberately chosen a 'high-specialization-strategy' to maximize labour income, not because they are employees per se; indeed, it is not difficult to think of a situation, where the specific knowledge of the employee may inflict serious damage on the employer in the event of his quitting, which would, if anything, redress the 'balance of power' in the employee's favour (see Klein et al 1978).

Through this type of reasoning - where equality of opportunity goes together with differences in talent and preferences among people - economics has been able to stave off most of the attacks on it for its alleged 'powerlessness'. But what if it can be shown empirically that there is no equality of opportunity among, for example, young people in poor and wealthy families in terms of the likelihood that they will be equally successful in mobilizing their full talents through the educational system? For a long time, we have observed in most developed countries recurring patterns of educational and occupational choice in the two categories, patterns that are not easily reconciled with the idea of free choice (or equality of opportunity): workers' children tend to become workers, employers' children tend to become 'supervisors'. Could this pattern in any way be said to reflect differences in power between these categories of children – and the corresponding groups of adults that the children will eventually grow into?

That depends. An economist trained in neo-classical economics would point out that the size and distribution of (basic) educational resources in market economies are typically determined through the political system, where each and every citizen has an equal right to give voice to his preferences on national educational policies. He might add that the bulk of public educational resources are, in fact, allocated according to a principle of equality of opportunity (compulsory, no private charge etc.), and so the differences in occupational choice and earning capacities cannot in any simple way be related to a discriminatory undersupply of educational resources to 'the poor' or a lack of political influence on their part. So, he might conclude, where is the power aspect of it? Might not differences in personal ability, rather than in (parental) power, explain a large part of the observed patterns of skewed occupational choices? Again, the argument rests on the independence and rationality of the individual, which deny power a role in economic analysis.

However, there are alternative interpretations of the skewed patterns referred to above. For instance, it would seem reasonable to infer that the longer a certain area of occupation is held on to by a family and its offspring, the less likely it would be that a situation of free choice really prevailed. If it could be established statistically that the family/time patterns of occupational choice did deny the 'hypothesis of free choice', the obvious question would seem to be why this situation (of non-free choice) had come about in the first place and why those affected by it had not reacted – or been able to react – to change the situation. True, there are many countries where – on the basis of the one-man-one-vote principle – the citizenry have opted for general educational policies that are clearly intended to reduce the inequality of opportunity among children. In addition, in most developed market economies the tax system has been fashioned in such a way as to modify the consequences of the remaining inequalities of opportunity. The results of these redistributive activities have not been very impressive, however, with the possible exception of the Scandinavian countries. I recall Professor Charles Lindblom stating in a lecture that, in his opinion, the American economic and political system had not been able to achieve any real redistribution of income and wealth in the United States since the turn of the century.

Is this where 'power' comes into the picture? Despite the professed ambitions on the part of what is perhaps a majority of the population to equalize opportunities for occupational choice among people with different backgrounds, progress seems slow (cf. the analogous issue of sex-based inequalities). Is there a structure of influence and are there mechanisms of persuasion behind it all that hold equalization back – and are they what we should understand by 'power'? Possibly – sociologists will offer a menu of varieties on the 'pane-et-circensis'-theme. The well-to-do and privileged will be ready to sacrifice some of their income through progressive taxation and to organize soothing entertainment of all sorts to give the losers a sense of being cared for. But this, of course, is only an 'investment' by the former in a comfortable (for them) structure of production, consumption and, if you will, distribution of 'power'. Clearly, it is this distributional conflict aspect of equality of opportunity which is the most obvious and hitherto most heralded in, for example, sociology.

Economics, however, has a language that will typically exclude this particular aspect from description and analysis. Here the universal propeller of scientific study is the (exogenously given) individual preference functions, whose bearers cannot in any meaningful way be grouped into 'privileged' and 'under-privileged'. Any such classification smells of arbitrariness and cannot be the object of rigorous scientific inquiry. So, to recapitulate what has already been said, the 'power' dimension remains outside economics.

Now I submit that this need not be so for ever if the allocation aspect of the problem of equality of opportunity in occupational choice were given more weight. Clearly, in economics, there is a case to be made for a kind of competition in the labour market, where each and every individual makes his occupational choice primarily on the basis of his – or her – potential talents for various professions, and not by 'force of habit' in the family. I fully realize that there is a host of statistical complications involved in establishing the extent to which the present situation (e.g. in Sweden) diverges from this ideal. I am also aware that any measures taken to close the gap would have to be of a long-run type, in order to reduce current adjustment costs, explain the virtues of the changes and so forth; it will be a huge pedagogical task to explain how the allocational (efficiency) gains materialize in the process and who will benefit from them. This will be a resource-demanding task, and so present the economist with an analytical set-up he – or she – will understand. Against the potential allocation efficiency gains from approaching a situation of free occupational choice in the labour market stand the costs of informing and motivating (a majority of the) people to accept the necessary measures to reap these gains. (So far the costs seem, in most countries, to have outweighed the perceived benefits).

The point I wish to make is simply, that anything in the nature of an 'economics of power' must have its starting point in a distribution of incomes, property or resource rights that can be given an economically (theoretically and empirically) meaningful interpretation, i.e. it must somehow relate to the efficiency properties of the allocation system. Power might then be defined in terms of the costs that must necessarily be incurred to bring reality closer to the ideal allocation system. This will be seen by many non-economists as a childish approach that does not accept the fundamental conflict of interest between the social groups under discussion. But this alternative, in my view, is simply not open to the economist.

More important, I think, the economist's perspective adds a dimension to the typical concept of power or power relations as a zero-sum game – 'the power of the employer is the powerlessness of the employee' etc. One needs little insight into social science to become aware of the enormous interrelatedness and complexity of the allocation system. All attempts to cut into, for instance, local organizations like the firm and define a new borderline between employer and employee in decision-making are likely to cause impact effects on consumers (who are likewise employees) and owners (who are likewise consumers) and others. Clearly, such effects also belong in an overall judgement of a 'power reform', though the zero-sum perspective is apt to disregard them. Even in a world of one archetypical firm (say, the joint stock company) it would be difficult to foresee these impact effects. In the real world – with a great many different types of firms of different sizes – it would be impossible to follow and measure these effects through all the various organizational structures.

The economist's perspective might largely avoid these complications by focusing on the individual's position in the labour market - or, more broadly, on his or her position with respect to occupational choice: is there or is there not an equality of opportunity among young people with different social backgrounds? If there is not, what can be done about it? This, clearly, is not really a zero-sum game of power. The question has an altogether different frame, the essence of which is 1) to inform everybody of the potential long-run gains in overall productivity from establishing the required equality of opportunity and 2) to introduce such changes in the working and living conditions of the underprivileged and less well-to-do that they would find it more natural and realistic to advise their sons and daughters to seek any occupation they wish.

I fully realize that there will - for obvious reasons - be no general consensus on the size and nature of the potential productivity gains. I am also aware that the 'changes in the working and living conditions' referred to may have consequences elsewhere that cannot be accepted. But this is beside the point. The point is that here is a field of discussion of alternative strategies to which economists could be invited. Where the sociologist would identify the obstacles as expressions of differences in power, the economist would see various costs and benefits associated with alternative strategies to reach a situation of equality of opportunity in occupational choice.

There are even costs in establishing the potential benefits of 'free choice'. Then there are costs associated with giving information about them in an intelligible way. But more interesting are the types of costs that may have to be incurred in order to develop attitudes among the less well-to-do which will make it 'more natural and realistic (for them) to advise their sons and daughters to seek any occupation they wish'. What measures could possibly serve this purpose, now that egalitarian educational policies and huge income redistributions have failed to do it?

I maintain that the crux of the matter has to do with the expectations for future occupational success and worklife satisfaction among the young. When hopes are high and there is self-confidence, any person would see a broader range of occupational choice than when he - or she - disbelieves in the future and himself (herself). Let it be assumed now that parents' 'hopes and self-confidence' exert a major influence on the expectations of the children and that this influence, in turn, is strongly related to how parents (and other grown-ups) look on their roles in production in general - and in the factory or workplace in particular. There is sociological research which indicates that the less satisfactory worklife conditions are deemed to be, the weaker the demand for increased influence and changes will be. (Gardell 1976). Might not the weakness in these demands be precisely a reflection of the low expectations for a change to the better?

So - what is the essence of a strategy for raising the expectations in occupational choice among the 'non-expecting'? It is to raise the status of the worker in the workplace.[1] This, in turn, can only be achieved by instituting arrangements that give workers/employees lasting incentives to improve their insights into their jobs, the relations between them and the jobs of others and, last but not least, the relationship between their whole workplace (or firm) and the rest of the economy. Man can never respect a phenomenon he does not fully understand - his position in a certain job? And where is the urge to ask for improvements in a situation whose meaning and ramifications are not clear to one?

My personal view is that, in corporations, minority shareholding among the employees might be an arrangement to serve the purpose just referred to. This will entail certain costs, both to subsidize employee purchases of shares and as a result of possible efficiency effects on the share market of congealed employee ownership. Other strategies will carry other costs, but I will not look further into them.

At this point, I want to refer back instead to the introductory 'powerless quotation'. I think we must agree with Alchian and Demsetz that it is not in the nature of the firm that the employer is more powerful than the employee. I also think economists are right in pointing out the difficulties in establishing operational concepts of power of any scientific rigour. But there are certain aspects of power that will come into the open even to the economist - if only he would start his analysis at a point which he could fill with operational meaning. This starting point is (always) efficiency of allocation, applied here to occupational choice in a competitive labour market. One 'certain aspect of power' is, as we have tried to show, the costs involved in dissolving long-standing structures of dissuasion and lack of self-confidence. And it is in the workplace that much of it must happen.

So, although based on efficiency arguments, economic reasoning about work and power can yield conclusions that do not seem too far apart from those based on ideas of justice and morality. This is as it should be - in a long-run perspective:

> ... while (men's) natural endowments differ profoundly, it is the mark of a civilized society to aim at eliminating such inequalities as have their source, not in individual differences, but in its own organization, and that individual differences, which are a source of social energy, are more likely to ripen and find expression if social inequalities are, as far as practicable, diminished. (Tawney 1931: 57).

Notes

<1> Some time ago I worked with a group of miners, carpenters, steel-workers and (occasionally) representatives of the management. It struck me that when I sent letters to the former it was under their home address, whereas management people had their office addresses on neat little cards.

23 A decade with employee representation on company boards: experiences and prospects for the future

BJØRN GUSTAVSEN

INTRODUCTION

In the Scandinavian countries, minority representation – roughly one third of the board members – was introduced in 1973. Details of the systems will not be given here, beyond the fact that even relatively small companies are included, 25 employees (Sweden) and 50 (Norway and Denmark). The purpose of this paper is to take a look at the impact of this system – which has now passed its first decade. Perhaps equally important is to identify what dimensions are relevant when talking about 'impact'.

REPRESENTATION AND INFLUENCE

There are several arguments for the introduction of employee representation on the board. In Gustavsen & Hunnius (1981:95) three such arguments are specified (see also Gustavsen 1976a; Englestad & Qvale 1977):

Firstly, the reason can be declarative. Representation is introduced not because it is believed that any specific 'measurable' effects will actually emerge, but simply to state that the employees are an interest group on the same level as capital and management.

Secondly, the argument can be to give the employees a position or a resource, which is not in itself decisive but which can play a role as one of a number of steps in a broader process of change. The employees can, for instance, gain access to new information and insight of possible value in several directions, e.g. for union work.

Only on the third level do we arrive at the argument that specific impacts on board behaviour and decisions are the point of the reform. Impact on the first level is achieved as a consequence of the introduction of the representative system as such. The question is to what extent the impact goes beyond this and, if so, how far.

It seems reasonably clear that the main impact is on the second level. SIND (1975:257) gives, for instance, the following summary:

A general impression (from an interview investigation) is that even though the reform has not contributed to any significant increase in the influence of the employees, it has definitely improved on employee insight (into company matters) and, perhaps most importantly, contributed to an improvement of the contacts between management on the one hand and the local unions on the other.

In a more recent study of representation in Swedish companies with 25-99 employees, Andersson & Lindroth (1979:20) draw the same general conclusion, which is also in agreement with what came out of a study of Norwegian boards (Englestad & Qvale 1977).

This does not imply that no impact can be found on the third level. In all investigations it is shown that the representatives bring before the board cases or issues that would otherwise not have been there. According to SIND (1975:180) approximately 40% of the employee representatives say that they have raised and argued at least one case before the board; Engelstad & Qvale (1977:118) found that in about half the boards covered by the study the employee representatives had brought new issues before the board.

To bring a case before the board is not the same as to be guaranteed a certain decision. Nor is the bringing of 'at least one case' an indicator of major influence. It seems, however, that when the employees raise and argue a case, the other board members rarely go against them. There may be several reasons for this. One is probably that the employer elected members do not want to face conflicts with the employees' representatives, provided that the number of cases raised by the employee representatives is moderate. The studies do not contain unambiguous data on this point but there is nothing to indicate that employee representatives frequently raise issues of their own, and there are a number of indicators that they do not.

It is probably more important than bringing in whole new cases for the representatives to introduce new points and arguments in relation to standard board cases. All investigations show that the representatives do so to a not inconsiderable extent. These considerations generally pertain to personnel, welfare, work environment and other internal issues, such as rationalisation (SIND 1975:173-178; Engelstad & Qvale 1977:80-82; Andersson & Lindroth 1979:108-110). From this, however, a major problem emerges. In a critical analysis of board representation as a chief approach to democratization, Emery & Thorsrud (1969) argued that the bringing in of these considerations constitutes an argument against board representation because personnel issues etc. are not appropriate matters on board level. At this point we will turn to a study of the general role of the boards (Gustavsen 1972, 1975, 1976b) which throws light on some aspects of this role.

THE ROLE OF THE BOARD

When board representation holds a certain amount of attraction as a solution to the problem of industrial democracy one reason is that the board seems to be 'at the top' of the enterprise. There is a general assembly 'above' the board, but this is seldom a very important and efficient decision-making body. Hence, the board seems to be the core unit in the decision-making structure of the enterprise. However, the situation is more complex.

One important aspect can be indicated by underlining the need to differentiate between the enterprise and the company. The enterprise can be defined as a substantial reality of men, machines and materials

(Emery 1959), while the company is something different. The company is a legal construction which in several important ways does not correspond to the enterprise.

The development of the company whose members' responsibility for the debt is limited by shares, was one of the major innovations that made the industrialization process possible. It is not as concrete as the Spinning Jenny nor as easily ascribable to a single inventor. Nevertheless, without it the industrialization process could hardly have taken place. Before the emergence of the modern company, capital generally had two characteristics:

- It was concrete in the sense that it was identical with specific real estate, a specific workshop, or the like
- It was bound to, or was an extension of, specific persons in families, sometimes other social groups.

The company breaks with both these characteristics. It can exist as a legal entity while the members change. This was made possible by the invention of the negotiable share. Its existence is, however, also independent of specific, physical resources: a company can sell all its production equipment and buy completely new equipment without any change of identity. These characteristics were made possible by the development of what can be called the enterprise as capital in its abstract form (Gustavsen 1972, 1976b, 1976c). By capital in its abstract form is meant material resources as measured in monetary value. Such value is an abstraction in the Marxian sense of the term in that it gives a selective picture of the object rather than a simplified one. The development of this particular way of defining productive resources made it possible to dissolve the link between wealth on the one hand and particular physical resources on the other. When this link was dissolved, companies could be established as 'legal persons' and, in turn, become independent of specific members. A company must have members in terms of shareholders, but it does not matter, in principle, who they are.

Company legislation is generally about these two phenomena: the abstraction and de-personification of capital. Historically, company law is not about enterprise organization, technology, personnel issues, etc. What it deals with, is shares, balance sheets and related issues. The role of the board follows from its location within this system of rules. Its responsibility must be defined with reference to the enterprise as capital in its abstract form and has to do with securing this capital against loss and - preferably - causing it to grow. It is the task of management to deal with the enterprise as capital in its concrete form: the obligations of management are generally not explicitly stated in company legislation, but have to be deduced - through so-called antithetical deductions - from the legislation.

Given this point of departure, the board of directors cannot become engaged in all types of issues. It has to delimit its engagement to those issues that are reasonably strongly related to the enterprise as capital in its abstract form. Table 1 presents some results from an empirical investigation pertaining to this issue.

Table 1. *The influence of the board over the acts of the enterprise in terms of aspects of cases*

Aspects	Score
Financial	0,70
Analysis/interpretation of economic results	0,64
Relationships to other enterprises	0,46
Relationships to shareholders	0,32
Personnel and organization (internal)	0,06
Technical aspects of technology to be acquired	0,04

Number of entrerprises: 25. The questionnaire contained a larger number of aspects than those included in the table, see Gustavsen (1972).

What is presented here, is a selection. SIND covers the same point and with parallel results (SIND 1975:131). The boards largely involve themselves in financial issues and issues pertaining to those relationships to the environment that are of particular importance to the enterprises as capital in its abstract form. Typical internal issues such as technological development, work organization and personnel draw little involvement. On the other hand, it is such issues to which the employees tend to give priority. Here, a conflict emerges pertaining to what are legitimate issues on the level of the board.

This conflict has various aspects. One of them has to do with prerequisites for making decisions. Given the responsibility of the board, it will have to take on a 'boundary role'. Its functions will be linked to transactions between the enterprise and (certain parts of) its environment. Figure 1 gives a picture of some of the main variables and relationships picturing the boards as decisionmaker:

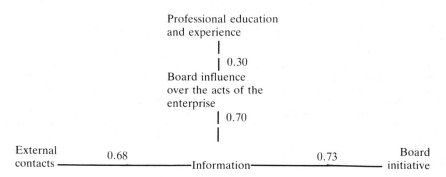

These are the core variables in an elementary linkage structure (McQuitty 1957) which contains a number of further variables more weakly correlated to those found in the figure. For a complete picture, see Gustavsen (1972).

Figure 1. *The linkage structure between (some of the) variables used to describe board behaviour and qualifications*

Information emerges as the core variable. Information is directly linked to three other variables: external contacts, initiative, and influence over the acts of the enterprise. Professional expertise – by which is meant expertise as lawyer, engineer, economist, etc. – is related to the other variables, but through a somewhat weaker relationship. This indicates that information gathered from sources outside the enterprise is more important than the type of competence gained through a professional education (for further discussion of this point, see Gustavsen 1975). Returning to the relationship between board decisions and the tendency among employee representatives to raise considerations emerging from 'inside' the enterprise, it is seen that the resulting difference has to do not only with what to decide but also with what information is relevant – actually, with what cognitive map is most appropriate.

Provided that broader changes in so-called capitalist society are not part of the reform strategy, it seems that the utilization of employee representation on the board of directors in a process of democratization must depart from the premiss that the board has to play a role as guardian of the enterprise as capital in its abstract form. If this task is taken away from the board it simply has to be taken over by someone else, e.g. the finance institutions. Rather than trying to make the board into a forum for debates about internal issues, the most constructive policy seems to be to accept its special responsibility and see to what extent development consistent with this responsibility can be created. To this issue we will now turn.

INDUSTRIAL DEMOCRACY AND THE NEED TO MANAGE THE ENTERPRISES AS CAPITAL IN ITS ABSTRACT FORM

From this point of departure, several possibilities present themselves, of which following four will be taken up here:

- To what extent employee representation can give rise to a network for capital management
- To what extent new criteria for investments emerge
- To what extent there is a process of 'de-privatization' of capital
- To what extent there are changes which are a logical consequence of the introduction of employee representation on the board.

Below, each of these possibilities will be discussed – albeit briefly, as space does not allow indepth treatment.

A New Network for Management of the Enterprises as Capital in its Abstract Form

Figure 1 shows that external contacts are the chief prerequisite for acting as a board member. Such contacts can be with other enterprises, finance institutions, raw material suppliers, public institutions, etc. They, however, also represent channels for other types of transactions such as approaches to mergers, to agreements in restraint of competition, etc. Such networks can be more or less well organized. There are several possibilities in this respect, ranging from loosely knit horizontal systems to one single monolithic structure. In Gustavsen (1976c) a review of some of the possibilities is given and a comparison between Norway and Sweden made, indicating that 'the capital system' in Sweden is more highly organized than the similar system in Norway. A board member is, in other words, not only an individual decision-maker but also part of a collective structure. Such a structure will carry certain types of knowledge, preferences, etc.

The question is to what extent employee representation can give rise to an alternative system. An alternative can compete with the existing system, but it can also imply an addition and hence more variety - a greater range of options in terms of ideas and criteria for investments. When employee representation was introduced in Norway in 1973, this author happened to participate in the development of a training programme for board members belonging to unions affiliated with the Federation of Trade Unions (LO). Together with a representative of the training organization of the labour movement, it was argued that network building should be the core element of the training programme. In course situations, most of the time should be used to discuss experiences from different boards and to see to what extent they could provide a basis for joint learning. We wanted, furthermore, to utilize some of the central figures in the labour movement who had experience from industrial policy, board memberships etc. as resource persons in this network. The idea did not, however, work out. It was commonly thought at the time that the key to a successful role as a board member was to be found in elementary training in law and economics. The network aspect was soon lost and the whole training programme was turned into a conventional exercise. To what extent an effort to go new ways would have been successful is, of course, an open question. To develop a network for investment policy is a difficult matter and it is far from certain that much would have come out of such an effort. Provided that its aims were modest - at least for the first decade - and largely defined as the provision of supplementary criteria and alternatives, it is my belief that something could have been achieved. At least, a process would have been started in the early 70's which could have provided some experience with which to confront the 80's, with rising unemployment and deep-going structural problems, not least in industry. Instead, the labour movement is still almost completely dependent upon the ability of the traditional system to make viable investments. Networks may, of course, have emerged through other mechanisms. To what extent this is the case, is not known. There is nothing to indicate that this is the case. Concerning Sweden, SIND (1975:161) covers external contacts for employee representatives and concludes by saying that such contacts exist to a very limited extent.

New Criteria for Investments

Given the responsibility of the board, investment decisions become the key task. Not, however, all types of investments. Investments can have various reference points (Gustavsen 1972). The board is primarily linked to those decisions that either involve substantial amounts of the total enterprise capital and/or imply redefinition of the characteristics of the enterprise.

Such investments can be made according to different criteria, ranging from those that are dealt with in economic theory to beliefs, rules of thumb of various types, etc. The concrete form of the total productive resources of a society expresses a certain range and combination of such criteria. The development of new criteria is, to a large extent, identical to the question dealt with before: the emergence of an alternative network for management of enterprises as abstracted capital. However, investment criteria also imply other issues.

230

If investment decisions are performed according to a more classical economic type of thinking, where the enterprise always moves towards the area where the profit seems to be highest, the result will be an enterprise whose concrete resources change very rapidly. Often, this will imply that no internal competence is developed, nor any deep going knowledge about any particular type of technology or market. This will, in turn, have a detrimental effect on the ability of the enterprise to make a profit because product quality and a number of other dimensions will be adversely affected. Consequently, there is a need to balance pure economic reasoning against various social and technological realities. In this process of balancing, the legal system presupposes that it is the task of management to put forward and argue those criteria that have to do with stabilizing internal resources, developing competence, etc. Generally, however, the employees will have an even stronger preference for stabilizing the enterprise in its given form. When employee representatives enter the board of directors, one can imagine a shift in the way flexibility derived from economic considerations is matched against the needs of the people working in the enterprise for security, stability and the preservation of existing competence. There are no clear empirical data on this issue. There are some pointers indicating that there has been some shift in this balance point, at least in Norwegian enterprises (Engelstad & Qvale 1977:130-132).

When economic considerations are pushed to the background, the risk increases that the enterprise can no longer show a profit. If profits fall below the critical limit, the investment criteria must be reversed or economic support systems created. In Norway, the oil revenues have generated new possibilities for protection of economically exposed enterprises. It is unclear to what extent Norway really has a total industrial policy that deviates a great deal from what other countries do to protect existing industry, but it is at least clear that Norway, today, uses fairly large amounts of money to maintain enterprises that would otherwise have gone out of business and that this amount has increased significantly since 1973. In 1973 it was 1,050 mill. Norw. crowns, in 1982 it had multiplied by eight to 8,193 mill. crowns (St. meld. nr. 88, 1982-83). More than half of this money goes, however, to a relatively small number of state owned enterprises which are supported for a broad set of reasons. On the other hand, there are further support systems which do not emerge from figures such as those quoted above, for instance in the form of electricity prices below what the publicly owned power plants could achieve in the market and also below the marginal costs of development of new plants. Development, expansion and maintenance of support systems often demand worker-management coalitions, or at least agreement, both locally and centrally. It is quite clear that such coalitions have emerged in a number of cases. This would probably have happened without board representation for the employees, but it seems as if this representation has strengthened and cemented particularly the local part of these coalitions.

While, on the one hand, a tendency towards freezing given investments can be seen, there is, on the other hand, in all probability also a tendency towards developing more open and flexible forms of internal organization, at least in parts of working life (Gustavsen 1983). This implies that what is lost at one point in terms of more rigid investment policies can be gained at another in terms of more flexible concrete resources able to deal with a broader range of functions, products and markets. A change in this direction is clearly positive, because it makes change and restructuring possible without going via plant closures and the building of wholly new plants – often at different locations – a socially very expensive pattern of adaptation.

De-privatization of Capital

'De-privatization' of capital is a concept introduced by, among others, Per Kleppe, a former minister of finance in Norway, presently secretary general of EFTA. Its primary expression was a change in the governing bodies of the commercial banks, where the parliament was given the right to elect the majority of members, at the expense of the share-holders. This system was reversed by a conservative government when it came into power in 1981.

The concept of de-privatization can, however, be used with reference to other issues. There are some data indicating that employee representation has led to more openness around the boards and more publicity (in the meaning of 'Öffentlichkeit') around investment decisions. More openness is also reflected in a number of shareholder elected board members being exchanged for new ones when the representative system was introduced (Engelstad & Qvale 1977:55–56) and it is reasonable to assume that those who went out, to a large extent, represented various forms of irrationality compared to the legal responsibility of the board, such as subjective, often historically given criteria for investment, the utilization of one company to gain profits in another, etc. Instead, people with a more professional profile generally came in.

De-privatization of investment decisions is helped by other mechanisms as well. In Norway, where the stock exchange has generally been of marginal importance, a change has taken place in recent years. More companies go public and the companies who want to be quoted on the stock exchange must follow certain rules which contribute to the abandonment of the more irrational investment policies. SIND (1975:152) notes that employee representatives acquire better information in enterprises quoted on the stock exchange than they do in enterprises which are not subject to this type of public scrutiny.

When board decisions become more open, they can be made subject to a more open dialogue and discussion on the level of society. Here, however, there is still a long way to go. In spite of their tremendous importance for employment, economy and other issues, even the biggest investments in a country like Norway are not made subject to much public debate and what little there is, suffers from lack of adequate information. This does not only pertain to private enterprises but is also the case where the state is heavily involved. When a large pulp factory (Tofte cellulose) developed jointly by industry, forest owners and the state – largely at the expense of the taxpayer – recently went bankrupt after a very brief period of operation, hardly any effort was made to scrutinize the decisions behind this venture publicly. Those who had made them were not asked to explain themselves publicly.

The boards as such have a number of characteristics which imply constraints on their ability to function in a democratic dialogue. A certain amount of secrecy must often be maintained, blocking a discussion involving more than an inner circle (SIND 1975:164–168; Engelstad & Qvale 1977:61–64). The information given the members is often of a formal and ritualistic kind. It does not give pro- and counterarguments but rather lists of figures interspersed with brief descriptions of a seemingly uncontroversial nature. The information is, in other words, not dialogue-oriented.

Constraints and limitations notwithstanding, de-privatization of investment decisions seems to be one of the main processes to which employee representation on the board has contributed and will contribute in the future.

Further Changes

A 'follow up' on board representation should result in further changes in the organization and management of capital in its abstract form. There are several possibilities, of which three will be touched upon here.

One is to increase the number of employee representatives on the board, a suggestion which was put forth by a committee appointed by the Norwegian Federation of Trade Unions to look into the issue of furthering democracy in working life (The Skytøen Committee 1980). This suggestion will probably not be acted upon in the near future. The suggestion does not imply worker parity, because it is presupposed that the chairman is chosen by the employer-elected members and that the chairman has a double vote in cases of ties.

Another type of change is to bring more of the investment capital under the control of the state. This can make capital more accessible to the employee representatives. A main asset of a board member is the ability to raise capital. The influence which a board member can exert over the enterprise is, to a large extent, a function of the dependence of the enterprise upon his endorsement of the enterprise as a worthy recipient of capital towards, for example, finance institutions. (Gustavsen 1972:99-129). Employee-elected members will have limited access to ordinary finance institutions. They will, however, often be in a better position in relation to capital controlled by the state. Social-democratic political networks can, for instance, become interwowen with the networks for allocation of capital. Hence, state funding of investments also changes the patterns of influence in enterprise bodies. In Norway, a relatively large proportion of the capital is state controlled (Gustavsen & Hunnius 1981:98) which is probably part of the explanation why wage earner funds have attracted much less interest from the unions than is the case in Sweden and Denmark.

Collectivization of the enterprises as capital in its abstract form, then, emerges as a third main alternative. There is a broad range of schemes and suggestions within this area, ranging from employee shares to the more radical versions of the idea of wage earner funds (for a review see Eidem & Öhman 1979). They have given rise to broad discussions which cannot be reviewed here. It is quite clear, however, that such a step as the introduction of wage earner funds (Meidner 1978) is a logical result of employee representation on the board of directors. It implies a further employee penetration of the core system of capitalism - the generation and management of 'the world as measured in money'. How it will work depends more specifically upon how the system is shaped. Even in Sweden, where the development of this idea has come a fairly long way, several aspects are still not clear. One point, however, seems reasonably well founded: the major challenge will be to develop an adequate investment policy. If the system of wage earner funds does not result in investments that meet a broad range of criteria covering the economic as well as the social field, it will probably be difficult to give it sufficient legitimation. Furthermore, unlike employee representation, which was introduced with a reasonable degree of consensus, wage earner funds may be met with explicit counter-strategies from the existing system, which will imply that the new system will have to meet even greater challenges. The Swedish labour movement must certainly perform a major feat of network building and development of new information systems and competence to carry the idea of wage earner funds through, at least if one wants to avoid watering it down to an uncontroversial but marginal contribution to the support of given industry.

24 The prospects for disalienation of work

BRANKO HORVAT

If the power over my work is exercised by somebody else, then my work and its products are alienated from me. Since work is an existential activity, its alienation has profound psychological and social effects upon society and its members. Alienation of work generates an alienated society.

Being an existential activity, work has ontological status, as Marcuse would say. Yet, to say that work is an ontological concept, though true, is not very helpful. The concept needs operationalization. One possibility is to provide a nested definition with several stages of increasing inclusiveness. Work is, first, a physiological and mental activity indispensible for the physical and mental health of human beings. It is, next, a productive activity generating goods and services that satisfy human needs. As productive activity, work can be independent (wage, slave, serf labour), free or repressive, depending on the social organization of work. This implies, thirdly, that work is always socially organized and that the social division of labour (with specialization, cooperation and competition) generates social relations at the micro (group) and macro (societal) level. One of these relations is particularly important, it dominates the others and defines the next stage of inclusiveness. That is work as a source of power in the political community. Fifthly, as a self-determining and self-realizing activity, work represents an essential human - not just physiological or mental - need. It gives meaning to life and at this stage of philosophical anthropology gains its ontological status. We have come back to Marcuse, but now in a structured and operationalized way. This paper deals with work at its fourth stage of complexity.

It is also possible to define work operationally in terms of its aspects as studied by various professions. Thus, work has physiological, economic, social, political and philosophical aspects. One may also follow Bengt Abrahamsson and say[1] that work is about survival, physical (first three aspects) and social (the next two). Here the last aspect is left out since philosophical anthropology is not a science - like anthropology - but philosophy; and the meaning of life, though of enormous importance, is not a proper subject for scientific research.

After these introductory remarks, let us resume our discussion of work in the context of power.

In class societies - such as the capitalist and etatist societies of 1984 - power is extremely unequally distributed. These societies are also extremely alienated. On the other hand, an examination of the possibilities of disalienation is, at the same time, an inquiry into what might help create a classless society. This is a grand theme which goes far beyond the scope of the present paper. Yet, the remarks which follow ought to be interpreted within such a grand framework.

I take it that the task assigned to me is not to describe what is happening in 1984. That is pretty well known and is not particularly inspiring. The really fascinating task is to try to discover what the prospects are for a not too distant future. Since human affairs are not strictly deterministic, the prospects are various depending on what course of action we happen to choose. I intend to analyse the prospects for disalienation of work. In other words, I would like to see what the historically given possibilities are for a substantial reduction of power over somebody else's work. This is not an entirely arbitrary choice. It may be shown that disalienation of work is a deeply felt need of modern man. Nevertheless, instead of proving this proposition, I shall take it for granted.<2>

Let me start the analysis by a review of the relevant facts.

- In the most developed countries manual workers constitute one third of the active population and their number is decreasing.

- University education is already accessible to 40% of the relevant cohort and this percentage is steadily increasing.

- There are some who change their occupation three (in the Soviet Union) to seven (in the USA) times during their active life.

- The working week is being reduced at an accelerating pace. If we consider a sufficiently large society (United States) over a sufficiently long period of time, the facts are as follows:

1800	78 hours	1940	44 hours
1850	70 hours	1960	39 hours
1910	55 hours	1975	36 hours

- At the same time the global productivity of factors of production in the United States is increasing at an accelerating rate (Horvat 1982:504-5):

1800	- 1855	0.3% per year
1855	- 1905	0.5% per year
1905	- 1927	1.5% per year
1927	- 1967	1.9% per year

As a result, the standard of living is increasing at an accelerating pace, too, in spite of the shortening of the working week. The trends are, of course, the same in other developed countries. Postwar economic growth was faster than in any comparable period in human history. If in the near future the development pace slows down, this will not be technological reasons.<3>

- Economic output is increasing substantially faster than its material input. In other words, the increasing share of information input is characteristic for modern products.

- Robotization is making the complete replacement of routine manual labour possible.

- As a consequence, postindustrial technology has the following characteristics:

(a) the concentration of labour at certain places called factories ceases to be necessary;
(b) fast changes and production to order make team work - teams being composed of various specialists - indispensable; as a consequence, the manager becomes functionally one of the specialists, namely the one specializing in co-ordination;
(c) the need for more education - education being also an information input - leads to a rapid homogenization of the work force.

- So far, work has been supervised by owners and their agents in capitalist countries and by the state and its agents in etatist countries. Private owners and the state buy labour power and issue work commands, workers sell their labour power and submit to the dictatorship at the work place. Owners and managers hold power not only over work but also - directly or indirectly - over crucial societal decisions.

It is quite obvious that this last organizational feature of contemporary societies is inconsistent with the technological trends described. We have the classical Marxian situation of the forces of production and production relations getting out of step. If economic development is to continue, the 'contradiction' between the two must be resolved. Its resolution means the emancipation of work.

Let us have a look at the possibilities implied.

- The decreasing share of manual work eliminates the social difference between manual and brain workers. In fact, manual work, such as in agriculture or in crafts, becomes desirable for its own sake.

- Changing occupations makes work more interesting and requires different and more complete education.

- Accessibility of education for everybody (education becomes a life-long process) increases the homogenization of the population in terms of educational and cultural standards. Although individuals will continue to differ qua individuals, it is no longer obvious why certain groups should dominate the rest of society.

- With a per capita income of 15,000 dollars per annum it is possible to provide all the ingredients - material and cultural - for a comfortable life for all members of society.

- Empirical research indicates that automation reduces work alienation and that technological complexity fosters self-management (Rus & Arzensèk 1984:123, 141).

- If the working week is reduced to 30 hours or less, one half of the working week becomes available for 'leisure' activities. Alienated work is psychologically exhausting and relatively modest leisure time has been used for relaxation, passive enjoyment (such as TV watching) and the consumption of cheap mass culture. If 'productive' labour becomes intrinsically interesting and free time substantially increases, its use will become very different. First of all, educated people will tend to participate in the general culture of their societies (both as producers and as consumers). And, secondly, self-conscious citizens will tend to engage in political activities. In other words, the style of life characteristic of the ruling classes will gradually be adopted by the population at large.

- If the satisfaction of existential needs is secured, people will become more concerned with their higher needs, with self-determination and self-realization. The life game ceases to be a zero sum and becomes a positive sum game: I benefit from personal development or other individuals. As a result, people become more tolerant and more resistant to any kind of hierarchy and domination.

- Information is not bulky and does not distort space; it is also clean and does not pollute the environment. But, above all, the information industry makes possible the radical decentralization of all activities, productive as well as civic.

- If concentration of labour is no longer necessary, the cancerous growth of cities might be stopped, and people might be given the opportunity to live in the more natural environments of small towns and villages, while still participating fully in the cultural and political activities of their countries. Besides, since robotization will take care of bulky production processes, what remains might be organized on the cottage industry basis. And working at home means that one controls the amount and the pace of one's work.

- In the technological and social environment described, the classical manager will cease to be functional. Instead of issuing orders, he will have to co-operate with other members of the team since they know what he does not and they may withold their knowledge. Thus an increase in productivity depends on group co-operation and not on the authoritarian discipline imposed by an omniscient boss or his agents.

- If there are no bosses, work organization will have to be based on self-management. And self-management implies an egalitarian distribution of power. The egalitarian distribution of power at the work place does not necessarily imply an egalitarian distribution of political and general societal power. But it is one of the preconditions for the latter.

The foregoing discussion exposes the fallacy of the widespread view that the increased spread of power conflicts with efficiency and rationalization. Not only does it not conflict with them, it is, on the contrary, the basic precondition for efficient production in the post-industrial era. Given the conditions described, the egalitarian distribution of power increases the total amount of power available for efficient decision making.

Yet, the spread of power conflicts, no doubt, with both private and state ownership. It thus encounters formidable vested interests. For this reason, functional considerations provide no guarantee that work will, in fact, be emancipated or that this will happen soon. Before they achieve substantial advances in the disalienation process, societies will have to pass through prolonged and probably not very gentle class struggles. Fortunately, this is no longer the task I have to worry about in this paper.

Notes

⟨1⟩ In a comment made in the symposium discussion.

⟨2⟩ For an extensive discussion see my <u>Political Economy of Socialism</u>, 1982.

⟨3⟩ And, indeed as the econometric study by Bowles, Gordon and Weisskopf shows, social variables were the major factor causing the slow-down of American productivity growth after 1966 (1984:66).

25 Notes on work and power

C. B. MACPHERSON

It is evident, from the discussion on the concept of work at the opening session, that there are many different concepts of work, and that different ones may be legitimate in different contexts. Thus the choice of a definition of work is not arbitrary but should depend on the context in which it is to be used.

This Symposium is about 'Work in 1984'. And in 1984 most of the world's nations either operate in capitalist relations of production or use capitalist techniques of work control in hopes of catching up with capitalist rates of productivity. What concept of work is most appropriate for such societies? Clearly, the concept which was produced by capitalism, that is, the concept of work as a disutility. In that view, work may be defined (following the neo-classical economists, e.g. Alfred Marshall) as any exertion of human energy not exerted entirely for the pleasure derived from the exertion. This is, of course, much narrower than Marx's concept, but it seems to be the appropriate one for any discussion of work as it actully is in 1984.

Power I shall define simply as the ability to get desired results. Thus, power <u>over</u> something is the ability to control it, or control its use, so as to produce a desired result. In this paper, I shall look briefly at only two problems concerning work and power: 1) the relation between control over one's own work and control over one's political government, and 2) the relation between control over one's own work and productive efficiency.

1.

Let us consider first the relation between power over (control of) one's own work and power over (one's share in the control of) one's political government.

At a first approximation we may hypothesize that the extent of one's control over one's own work determines the extent of one's control over the government of one's political society. Thus, the extent of one's share in the control over one's government would be proportional to the extent of one's control over one's work. Does this relationship hold for all known and conceivable types of society, types classified by the prevailing relations of production, i.e. societies in which material production is carried on predominantly by slaves, by serfs, by free wage-labour, and by co-operative labour under communal ownership?

241

It clearly holds in a slave society: the slave's control of his own work and his share in the government are both effectively zero. In a feudal society the relationship is less clear. The serf has some control over part of his work, but seems to have no share of political power. Yet he has some political power, in that custom gives him some rights which the lord cannot infringe without the risk of a rebellion. Where free wage-labour is the prevalent type of work, i.e. in capitalist society, the extent of the worker's control over his own work is different at different stages of capitalist development.

We may distinguish three stages: pre-industrial mercantile capitalism, industrial capitalism, and post-industrial capitalism. In the first stage, the labour force consists partly of independent yeomen and craftsmen and partly of wage-earners: the former have some political weight; the latter have none. In the second stage, almost the whole labour force is wage-earning, and at the beginning they have no share in political power. Later, they do win the vote. But by the time they have won it, the party system has generally rendered their political control of the government largely ineffective (see Macpherson 1977:64 et seq.): such power as they then have is only the industrial power they have by virtue of their organization in trade unions.

The third stage (the post-industrial) is reached when technological advance has moved much current labour from the production of material goods to the production of services. At this stage, an increasing share of the whole work of the society is done by white-collar workers, technicians, and middle-management. Their work does not need to be so closely controlled from above as does the work of the blue-collar worker. The former jobs permit, and may even require, some self-direction or autonomy. According to our first hypothesis, therefore, they should also have more control over their governments, that is, more power as voters. But, as I have argued, the party system has reduced the voters' political control over the government to a negligible amount: the amount of their control over government is only the amount of their unionized power. And since white-collar workers, technicians, and middle management are generally less unionized than the blue-collars, their unionized power, and hence their control over the government, is less. Thus in post-industrial capitalism, to the extent that the labour force has changed in the way just described, the political power of the workers appears to vary inversely with their control over their own work.

However, if we consider capitalist society in general, in contrast to a model of a fully communal society where work is under the communal control of the workers (and which, like post-industrial capitalism, would mainly be producing services), it appears that what determines the workers' political power is not the type of production (services versus tangible material objects) but the relation of the worker to capital.

Control of capital, not control of one's work, is what gives political control. Or, if you prefer, control over one's own work requires either control over one's own working capital (as in petit-bourgeois production) or an effective share in the control of the whole society's capital (as in a fully socialist model). It follows that in a fully capitalist model, where no workers own any capital, no workers have any control over their own work. And in that model, as we have seen, the exigencies of the party system give the workers, as voters, no effective political control. Effective political control remains with capital.

Thus, in the full capitalist model, one's share of political control is proportional to one's control over one's own work (both being close to zero). And paradoxically we may also say that in that model one's share of political control is proportional to one's control over others' work (the capitalists having effective political control over the whole society because they control others' work). It would be misleading to assert, without a precise explanation, that, therefore, in the full capitalist model, work and power are inversely proportional. For what is inversely proportional to the amount of one's share in political control is not the amount of control one has over one's work but the amount of work one is compelled to do. Only in this sense are work and power inversely proportional in capitalist society. That they were so was acknowledged in the classical liberal tradition: Bentham, for instance, while asserting that the great mass of citizens would never have any resource except their daily industry, and consequently would be always near indigence, remarked that wealth and power are each an instrument of production of the other (as quoted in Macpherson 1977:28, 26); and John Stuart Mill recognized that men's incomes were almost inversely proportional to labour expended (Macpherson 1977:53).

2.

We may now look briefly at the relation between workers' participation in the control of production and productive efficiency. Is widespread workers' participation incompatible with efficient production?

At the micro level (plant, firm, or single enterprise) there is no evidence of a necessary conflict between workers' participation and productive efficiency. Indeed, the evidence in capitalist firms where there is some workers' participation indicates that it sometimes increases productive efficiency. The only incompatibility between workers' participation and efficiency is that between workers' control (the workers having parity with or a veto over the management) and capitalist efficiency (measured by rates of profit and of capital accumulation). Private capital cannot be expected to give up its control of the planning and execution of production in its own enterprises.

At the macro level (a whole national or regional economy) the evidence suggests an inherent conflict between state bureaucratic control and productive efficiency, but not between workers' control and productive efficiency. For evidence on this we can look only at socialist countries, since the state bureaucracies of capitalist countries do not yet fully control the economy.

The extent of conflict between state control of production and productive efficiency may be said to depend on the extent to which state policy is dominated by desire to catch up with the productivity of the most advanced capitalist countries. In those countries, productivity is seen to depend on the high ratio of capital to labour, and hence on a high rate of capital accumulation. Therefore, the central state apparatus in a socialist country is tempted to achieve a high rate of productivity and capital accumulation by adopting capitalist methods of maximizing the efficiency of labour: the most striking example is Lenins's acceptance of Taylorism.

Thus a socialist state which gives priority to catching up with capitalist rates of productivity will be as hostile to workers' control or industrial democracy as any capitalist state. Indeed, a socialist state intent on catching up may be more hostile, for in advanced capitalist societies the state may have to step in to require some industrial democracy, whereas in a socialist catching-up society it is precisely the state which will oppose any measure of workers' control which is deemed incompatible with industrial efficiency and high productivity. This is not to say that every socialist state which would like to catch up with the productivity of the most advanced capitalist countries will be hostile to workers' control. It is only to say that a socialist state whose policy is dominated by the desire to catch up, sacrificing any humanistic values, will be so hostile.

We may conclude, then, that at both micro and macro levels there is no necessary incompatibility between workers' participation and productive efficiency.

Bibliography

PART I   THE CONCEPT OF WORK

1. LIEDMAN

Gehlen, A. (1980): Man in the Age of Technology. New York: Columbia
    University Press
Heller, Agnes (1981): 'Paradigm of Production: Paradigm of Work'.
    Dialectical Anthropology, Vol. 6, No. 1
Kosík, Karel (1976): Dialectics of the Concrete. Dordrecht: D. Reidel
Marcuse, Herbert (1933): 'Über die philosophischen Grundlagen des
    Wirtschaftswissenschaftlichen Arbeitsbegriffs'. Archiv für
    Sozialwissenschaft und Sozialpolitik, Vol. 69, No. 3
Marx, Karl (1973): Grundrisse. Foundations of the Critique of Political
    Economy. Harmondsworth: Penguin

2. CORNELL, KARLSSON AND LINDQVIST

Antony, P.D. (1977): The Ideology of Work. London: Tavistock
Braude, Lee (1963): 'Work: A Theoretical Clarification'. The Sociological
    Quarterly, Vol. 4, No. 4
Brinkman, Gerhard (1981): Ökonomik der Arbeit I. Stuttgart: Klett-
    Cotta
Cohen, G.A. (1978): Karl Marx's Theory of History. A Defence. Oxford:
    Clarendon Press
Cornell, Lasse and Jan Ch Karlsson (1983): 'Arbetets sociala former'.
    (Social Forms of Work). Historisk Tidskrift, No 4/1983
David, Rosalie A. (1975): Egyptian Kingdoms. Oxford: Elsvier Phaidon
Dubin, Robert (1965): The World of Work. Englewood Cliffs: Prentice
    Hall
Duby, Georges: (1973): Guerriers et paysans. Paris: Gallimard
Elster, Karl (1919): 'Was ist "Arbeit"?' Jahrbücher für Nationalökonomie
    und Statistik, Vol. 112
Finley, M.I. (ed.) (1960): Slavery in Classical Antiquity. London:
    Heffer
-            (1981): Economy and Society in Ancient Greece. London:
    Chatto & Windus
Friedmann, Georges (1960): 'Qu'est-ce que le travail?' Annales, Vol. 15,
    No. 4
Friedmann, Harriet (1978): 'World Market, State, and Family Farm:
    Social Bases of Household Production in the Era of Wage Labor.'
    Comparative Studies in Society and History, Vol. 20, No. 4

Geremek, Bronislav (1968): Le salariat dans l'artisanat parisien aux XIIIe-XVe siècles. Paris: Mouton

Gross, Edward (1958): Work and Society. New York: Thomas Y. Crowell

Gustafsson, Bo (1980): 'Hur arbetet skapar människan – arbetet i marxismens perspektiv' (How Work Creates Man – Work from a Marxist Perspective), in Arbetets värde och mening. Stockholm: Riksbankens Jubiléumsfond

Heller, Agnes (1981): 'Paradigm of Production: Paradigm of Work', Dialectical Anthropology, Vol. 6, No. 1

Hilton, Rodney (1973): Bond Men Made Free. London: Methuen

Ingelstam, Lars (1980): Arbetets värde och tidens bruk (The Value of Work and the Customs of the Time). Stockholm: Liber

Kaiser, Edwin G. (1966): Theology of Work. Westminster, Maryland: Newman

Karlsson, Jan Ch. (1983): 'Concepts of Work in Social Science'. (Unpublished paper, University of Karlstad).

Kosík, Karel (1976): Dialectics of the Concrete. Dordrecht: D Riedel

Kwant, Remy C. (1960): Philosophy of Labor. Pittsburgh: Duquesne

Lange, Oskar (1971): Political Economy II. Oxford: Pergamon Press

Lee, Richard Borshay (1979): The !Kung San. Men, Women, and Work in a Foraging Society. Cambridge: Cambridge University Press

Lewenhak, Sheila (1980): Women and Work. New York: St. Martin's Press

Lukács, Georg (1973): Zur Ontologie des gesellschaftlichen Seins. Die Arbeit. Darmstadt: Luchterhand

Lutz, Mark A. (1980): 'Towards a More General Economic Theory of Work'. International Social Science Journal, Vol. 32, No. 3

Marcuse, Herbert (1933): 'Über die philosophischen Grundlagen des wirtschaftswissenschaftlichen Arbeitsbegriffs'. Archiv für Sozialwissenschaft und Sozialpolitik, Vol. 69, No. 3

Marx, Karl (1968): Theorien über den Mehrwert III. (MEW 26:3) Berlin: Dietz Verlag

–   (1969): Das Kapital I. (MEW 23) Berlin: Dietz Verlag

Marshall, Alfred (1907): Principles of Economics. London: Macmillan

Maslow, Abraham (1954): Motivation and Personality. New York: Harper & Row

Mathaei, Julie A. (1982): An Economic History of Women in America. Brighton: Harvester Press

Mendelsohn, I. (1949): Slavery in the Ancient Near East. New York: Oxford University Press

Mills, C. Wright (1951): White Collar. New York: Oxford University Press

Murra, John V. (1980): The Economic Organisation of the Inka State. (Research in Economic Anthropology, Suppl. 1). Greenwich, Conn.: JAI Press

Novarra, Virginia (1980): Women's Work, Men's Work. London: Marion Boyars

O'Connor, James (1975): 'Productive and Unproductive Labor'. Politics and Society, Vol. 5, No 3

Oliva, Pavel (1961): 'On the Problem of the Helots'. Historica, Vol. 3

Ruben, Peter and Camilla Warnke (1979): 'Arbeit – Telosrealisation oder Selbsterzeugung der mennschlichen Gattung?' Deutsche Zeitschrift für Philosophie, Vol 27, No. 1

Stein, Stanley J, (1957): Vassouras: A Brazilian Coffee County, 1850–1900. Cambridge, Mass.: Harvard University Press

Tilly, Louise and Joan W. Scott (1978): Women, Work and Family. New York: Holt, Rinehart and Winston

Tvarnø, Henrik (1982): Det romerske slaveri – i europeisk forskning
efter 2. verdenskrig (Roman Slavery – in European Research after
World War II). (Studier fra sprog- og oldtidsforskning, No. 302).
Copenhagen: Museum Tusculanum Forlag
Udy, Stanley H. (1970): Work in Traditional and Modern Society.
Englewood Cliffs: Prentice-Hall
Wadel, Cato (1977): 'Hva er arbeid?'(What is Work?) Tidskrift for
samfunnsforskning. Vol. 18, No 5-6
-             (1979): 'The Hidden Work of Everyday Life', in Sandra
Wallman (ed.): Social Anthropology of Work. London: Academic Press
Work in America. (1973). Cambridge, Mass.: MIT Press

3. EYERMAN

Arendt, H. (1958): The Human Condition. Chicago: University of
Chicago Press
Berger, P. (ed.) (1964): The Human Shape of Work. New York:
Macmillan
Braverman, H. (1974): Labor and Monopoly Capital. New York: Monthly
Review Press
Gamarnikov, E. et al (eds.) (1983): The Public and the Private.
London: H.E.B.
Gehlen, A. (1980): Man in the Age of Technology. New York: Columbia
University Press
Godelier, M. (1980): 'Work and its Representations...', History Workshop
Journal. No 10
Goldthorpe, J., O.Lockwood et al, (1968, 1969): The Affluent Worker,
(3 vols.). Cambridge: Cambridge University Press
Gorz, A. (1982): Farewell to the Working Class. London: Pluto Press

4. TABUKASCH

Arnason, J.P (1976): 'Produktivkräfte und Produktionsverhältnisse', in
I. Fetscher (ed.): Grundbegriffe des Marxismus. Hamburg: Hoffmann
und Campe
-             (1980): 'Marx und Habermas', in A. Honneth and U. Jaeggi
(eds.): Arbeit, Handlung, Normativität. Frankfurt/Main: Suhrkamp
Autorenkollektiv (1980): Entfremdung und Arbeit. Hamburg: VSA
Bahr, H-D (1970): Kritik der 'Politischen Technologie'. Frankfurt/Main:
EVA
Habermas, J. (1968): Technik und Wissenschaft als 'Ideologie'.
Frankfurt/Main: Suhrkamp
-             (1971): Theorie und Praxis. Frankfurt/Main: Suhrkamp
-             (1973): Erkenntnis und Intresse. Frankfurt/Main: Suhrkamp
-             (1976): Zur Rekonstruktion des Historischen Materialismus.
Frankfurt/Main: Suhrkamp
Honneth, A. (1980): 'Arbeit und instrumentales Handeln', in A. Honneth
and U. Jaeggi (eds.) Arbeit, Handlung, Normativität. Frankfurt/-
Main: Suhrkamp
Krämer-Badoni, T. (1978): Zur Legitimität der bürgerlichen Gesellschaft.
Frankfurt/Main: Campus
Lukács, G. (1973): Zur Ontologie des gesellschaftlichen Seins. Die
Arbeit. Darmstadt: Luchterhand
Marx, K. (1842): 'Über die ständischen Ausschüsse in Preussen', in
MEW 1

Marx, K. (1844): 'Ökonomisch-philosophische Manuskripte', in MEW
    Erg.Bd. 1
-        (1844b): 'Auzzüge aus James Mill', in MEW Erg. Bd. 1
Marx, K. and F. Engels (1844): Die heiligen Familie. (MEW 2)
Marx, K. (1845): 'Über Friedrich List', taken from H. Reichelt and R.
    Zech (1983)
-        (1845b): 'Thesis on Feuerbach', in Marx, K. and F. Engels:
    Selected Works. London (1968): Lawrence and Wishart
Marx, K. and F. Engels (1846): Die deutsche Ideologie. (MEW 3)
Marx, K. (1970): Das Kapital I. (MEW 23)
-        (1972): Das Kapital III. (MEW 25)
-        (1973): Grundrisse. Foundations of the Critique of Political
    Economy. Harmondsworth: Penguin
McCarthy, T. (1978): The Critical Theory of J.Habermas. Cambridge:
    Harvard
Mészáros, J. (1975): Marx's Theory of Alienation. London: Merlin Press
MEW - Marx-Engels-Werke in 39 vol. and a supplementary vol. in 2
    parts. Berlin: Dietz Verlag
Reichelt, H. and R. Zech (1983): Karl Marx: Produktivkräfte und
    Produktionsverhältnisse. Frankfurt/Main: Ullstein
Reichelt, H. (1983): 'Zur Dialektik von Produktivkräften und Produk-
    tionsverhältnissen, Versuch einer Rekonstruktion', in H. Reichelt and
    R. Zech (1983)
Schmid-Kowarzik, W. (1981): Die Dialektik der gesellschaftlichen Praxis.
    München: Verlag Karl Alber
Tabukasch, M. (1978): 'Zur Arbeitsteilung bei Marx'. Unpublished
    paper: University of Bremen
-        (1980): Die Gesellschaftlichkeit der Technik. (Diplom-
    thesis): University of Bremen
Van Niekerk, P.J. (1982): Demokratie und Mündigkeit, (Doctoral thesis):
    University of Frankfurt
Vergara, C. (1974): Zur Problematik und Entwicklung des Begriffs des
    Wesens in den Frühschriften von Karl Marx. (Doctoral thesis):
    University of Frankfurt
Weihe, U. (1979): Diskurs und Komplexität. Stuttgart: Hochschulverlag
Zech, R. (1983): 'Produktivkräfte und Produktionsverhältnisse in der
    Kritik der politischen Ökonomie', in H. Reichelt and R. Zech (1983)

5. WALLMAN

Apter, David (1964): 'Ideology and Discontent', in D. Apter (ed.)
    Ideology and Discontent, Glencoe, Illinois: Free Press
Banton, M. (ed.) (1966): The Social Anthropology of Complex Societies,
    (ASA Monograph No. 4), London: Tavistock
Belshaw, C. (1954): Changing Melanesia. Melbourne: OUP
-        (1967): 'Theoretical Problems in Economic Anthropology' in
    M. Freedman (ed.): Social Organisation: essays presented to Raymond
    Firth, London: Frank Cass.
Beynon, H. and R.M. Blackburn (1972): Perceptions of Work: Variations
    within a Factory. (Cambridge Papers in Sociology No. 3). Cambridge:
    Cambridge Univ. Press
Bourdieu, Pierre (1977): Outline of a Theory of Practice. Cambridge:
    Studies in Social Anthropology
Cohen, A.P. (1979): 'The Whalsay Croft; traditional work and customary
    identity in modern times', in Wallman (ed.) (1979b)
-        (ed.) (1980): Belonging, Manchester: Manchester University
    Press

Fagin, L. and A. Little (1984): The Forsaken Families. Harmondsworth: Penguin

Firth, R. (1967): Themes in Economic Anthropology, (ASA Monograph No. 6), London: Tavistock

— (1979): 'Work and Value: Reflections on ideas of Karl Marx', in Wallman (1979b)

Frankenburg, R. (1966): 'British community studies: problems of synthesis', in Banton (ed.) (1966)

Fred, M. (1979): 'How Sweden Works: a case from the bureaucracy', in Wallman (ed.) (1979b)

Gellner, E.A. (1982): Language, State and Culture, (6th Radcliffe Brown Memorial Lecture in Social Anthropology). London: The British Academy

Gershuny, J.I. (1979): After Industrial Society? London: Macmillan

Godelier, M. (1972): Rationality and Irrationality in Economics, London: NLB

Hannerz, Ulf (1980): Exploring the City, New York: Columbia U.P.

Harrison, G.A (1979): 'Views from three other disciplines: biological anthropology', in Wallman (ed.) (1979b)

Hawlyryshyn, O. (1978): The measurement of household production. Ottawa: Statistics Canada

Jahoda, M., F. Lasarsfeld and H. Zeisel (1972): Marienthal: the sociography of an unemployed community. London: Tavistock

Jahoda, M. (1982): Employment and Unemployment. Cambridge: Cambridge University Press

Klein, L. (1976): New Forms of Work Organisation. Cambridge: Cambridge University Press

Kosmin, B.A. (1979): 'Exclusion and Opportunity: traditions of work among British Jews' in Wallman (ed.) (1979a)

Loudon, J.B. (1979): 'Workers, Lords and Masters: the organisation of labour on South African farms', in Wallman (ed.) (1979b)

McGee, T.G. (1974): The Persistence of the Protoproletariat: occupationalstructures and planning of future world cities. Mimeo: Australian National University, Research School of Pacific Studies, Dept. of Human Geography

Marsden, D. and E. Duff (1975): Workless: some unemployed men and their families. Harmondsworth: Penguin

Miner, H. (1956): 'Body Ritual among the Nacerima'. American Anth. Vol. 58

Nadel, S.F. (1957): The Theory of Social Structure. London: Cohen and West

Pahl, R.E. and J.I. Gershuny (1979-80): 'Work Outside Employment: some preliminary speculations', New Universities Quarterly, Vol. No. 34, No 1

Pahl, Ray (1980): 'Employment, Work & the Domestic Divison of Labour', International J. Urban and Regional Research, Vol. 4, No. 1

Paine, R. (1970): 'Informal Communication and Information Management'. Can. Rev. of Sociology and Anthropology, Vol. 7, No. 3

— (1974): Second thoughts about Barth's models. (R.A.I. Occasional Paper No. 32). London: R.A.I.

— (1976): 'Two modes of exchange and mediation', in B. Kapferer (ed.) Transaction and Meaning. (A.S.A. Studies Vol. 1). Philadelphia: I.S.H.I.

Piccone-Stella, S. (1979): 'Rapports sugli intellettuali italiani: le condizioni di lavoro'. La Critica Sociologica, Vol. 10, No. 2

Sahlins, M. (1974): Stone Age Economics, London: Tavistock

Saifullah, Khan, V. (1979): 'Work and Network: South Asian women in South London', in Wallman (ed.) (1979a)

Santos, Milton (1979): 'Circuits of Work', in Wallman (ed.) (1979a)

Schwimmer, E. (1979): 'The Self and the Product: concepts of work in comparative perspective', in Wallman (ed.) (1979b)

-        (1980): 'The Limits of Economic Ideology: a comparative study of work concepts'. International Social Science Journal, Vol. 33

Searle-Chatterjee, M. (1979): 'The Polluted Identity of Work: a study of Benares Sweepers', in Wallman (ed.) (1979b)

Wadel, C. (1973): 'Now whose fault is that?' The struggle for self-esteem in the face of chronic unemployment. St. John's, Newfoundland: Memorial University ISER.

-        (1979): 'The hidden work of everyday life', in Wallman (ed.) (1979b)

Wallman, S. (1965): 'The communication of measurement in Basutoland'. Human Organisation, Vol. 24, No. 2

-        (1969): Take Out Hunger: two case studies of rural development in Basutoland, (LSE Monographs No. 39). London: Athlone

-        (1977) (ed.): Perceptions of Development. Cambridge: Cambridge Univ. Press

-        (1979a) (ed.): Ethnicity at Work. London: Macmillan

-        (1979b) (ed.): Social Anthropology of Work. (ASA Monograph No. 19)

-        (1982): 'Time and Affect: facets of the social anthropology of work', in G.A. Harrison (ed.) Energy of Effort. (Symposia of the Society for the Study of Human Biology, Vol. XXII). London: Taylor & Francis

-        (1984): Eight London Households. London: Tavistock

Willis, P. (1977): Learning to Labour. Farnborough: Saxon House

PART II   WORK AND TECHNOLOGY

7. BERGGREN

van Beek, H.G.(1964): 'The Influence of Assembly Line Organization on Output, Quality and Morale. Occupational Psychology, 38, 1964: 161-172

Berggren, C. (1983): Tio år efter Kalmarverken - vad händer med arbetsformer och produktionsutformning i bilindustrin? (Ten years after Volvo Kalmar: What is happening with job design and production systems in the automotive industry), Gothenburg: Chalmer's Institute of Technology

Berggren, C. & T. Engström, (1983): Framtida produktionssystem. (Production Systems of the Future). Gothenburg: Chalmer's Institute of Technology

Erixon, L.A, et.al. (1983): Arbetsorganisation i komponenttillverkning. En studie av fem underleverantörer i bilindustrin. (Work Organization in Component Production. A Study of Five Automotive Subcontractors.), Gothenburg: Chalmer's Institute of Technology

Karlsson, U. (1979): Alternativa produktionssystem till line-produktion. (Alternative Production Systems to Line Production.) Gothenburg: University of Gothenburg

Kern, H. & M. Schuman (1977): Industriearbeit und Arbeiterbewusst-sein. Frankfurt a M: Suhrkamp.

Wild, R. (1975): 'On the Selection of Mass Production Systems'. International Journal of Production Research, no 5, 1975

8. EDQUIST

Edquist, Charles (1977): Teknik, samhälle och energi (Techniques, Society and Energy), Lund
- (1980): Approaches to the Study of Social Aspects of Techniques - Summary of a doctoral thesis, Lund
- (1984): Capitalism, Socialism and Technology - A Study of Cuba and Jamaica. (To be published by Zed Books, London, in early 1985.)
Edquist, Charles & Olle Edqvist (1979): Social Carriers of Techniques for Development, published as SAREC Report R3:1979 by the Swedish Agency for Research Cooperation with Developing Countries, SIDA, Stockholm. (A somewhat abridged version was published under the same title in Journal of Peace Research, Vol XVI, 1979. In Swedish the study has been published as Zenit Häften 5, 1980.)
Edquist, Charles & Staffan Jacobsson (1984): Trends in the Diffusion of Electronics Technology in the Capital Goods Sector. Discussion Paper No. 161, Research Policy Institute, University of Lund, August 1984. (Also to be published by UNCTAD, Geneva, during 1984.)
Fauconnier, R. (1983): 'Standard of living and degree of mechanization of sugar cane harvesting'. Paper presented at the International Society of Sugar Cane Technologists, XVIII Congress, Cuba, 1983
Marx, Karl (1967): Capital. A Critical Analysis of Capitalist Production, Volume 1, New York (International Publishers)
Palmer, Lesley, Charles Edquist and Staffan Jacobsson (1984): Perspectives on Technical Change and Employment. Discussion Paper No.167, Research Policy Institute, University of Lund, September 1984.

9. HAUG

Haug, Frigga (1982): 'Werte und Bedürfnisse in der Automatisierung' in Rapp 1982:13-26
Haug, Frigga & Uwe Gluntz, Rolf Nemitz, Werner van Treeck, Gerhard Zimmer (1975): 'Automation führt zur Höherqualifikation. Thesen über Hand- und Kopfarbeit' in Demokratische Erziehung, 1975, Jg. 1, Heft 4; reprinted in Projektgruppe Automation und Qualifikation: Bildungs-ökonomie und Bildungsreform. Aufsatzsammlung. Argument-Verlag, Berlin 1980
Holzkamp, Klaus (1983): Grundlegung der Psychologie. Frankfurt/M: Campus Verlag
Kelley, Ch. R. (1972): 'Display Layout' in Bernotat, R.K. und K.-P. Gärtner (eds): Displays and Controls. The Proceedings for an Advanced Study Institute held at Berchtesgaden in March, 1971, sponsored by the NATO Scientific Affairs Division and the Federal Republic of Germany. Amsterdam
Kern, Horst & M.Schumann (1984): Das Ende der Arbeitsteilung, München: Beck Verlag
Negt, Oskar (1984): 'Lebendige Arbeit, enteignete Zeit' in TAZ 11.2.84
Projekt Automationsmedizin (1981): 'Automationsarbeit under Gesundheit - Perspektiven der Arbeitsmedicin' in Prävention. Argumente für eine soziale Medizin IX, Berlin: Argument-Verlag, (AS 64)
Projekt Automation und Qualifikation (1980-83): Automationsarbeit. Empirische Untersuchungen Teil 1. 1980 (AS 43); Teil 2. 1981 (AS 55); Teil 3. 1981 (AS 67); Teil 4: Zerreissproben. Automation im Arbeiterleben. 1983 (AS 79), Berlin: Argument-Verlag

Willis, Paul (1977): <u>Learning to labour. How working class kids get working class jobs</u>. Saxon House

10. PANG

Bylinsky, Gene (1979): 'Those Smart Young Robots on the Production Line', <u>Fortune, 17 December 1979</u>
Cluttenbuck, David & Roy Hill (1981): <u>The Re-Making of Work</u>, London: Grant McIntyre Ltd.
Davis, Louis E. & Eric L. Trist (1974): 'Improving the Quality of Work Life: Sociotechnical Case Studies', in James O'Toole (ed.), <u>Work and the Quality of Life</u>, Cambridge: The MIT Press
Evans, Christopher (1980): <u>The Mighty Micro</u>, London: Coronet Books
Jones, Barry (1982): <u>Sleepers, Wake!</u>, Melbourne: Oxford University Press
Lim, Linda & Pang Eng Fong (1984): 'Labour Strategies for Meeting the High-Tech Challenge: The Case of Singapore', <u>Euro-Asia Business Review</u>, vol. 3, no. 2, April 1984
Lim, Linda & Pang Eng Fong (1981): <u>Technology Choice and Employment Creation: A Case Study of Three Multinational Enterprises in Singapore</u>, ILO Multinational Enterprises Programme Working Paper No. 16, Geneva: ILO
Naisbitt, John (1982): <u>Megatrends</u>, New York: Warner Books
Riche, Richard W. (1983): 'The Impact of Technological Change', <u>Economic Impact</u>, No. 41, 1983/1
Walton, Richard E. (1974): 'Alienation and Innovation in the Workplace' in James O'Toole (ed.), <u>Work and the Quality of Life</u>, Cambridge: the MIT Press
Weber, Arnold R. (1967): 'Manpower Adjustments to Technological Change: An International Analysis', in Solomon Barkin et.al. (eds.), <u>International Labor</u>, New York: Harper & Row
Wilkinson, Barry (1983): <u>The Shopfloor Politics of New Technology</u>, London: Heinemann Educational Books
Zuboff, Shoshana (1983): 'Computer-Mediated Work: A New World', <u>Economic Impact</u>, No. 41, 1983/1

PART III WORK AND CULTURE

11. DAHLKVIST

Ahrne, G. (1981): <u>Vardagsverklighet och struktur</u> (Everyday Reality and Structure), Uddevalla: Korpen
Barret, M. (1980): <u>The Oppression of Women Today</u>, London: Verso
Bell, D. (1973): <u>The Coming of Post-Industrial Society</u>, New York: Basic Books
Boccara, P. (1972): <u>Der Staatsmonopolistische Kapitalismus</u>, Berlin: Dietz
Dahlkvist, M. (1978): <u>Att studera 'Kapitalet'</u> (Studying 'Capital'), Köthen: Cavefors/Arkiv
–   (1982): <u>Staten som problem</u> (The State as the Problem), Lund: Arkiv
Dahlkvist, M. & H. Nordlöf (1982): 'The Mixture of the Mixed Economy', unpublished research-plan, Institute of Political Science, Gothenburg University
Dürkheim, E. (1960a): <u>De la Division du Travail Social</u>, Paris: PUF
–   (1960b): <u>Le Suicide: Etude Sociologie</u>, Paris: PUF

Flora, P.. & A.J. Heidenheimer (1981): The Development of Welfare
   States in Europe and America, New Brunswick: Transaction Books
Foucault, M. (1976): L'Histoire de la Sexualité. Vol I, Paris: Gallimard
Friedman, M. (1962): Capitalism and Freedom, Chicago: Univ. of
   Chicago Press
Galbraith, J.K. (1967): The New Industrial State, Aylesbury: Penguin
Giddens, A. (1973): The Class Structure of the Advanced Societies,
   London: Hutchinson
Habermas, J. (1962): Strukturwandel der Öffentlichkeit, Neuwied under
   Berlin: Luchterhand
Heckscher, E.F. (1955): Mercantilism 1-2, London
Hilton, R. (ed.) (1976): The Transistion from Feudalism to Capitalism,
   Thetford: New Left Books
Hobbes, Th. (1651): Leviathan, Aylesbury, Penguin, 1968
Ingelhart, R. (1977): The Silent Revolution, Princeton: Princeton
   University Press
Korpi, W. (1978): The Working Class in Welfare Capitalism, London:
   Routledge and Kegan Paul
Locke, J. (1690): Two Treatises on Government, Letchworth: Dent,
   Dutton, 1975
Mandel, E. (1975): Late Capitalism, London: New Left Books
Marx, K. (1867): Das Kapital. Kritik der politischen Ökonomie,
   Hamburg: Otto Meisner
Millet, K. (1971): Sexualpolitiken (Sex Policies)
Parsons, T. & N.J. Smelser (1956): Economy and Society, Glencoe
Polanyi, K. et al. (1956): Trade and Market in the Early Empires, New
   York: The Free Press
Poulantzas, N. (1968): Pouvoir Politique et Classes Sociales, Paris
Schonfield, A. (1965): Modern Capitalism, Oxford University Press
Therborn, G.: The Ideology of Power and the Power of Ideology,
   London: Verso
-               (1984): 'Den svenska socialdemokratin träder fram'
   (Swedish Social Democracy Emerges), Arkiv nr 27-28
Weber (1946): From Max Weber, edited and introduced by Gerth, H.H. &
   C.W. Mills, London: Routledge and Kegan Paul
Østerud, Ø. (1978): Utvidklingsteori og historisk endring (The Theory
   of Evolution and Historical Change), Oslo: Gyldendal

12. ANTHONY

Child, J. and B. Partridge (1982): 'Lost Managers, Supervisors in
   Industry and Society'. SSRC., Cambridge University Press
Dalton, Melville (1959): Men Who Manage. New York: John Wiley
Earl, Michael (1983): 'Accounting and Management', in Earl, M.J. (ed.)
   Perspectives on Management. Oxford: Oxford University Press
Gowler, D. and Karen Legge (1983): 'The Meaning of Management and
   the Management of Meaning: a view from social anthropology', in Earl,
   M.J. (ed.), Perspectives on Management. Oxford: Oxford University
   ·Press
Hardy, Barbara (1975): Tellers and Listeners, the narrative imagination.
   London: University of London, The Athlone Press
Kerslake, P.S and P.J Radcliff (1980): 'Inward Bound - A New Direction
   for Outward Bound', in Beck, John och Charles Cox, (eds.),
   Advances in Management Education. Chichester: John Wiley
Kotter, John P. (1982): The General Managers. New York: The Free
   Press

Leavitt, Harold J. (1983): 'Management Education in the West: What's
Right and What's Wrong?', The Stockton Lecture, London Business
School, 16th March 1983, Unpublished

MacIntyre, Alasdair (1981): After Virtue, a study in moral theory.
London: Duckworth

Redfield, Robert (1980): The Little Community and Peasant Society and
Culture. Toronto: University of Chicago

Stewart, Rosemary (1983): 'Managerial Behaviour: how research has
changed the traditional picture', in Earl M.J. (ed.), Perspectives on
Management. Oxford: Oxford University Press

13. BENERIA

Barrett, Michele (1980): Women's Oppression Today, London: Verso
Editions

Benería, Lourdes (ed.) (1982): Woman and Development: The Sexual
Division of Labor in Rural Societies, New York: Praeger

–   (1984): 'Overcoming Dualisms; Gender, Jobs and Skill',
unpublished manuscript

Benería, Lourdes and Gita Sen (1982): 'Accumulation, Reproduction, and
Women's Role in Economic Development: Boserup Revisited', Signs,
Vol. 7, No. 2 (Winter): 279–98

Boserup, Ester (1970): Woman's Role in Economic Development, New
York: George Allen & Unwin

Deere, Carmen Diana (1977): 'Changing Social Relations of Production
and Peruvian Peasant Women's Work', Latin American Perspectives,
Winter–Spring: 48–49

Engels, Frederick (1975): The Origin of the Family Private Property and
the State, New York: International Publishers

Heyzer, Noeleen (1982): 'From Rural Subsistence to an Industrial
Peripheral Workforce: An Examination of Female Malaysian Migrants
and Capital Accumulation in Singapore', in Benería (ed.)

Himmelweit, Susan and Simon Mohun (1977): 'Domestic Labor and
Capital', Cambridge Journal of Economics, 1:15–31

Hochchild, Arlie (1983): 'Illich: The Ideologue in Scientist's Clothing,
Feminist Issues, Vol 3, No. 1 (Spring): 6–11

Illich, Ivan (1982): Gender, New York: Pantheon Books

Molyneux, Maxine (1982): 'Socialist Societies: Progress Towards Women
Emancipation?', Monthly Review, July–August: 56–100

Pleck, Joseph and Michael Rustard (1980): 'Husbands' and Wives' Time in
Family Work and Paid Work in the 1975–76 Study of Time Use',
Working paper, Wellesley College Center for Research on Women.

Reitner, Rayna Rapp (1977): 'The Search for Origins: Unraveling the
Threads of Gender Hierarchy', Critique of Anthropology, Vol 3, 9 &
10: 5–24

Safilios-Rothschild, Constantina (1982): 'The Persistence of Women's
Invisibility in Agriculture: Theoretical and Policy Lessons from
Lesotho and Sierra Leone', New York: Population Council.

Scheper-Hughes (1983): 'Vernacular Sexism: An Anthropological
Response to Ivan Illich', Feminist Issues, Vol. 3, No. 1: 28–37

Tilly, Louise and Joan Scott (1978): Women, Work and Family. New
York: Holt, Reinhart and Winston

Wiegersma, Nancy (1981): 'Women in the Transition to Capitalism;
Nineteenth to Mid-twentieth Century Vietnam', in Research in Political
Economy, edited by Paul Zarembka, Greenwich, Ct.: JAI Press, Vol.
4: 1–28

Zaretsky, Eli (1976): Capitalism, the Family and Personal Life, London:
Pluto Press

15. WINGREN

Agrell, Göran (1976): Work, Toil and Sustenance. An Examination of the
View of Work in the New Testament. Lund-Stockholm: Verbum
Krusche, Werner (1957): Das Wirken des Heiligen Geistes nach Calvin.
Berlin-Göttingen: Evang. Ver.-Anst.
zur Mühlen, Karl-Heinz (1978): 'Arbeit VI', in Theologische
Realenzyklopädie III. Berlin-New York: Walter de Gruyter
Niebuhr, Reinhold (1932): Moral Man and Immoral Society. London-New
York: C. Scribner's sons
Troeltsch, Ernst (1923): Die Soziallehren der christlichen Kirchen und
Gruppen. 3rd ed. Tübingen: J.C.B. Mohr (Paul Siebeck)
Vontobel, Klara (1946): Das Arbeitsethos des deutschen Protestantismus
(Beiträge zur Soziologie und Sozialphilosophie 2) Bern: A. Francke
AG
Weber, Max (1947): Die protestantische Ethik und der Geist des
Kapitalismus. Tübingen: J.C.B. Mohr
Wolf, Hans Heinrich (1958): Die Einheit des Bundes (Beiträge zur
Geschichte und Lehre der reformierten Kirche 10). Neukirchen: Kr.
Moers:Verl. d. Buchbehandlung d. Erziehungsvereins
Wingren, Gustaf (1957): Luther on Vocation. Philadelphia: Muhlenberg
Press
-          (1980): 'Beruf II', in Theologische Realenzyklopädie V.
Berlin-New York: Walter de Gruyter

PART IV   WORK AND EDUCATION

16. BROADY

Bourdieu, Pierre (1979): La distinction. Critique sociale du jugement,
Paris: Ed. de Minuit
Jánossy, Ferenc (1966): A gazdasági fejlödés trendvonalai és a
helyreállitási periódusok (The Trend of Economic Development and
Periods of Restitution), Budapest: KJK. English translation in Eastern
European Economics, Vol X, 1971
Kern, Horst & Michael Schumann (1970): Industriearbeit und Arbeiter-
bewusstsein, Frankfurt/Main: Europäische Verlagsanstalt
-          (1984): Das Ende der Arbeitsteilung?,
München: Verlag C.H. Beck
Kluge, Alexander & Oskar Negt (1981): Geschichte und Eigensinn, 3rd
edition, Frankfurt/Main: Zweitausende ins
Mathiesen, Anders (1979): Uddannelsespolitikken, uddannelsesfordelingen
og arbejdsmarkedet (Educational Policies, the Distribution of Education
and the Labour Market), Copenhagen: Lavindkomstkommissionen,
Arbejdsnotat 4
Negt, Oskar (1968): Soziologische Phantasie und exemplarisches
Lernen, Frankfurt/Main: Europäische Verlagsanstalt

17. CARNOY

Aronowitz, Stanley (1973): False Promises: The Shaping of American
Working-Class Consciousness. New York: McGrow
Bowles, Samuel and Herbert Gintis (1982): Schooling in Capitalist
America. New York: Basic Books

Carnoy, Martin (1980): 'The Challange of Democracy'. Social Policy, Vol. 11, No. 2
Carnoy, Martin and Derek Shearer (1980): Economic Democracy. New York: Pantheon
Carnoy, Martin, Derek Shearer and Russell Rumberger (1983): A New Social Contract. New York: Harper & Row
Gordon, David M., Richard Edwards and Michael Reich (1982): Segmented Work, Divided Workers. Cambridge: Cambridge Univ. Press
Hartmann, Heidi (1976): 'Capitalism, Patriarchy and Job Segregation by Sex'. Signs, Vol. 1, No. 3
James, Thomas and Henry M. Levin (eds.) (1983): Public Dollars for Private Schools. Philadelphia: Temple Univ. Press
National Journal, May 5, 1979
O'Connor, James (1973): The Fiscal Crisis of the State. New York: St. Martin's Press

18. HABER

Antal, László and Júlia Szalai (1982-83): Ifjúság élet, egészség (Youth, Life, Health), Manuscript
Jánossy, Ferenc (1966): A gazdasági fejlödés trendvonalai és a helyreállitási periódusok (The Trend of Economic Development and Periods of Restitution). Budapest: KJK
Szénai, Márta (1983): Segédmunkás pályakezdö fiatalok (Entering a Career as Unskilled Workers). Manuscript
1980 Census on the basis of a 2 per cent sample, Budapest:KSH.

19. HOLMER

Abrahamsson, Bengt (1981): 'Socialisationsteori utan funktionalism?'. (Theory of Socialization without Functionalism?) in UHÄ report 1981:7: Empirisk kvalifikationsforskning. (Empirical Qualification Research). Stockholm
Abrahamsson, Kenneth, Lillemor Kim and Kjell Rubensson (1980): The Value of Work Experience in Higher Education. Institute of Education, Högskolan för lärarutbildning in Stockholm
Andersson, Ingemar, et al (1981): Varvsarbetare trots allt. (Shipyard Work Despite the Odds). Project carried out for the course 'Shipyard crisis, employment and commercial policy'. Centre for Interdisciplinary Studies, Gothenburg University
Axelsson, Sten (1982): Kvalifikationsstrukturens utveckling - effekter på sysselsättning av strukturomvandling. (The Development of the Structure of the Qualification System - the Effects of Structural Changes on Employment). Expertgruppen för Forskning om Regional Utveckling (ERU)
Beckholmen, Kuno (1979): Torpet (The Cottage.) Report commissioned by the Eriksberg shipyard's trade union branch in conjunction with the shutdown of the branch and the shipyard. Gothenburg
Bengtsson, Jari and Kjell Härnqvist (1972): 'Utbildningsreformer och jämlikhet'. (Educational Reforms and Equality), in G.R. Nordenstam et al: Värde, välfärd och jämlikhet. (Value, Welfare and Equality). Lund: Studentlitteratur
Berger, Peter and Thomas Luckman (1966): The Social Construction of Reality. Whitstable: Penguin

Boglind, Anders, et al (1981): Slutrapport. Fack i företagskris. (The Union in Corporate Crisis: final report). Department of Sociology, Gothenburg University

Borgström, Lena and Lars-Erik Olofsson (1980): Participation in Study Circles and the Creation of Individual Resources. Institute of Education, Högskolan för lärarutbildning in Stockholm

Broady, Donald (1978): Utbildning och politisk ekonomi. (Education and Political Economics). Insstitute of Education, Högskolan för lärarutbildning in Stockholm

- (1981): 'Arbetslivsperspektiv på utbildning och socialisationsteorins användbarhet' (The Perspective of Working Life on Education and the Usefulness of the Theory of Socialization), in UHÄ-rapport 1981:7: Empirisk kvalifikationsforskning. (Empirical Qualification Research). Stockholm

Bulmer, Martin (1975): Working-class Images of Society. London: Routledge & Kegan Paul

Conert, Hansgeorg (1978): 'Probleme und Grenzen der Verwirklichung der Negtschen Konzeption von Arbeiterbildung', in A. Brock et al: Arbeiterbildung. Soziologische Phantasie und Exemplarisches Lernen. Hamburg: Rowohlt

Eriksson, Kjell and Jan Holmer (1982): Högskolan och facklig kunskaps utveckling. (Higher Education and Learning via the Trade Union). Department of Sociology, Gothenburg University

- (1981): 'A Local Labour Union and Professionals from the University: Experiences of Cooperation'. Acta Sociologica 1981 (24) 1-2:93-97

- (1978): Året med varvscirklarna. Fack i företagskris. (One Year of Shipyard Study Circles. The Union in Corporate Crisis). Department of Sociology, Gothenburg University

Grimm, Susanne (1966): Die Bildungsabstinenz der Arbeiter. Munich: Barth

Huch, Kurt (1977): Vägen in i klassamhället. (The Way into the Class Society). Stockholm: Wahlström & Widstrand

Hultengren, Eva and Henning S. Olesen (1978): Eksemplarisk indlaering og arbejderuddannelse. (Exemplary Learning and Worker Education). Aalborg universitetscenter

Isling, Åke (1980): Kampen för och mot en demokratisk skola. (The Battle for and against Democratic Education). Stockholm: Sober

Johansson, Lena (1970): 'Utbildning: Resonerande del'. (Education: Discussion Section). Draft of Ch. 7. Låginkomstutredningen. (Low Income Commission Study). Stockholm: Allmänna Förlaget

Johansson, Lena and Hedvig Ekerwald (1976): Vuxenstudier och livssituation. (Adult Students and their Way of Life). Falköping: Prisma

Korpi, Walter (1978): Arbetarklassen i välfärdskapitalismen. (The Working Class and Welfare Capitalism). Kristianstad: Prisma

LOFO 1 (1980): Forskning för arbete och demokrati. (Research for Work and Democracy). Stockholm: LO/Tiden

Lorenzer, Alfred (1976): En materialistisk socialisationsteori. (A Materialistic Theory of Socialization). Stockholm: Gidlunds

Negt, Oskar (1977): Sociologisk fantasi og eksemplarisk indlaering. (Sociological Imagination and Exemplary Learning). Roskilde universitetsforlag

- (1978): 'Marxismus und Arbeiterbildung - Kritische Anmerkungen zu meinen Kritikern; in A. Brock et al: Arbeiterbildung. Soziologische Phantasie und Exemplarisches Lernen. Hamburg: Rowohlt

Nelsson, Olof (1982): Studerande på enstaka kurser. (Non-matriculated Students). Pedagogiskt utvecklingsarbete vid Lunds universitet

Popitz, Heinrich, et al (1957): Das Gesellschaftsbild des Arbeiters. Tübingen: Mohr

Reuterberg, Sven-Eric and Allan Svensson (1983): Studiemedel som rekryteringsinstrument och finansieringskälla. (Student Grants as a Recruitment Tool and a Source of Financing). Stockholm: UHÄ

Sjöstrand, Wilhelm (1968): Pedagogiska grundproblem i historisk belysning. (A Historical Perspective on Basic Problems in Education). Lund: Gleerups

Stange, Jan and Owe Ivarsson (1981): Forskning för demokrati. (Research for Democracy). Stockholm: Arbetarskyddsfonden

Svensson, Allan (1980): 'On Eduality and University Education in Sweden'. Scandinavian Journal of Educational Research, vol. 24, No. 1

Willén, Birgitta (1981): Distance Education at Swedish Universities. Uppsala: Acta Universitatis Upsaliensis

20. MATHIESEN

Indsatsen mod Ungdomsarbejdsløsheden 1978 (Measures against Youth Unemployment 1978), Copenhagen: Arbejdsministeriet (1979)

Indsatsen mod Ungdomsarbejdsløsheden 1982 (Measures against Youth Unemployment 1982), Copenhagen: Arbejdsministeriet (1983)

Lavindkomstkommissionens Betaenkning nr 946 (The Report of the Low-Income Commission), 1981

Lutz, Burkart (1969): 'Produktionsprozesse und Berufsqualifikation', in T.W. Adorno: Spätkapitalismus oder Industriegesellshaft?, Stuttgart: Ferdinand Enke Verlag

Mathiesen, Anders (1980): 'Velfaerdsfordeling eller fordeling af arbejdskraft' (Distribution of Welfare or Distribution of Labour), Økonomi og Politik. Vol 54, no. 4

–   (1979): Uddannelsespolitikken, uddannelsesfordelingen og arbejdsmarkedet (Educational Policies, the Distribution of Education and the Labour Market), Arbejdsnotat 4. Lavindkomstkommissionens Sekretariat

Sørensen, John Houman et al. (1983): Laerlingeuddannelse og udbytning 1-3 (Apprentice Training and Exchange). Aalborg: Aalborg Universitetsforlag

PART V   WORK AND POWER

21. LANTZ

Berg, E. (1978): 'Democracy and Self-Determination', in Birnbaum, Liverly & Parry: Democracy, Consensus & Social Contract. London: Sage

Blumberg, P. (1968): Industrial Democracy; the Sociology of Participation. London: Constable

Espinosa, J.G. & A.S. Zimbalist (1978): Economic Democracy. Workers' Participation in Chilean Industry 1970-1973. New York: Academic Press

Lindblom, C.E. (1977): Politics & Markets. New York: Basic Books

Oakeshott, R. (1978): The Case for Workers' Co-ops. London: Routledge & Kegan Paul

Wolff, R.P. (1969): The Poverty of Liberalism. Boston: Beacon

22. EIDEM

Abrahamsson, B. (1982): 'Transaktionsanalys: en länk mellan nationalekonomi och organisationsteori' (Transaction Analysis: a Link between Economics and Organisation Theory). Ekonomisk Debatt 7:463-470

Alchian, A.A. and H. Demsetz (1972): 'Production, Information Costs and Economic Organization'. American Economic Review 62:777-795

Calabresi, G. and A.D. Melamed (1972): 'Property Rules, Liability Rules and Inalienability: One View of the Cathedral'. Harvard Law Review, Vol. 85, No.6: 1088-1128

Gardell, B. (1976): Arbetsinnehåll och livskvalitet (Work Content and the Quality of Life), (in particular chapter 10), Stockholm: Prisma

Hahn, F. (1981): 'General Equilibrium Theory', in Bell, D. and I. Kristol (eds.), The Crisis in Economic Theory, New York: Basic Books

Hernes, G. (ed.) (1978): Forhandlingsökonomi og blandingsadministrasjon (The Economics of Negotiation and Mixed Administration), Oslo: Universitetsforlaget

Klein, B., R.G. Crawford and A.A. Alchian (1978): 'Vertical Integration, Appropriable Rents, and the Competitive Contracting Process', The Journal of Law and Economics, Vol. XXI, No. 2: 297-325

Tawney, R.H. (1975 (1931)): Equality, London: Allen & Unwin

23. GUSTAVSEN

Anderson, A. & C. Lindroth (1979): Styrelserepresentation för anställda i företag med 25-99 anställda (Board Representation for Employees in Companies with 25-99 Employess). Stockholm: Arbetslivscentrum

Eidem, L.R. & B. Öhman (1979): Economic Democracy Through Wageearners Funds. Stockholm: Arbetslivscentrum

Emery, F.E. (1959): Characteristics of Socio-technical systems. Doc. No. 527. London: Tavistock Institute

Emery, F.E & E. Thorsrud (1969): Form and Content in Industrial Democracy. London: Tavistock Publications

Engelstad, P.H. & T.U. Qvale (1977): Innsyn og innflytelse i styre og bedriftsforsamling (Insight and Influence in Company Boards). Oslo: Tiden

Gustavsen, B. (1972): Industristyret (Managing Industry). Oslo: Tanum
- (1973): 'Environmental requirements and the democratisation of industrial organizations'. Participation and Self-Management. Vol 4. Zagreb
- (1975): 'Redefining the role fo the board'. Journal of General Management. Vol. 2. No. 3
- (1976a): Styrearbeid (Work on Boards). Bedriftsdemokrati, hefte 2. Oslo: Arbeidernes Opplysningsforbund
- (1976b): 'The Board of Directors, Company Policy and Industrial Democracy' in Dubin, R. (red.): Handbook of Work, Organization and Society, pp. 447-461. Chicago: Rand McNally
- (1976c): 'The Social Context of Investment Decisions'. Acta Sociologica. Vol. 19. No. 3

Gustavsen, B. & G. Hunnius (1981): New Patterns of Work Reform. The Case of Norway. Oslo Univ. Press

Gustavsen, B. (1983) Sociology as action: On the constitution of alternative realities. Draft, Oslo: Work Research Institutes

McQuitty, L.L. (1957): 'Elementary linkage analysis for isolating orthogonal and ablique types and typal relevancies'. Educational and Psychological Measurement. Vol. 17

Meidner, R. (1978): Employee Investment Funds: An Approach to Collective Capital Formation. London: Allen & Unwin

SIND (1975): Statens Industriverk: Styrelserepresentation för anställda (Board Representation for Employees). Utredningar, nr. 4

Skytøen Committee (1980): LO-DNA: Vidareutvikling av bedriftsdemokrati (LO-DNA: Further Development of Company Democracy). Utredning og innstilling fra en felleskomité, Oslo

24. HORVAT

Bowles, S., D. Gordon & T. Weisskopf (1984): 'A Social Model for US Productivity Growth', Challenge No. 1

Horvat, B. (1982), Political Economy of Socialism, New York: Sharpe

Rus, V. & V. Arzensèk (1984): Rad (Work), Zagreb: SNL

25. MACPHERSON

Macpherson, C.B. (1973), Life and Times of Liberal Democracy, Oxford: Oxford University Press

Contributors

Anthony, P.D., Dept. of Industrial Relations and Managment Studies, University College, Cardiff, UK

Benería, Lourdes, Dept. of Economics, Rutgers University, New Brunswick, NJ, USA

Berggren, Christian, Laboratory of Industrial Ergonomics, The Royal Institute of Technology, Stockholm, Sweden

Broady, Donald, Dept. of Education, Teachers' Training College, Stockholm, Sweden

Carnoy, Martin, School of Education, Stanford University, Stanford, Cal., USA

Cornell, Lasse, Dept. of Economic History, Gothenburg University, Sweden

Dahlqvist, Mats, Dept. of Political Science, Gothenburg University and University of Karlstad, Sweden

Edquist, Charles, Research Policy Institute, Lund, Sweden

Eidem, Rolf, The Swedish Centre for Working Life, Stockholm, Sweden

Eyerman, Ron, Dept. of Sociology, Lund University, Sweden

Galtung, Johan, Université Nouvelle Transnationale, Paris, France

Gustavsen, Bjørn, Work Research Institutes, Oslo, Norway

Háber, Judit, Inst. of Sociology, Hungarian Academy of Sciences, Budapest, Hungary

Haug, Frigga, Freie Universität, Berlin, Federal Republic of Germany

Holmer, Jan, Dept. of Education, Gothenburg University, Sweden

Horvat, Branko, Dept. of Economics, University of Zagreb, Yugoslavia

Karlsson, Jan Ch., Dept. of Sociology, University of Karlstad, Sweden

Lantz, Göran, Dept. of Theology, Uppsala University, Sweden

Liedman, Sven-Erik, Dept. of History of Ideas and Sciences, Gothenburg University, Sweden

Lindqvist, Ulla, Dept. of Sociology, University of Karlstad, Sweden

Macpherson, C.B., Dept. of Political Science, University of Toronto, Canada

Mathiesen, Anders, Inst. of Education Research, Roskilde University Centre, Denmark

Pang Eng Fong, School of Management, National University of Singapore, Singapore

Tabukasch, Michael, Socialwissenschaft, Universität Bremen, Federal Republic of Germany

Thorsrud, Einar, Work Research Institutes, Oslo, Norway

Wallman, Sandra, The London School of Economics and Political Science, London, UK

Wingren, Gustaf, Dept. of Theology, Lund University, Sweden

261

Editors

Gustavsson, BengtOve, Dept. of Sociology, University of Karlstad,
    Sweden
Karlsson, Jan Ch., Dept. of Sociology, University of Karlstad, Sweden
Räftegård, Curt, Dept. of Labour Science, University of Karlstad,
    Sweden